The
Chain
Gang

The Chain Gang

One Newspaper
versus the
Gannett Empire

Richard McCord

University of Missouri Press
Columbia and London

Copyright © 1996 by Richard McCord
University of Missouri Press, Columbia, Missouri 65201
Printed and bound in the United States of America
5 4   00 99 98 97

Library of Congress Cataloging-in-Publication Data

McCord, Richard, 1941–
    The chain gang : one newspaper versus the Gannett empire / Richard McCord.
      p. cm.
    Includes index.
    ISBN 0-8262-1064-3 (alk. paper)
    1. McCord, Richard, 1941– . 2. Journalists—United States—20th century—
Biography. 3. Green Bay news-chronicle. 4. Gannett Company. I. Title.
PN4874.M3717A3   1996
070'.92—dc20
  [B]   96-7382
                                                      CIP

∞ ™ This paper meets the requirements of the
American National Standard for Permanence of Paper
for Printed Library Materials, Z39.48, 1984.

Designer: Stephanie Foley
Typesetter: BOOKCOMP
Printer and binder: Thomson-Shore, Inc.
Typefaces: Schneidler and Times

To Laurie, my partner

Contents

Acknowledgments

EVEN AFTER YEARS IN JOURNALISM, writing this first book was a formidable venture with difficult barriers, internal and external. Without the essential support of many people the book would not have happened. Listing all who helped is beyond the scope of this page. But let me note a few, whose contributions were indispensable. Heartfelt thanks to:

Paula Colson McCord, who prepared me for the work. Roger Morris, who said: "Whatever else you're doing, put it aside and make this into a book." Ann Marie McNamara, my only work-in-progress reader, who did so much to keep the work progressing. Marjorie Miller-Engel, who clarified: "It is not a book about journalism—it is a book about values." Peter Shepherd, who doggedly stayed on a discouraging trail. Michael Shnayerson, who knew what was needed to provide a push. Beverly Jarrett and her impressive team, generous with talent, enthusiasm, and courage. The Woods, who lived the story I wrote. And all who put up with me while I was putting it down.

Without each one of you, this story might not have been told.

The
Chain
Gang

Behind every great fortune is a great crime.

—Balzac

Prologue

THE TRADE JOURNAL HEADLINE BROUGHT a sense of déjà vu: "Community Papers Sue Gannett Daily in Illinois." Knowing what would follow, I read on. "Gannett Company's Rockford (Ill.) *Register Star* competes unfairly and illegally, a chain of community papers has charged in a federal lawsuit," the article began. It continued: "In a suit filed Oct. 21, 1992, in U.S. District Court in Rockford, Rock Valley Community Press Inc. charged the 75,944-circulation *Register Star* with violating federal and Illinois law by repeatedly lying about the competitive weeklies."

Oh yes, oh yes. I knew the story well. Though no longer a working journalist, though now withdrawn into my New Mexico home, thirteen hundred miles from Rockford, Illinois, I knew all about Gannett, the biggest newspaper chain in the land—and about small papers that get in the way.

" 'We have taken the dramatic step of filing a major lawsuit because we are firmly convinced the *Register Star* has gone well beyond fair competition by actively misrepresenting our publications and programs and actively disparaging us in ways that are not permissible under the law,' said Steven R. Haught, president and publisher of the *Rock Valley Community Press.*" Amazing: even the name *Community Press.*

"In an editorial Rock Valley charged that 'Gannett's tactics here in Rockford seem to be in concert with tactics Gannett has used to monopolize the publishing market in communities across the country.' " You're onto something there.

" 'We do not believe a huge national conglomerate has the right to run us out of business with illegal business tactics.' " Nor do I, my unmet friends. But I know what you're up against, and stopping them will not be easy. Good luck.

"*Register Star* spokesmen said the paper would have no comment on the lawsuit." That too. The stonewalling, the official silence. Yes, it all seemed so familiar.

1

Part I
Salem, Oregon

A Call in the Night

"THEY ARE THE DEVIL INCARNATE!"

As usual, the voice on the telephone did not identify itself, but I recognized it as that of my friend and fellow newspaper publisher Frank Wood. A big man with a curiously soft voice, Frank Wood was instantly recognizable, embodied or disembodied. Nor did I need to wonder what he was complaining about. It was a theme I had heard before, in numerous variations. No doubt his small, struggling daily in the football city of Green Bay, Wisconsin, was feeling some new squeeze from its giant competitor, the nation's largest newspaper chain, Gannett.

Frank tended to be passionate on the subject, and sometimes he got a little carried away—as he seemed to be now. But he did have real problems with Gannett, and he was a friend. So I prepared to lend a sympathetic ear, as I had often done before. And for once, I had plenty of time to listen.

After fourteen years of grueling, exhausting, mind-grinding, sixty-hour workweeks and all-night stands—offset by the rewards and freedoms that come only to those who run their own newspapers—I had recently let the torch pass. Four months earlier my weekly journal had been bought by an eager new owner. So in October 1988, as I sat at my desk at the *Santa Fe Reporter* in New Mexico's capital city, my only remaining obligation was to leave a clean office when I vacated the premises at the end of the year. Old habits die hard, however. Despite my vanished workload, most evenings still found me at my desk, tying up final details of the sale, writing letters, and musing over faded copies of the *Reporter* from the years when it was mine to shape as best I could.

Night had fallen when Frank's call came. No one else was in the building. My office window opened onto Santa Fe's marvelous autumn air. There was no pressing deadline to cut the conversation short, and I was at last out from under the eternal backlog of untended items on my desk. I leaned back in my swivel chair, ready to let Frank get it off his chest.

"Have you been following *Editor & Publisher*?" he asked.

"More or less," I replied, although in truth I had not paid close attention to the newspaper industry's leading trade journal since the *Reporter*'s sale in June. It was one of the little bonuses of letting go.

"Have you seen what they're doing in Little Rock?" Frank pressed on, indignation sharpening his voice. "Have you seen what they're doing in Detroit?"

"Yeah, Frank, I noticed."

"They're giving it away in Little Rock! No paper in the country can make money selling subscriptions for eighty-five cents a week. Their only purpose is to drive the *Democrat* under."

"Tha-at's right."

"And in Detroit! I've never seen such hypocrisy! They've filed for a joint operating agreement with Knight-Ridder's *Free Press*. That entire 'newspaper war' between the *News* and the *Free Press* has been nothing but a sham. Nothing but a sham!"

"Sure looks that way, doesn't it?"

"Once they stake out a market, they'll stop at nothing!"

"So what's new, Frank?"

"It's getting worse every day in Green Bay," he said, in a voice that sounded like a moan. "They're closing in on me, Dick, and I'm afraid they're going to get me. I'm afraid I won't be able to hold the *News-Chronicle* together."

Frank had talked like this before, but never until now had I heard the edge of desperation. For as long as I had known him, some six years, he had been struggling to hold his *News-Chronicle* together, and for half a decade before we met. His situation sounded familiar—but not his tone of voice.

Frank Wood had entered my life, characteristically by telephone, one Tuesday afternoon in 1982 as I rushed to close that week's issue of the *Reporter.* Like every other fellow journalist who ever was just passing through town and wanted to drop by for a visit, Frank called right on my hard deadline. "Look, I'd like to meet you," I said to this unknown colleague from Wisconsin, "but my paper goes to the printer in six hours, and I've got at least nine hours' worth of work to do before it closes."

Though I enjoyed the company of newspaper people, small-town or big-city, I had difficulty being gracious to anyone during the final stages of deadline. Each week as the carefully laid plans for that issue unraveled before my eyes, I whipped myself into a low-level frenzy, which always somehow got the job done but was seldom good to be around. "There is no way to try to meet today," I almost snapped at my caller, "and if you're leaving town tomorrow morning, I'm afraid it just won't happen." Watching the seconds pass, I did not care if we connected or not. I needed to get back to work.

"I understand," came the soft reply. "I'm in the business myself. Well, Agnes and I are enjoying Santa Fe. We wouldn't mind staying another day. Let us take you to lunch tomorrow, when you're off the hook." It was my first exposure to Frank Wood's remarkable persistence.

As we shook hands just inside Tomasita's Restaurant, I was not surprised that this man looked nothing like what I had imagined. Nobody ever does. A big guy, maybe six-feet-three and 220 pounds, he seemed oversize for the single-brim cap he wore. Under it his close-cut reddish hair was graying here and there. I took him to be in his early fifties, maybe ten years older than I. His wife, Agnes, was an interesting contrast. Petite where he was large, neat where he was rumpled, trim where he tended to bulge, quiet where he was outgoing, she seemed quick to defer. Her eyes showed she was always tracking the conversation, but she let him do most of the talking.

More than anything else, Frank wanted to talk about coexisting with the Gannett chain. Like his *News-Chronicle* in Green Bay, the *Santa Fe Reporter* faced a much larger Gannett-owned paper, which worked tirelessly to lock up all the business in town. He assumed, he said, that we had much in common. He had learned of the *Reporter* in trade journals that had written about the situation in Santa Fe. Sensing an ally, he wanted to meet me and hear about our operation. And he wanted to tell me about his.

In 1953 at the age of twenty-four, Frank Wood became a newspaper publisher. With his life savings of $700 and four loans totaling $17,460, he bought the weekly newspaper in a tiny Wisconsin farming village named Denmark. Now he was running a $14 million enterprise called Brown County Publishing Company, with more than a dozen publications and two printing plants, all in northeastern Wisconsin. At the center was the city of Green Bay, twenty miles away from his modest origins in Denmark.

In 1976, he had taken on his biggest challenge: the *Green Bay News-Chronicle*. Four years earlier, forty-two striking members of the local pressmen's union had started it to compete with the city's established daily. But the new paper faced grim financial odds. When Frank stepped in, it was losing four hundred thousand dollars a year. First as a major shareholder and finally as outright owner, Brown County Publishing Company began running the *News-Chronicle*. Frank himself took charge, often working past midnight. He vowed not to shave until the paper had a profitable month. Seventeen months later, with his beard near his waist, a tiny profit came. On an annual basis the losses had continued, he confided over lunch. But each year they were getting smaller. The break-even point now seemed attainable. If only Gannett would lighten up on him, he said, he just might get there.

"What are they doing to you?" I asked.

"Oh, the usual," he replied. "Hell, Dick, you know."

Yes, I knew.

Lunch ended, and Frank and Agnes flew back to Wisconsin. I had liked them well enough, but did not expect anything much to flow from the meeting. All around the country there were struggling publishers whose ill fortune it was to compete with Gannett. Already I was in touch with a dozen others. Those of us trying to coexist with the nation's largest chain were a special fellowship. But we had no meetings, no officers, no agenda. We were too busy just surviving. From time to time we connected with one another, usually by mail or telephone, occasionally over a vacation lunch or at a newspaper conference. But mainly what we gave each other was sympathy.

The most I might have predicted from meeting Frank Wood was a phone call now and then, perhaps a Christmas card. Instead the connection between us grew steadily, always at his instigation. Just months after his first appearance he was back in Santa Fe, careful to avoid my deadline day. He was visiting an old friend in Arizona—and New Mexico was on the way. How about lunch? Several weeks later he was in town again, to enroll a son in the College of Santa Fe. Then he and Agnes returned for another getaway. He never called to say he was coming, he called to say he was here—let's get together.

Before long he was inviting me to Wisconsin, to see his operation, to meet his family and friends, to spend a weekend in the primitive cabin he owned in the northern woods. And whenever I found myself in Chicago, he insisted, I must stay in the small apartment he kept in the John Hancock Building. If he and Agnes were there at the same time, we would share the place. If they were elsewhere, the apartment was mine.

Each time we met I learned more about Frank. He was a man of many parts. One part was adventurous, as when he had taken his family of eight children—the youngest still an infant, most of the others not yet teenagers—off for a year in the high Andes of Peru. One part was devout, evidenced by a lifetime in the Catholic faith. One part was loyal, to his wife, his family, his company, to all his commitments.

Two parts that blended were his academic and business sides. Several years after buying the village paper in Denmark, he entered the University of Chicago for a graduate degree in business. Most of his subsequent success he credited to the knowledge he gained there. Now, for many years, he had been a tenured associate professor of humanities at St. Norbert College, a small, highly regarded liberal arts school near Green Bay.

Frank was a friendly man—or more precisely, he was a man of deep friendships. A few of them traced back to his childhood in a small town on Michigan's Upper Peninsula. A number came from near or distant relatives in his and Agnes's families. Some were with classmates from business school. Many were with fellow faculty members at the college. Others were with longtime employees of his Brown County Publishing Company. Quite a few came from Agnes's activities, which were numerous. And several friends who felt the deepest bonds were those Frank had helped when they were in need.

Perhaps more than anything else, Frank was a paternal man. First he had been father to his own children, through the full range of catastrophes that assail most families, plus some: illness, birth defects, drugs, deaths of friends, divorce. He had guided all eight into adulthood, with college for those who wanted it, and had helped them get started in their careers.

Beyond his family, he had been a father figure to a generation of students at St. Norbert College, and to virtually everyone who had ever worked at Brown County Publishing—some three hundred employees at that time, thousands more over the years. He felt a personal responsibility for the well-being of every man and woman employed by his company, and had demonstrated it time and again: with generous and innovative benefits, with extraordinary measures to preserve jobs at all costs, with assistance out of his own pocket in times of crisis.

There was in Frank a humanitarian streak I had not often seen in the newspaper business—or in any business, for that matter. He came along just when I was ready to believe the worst about the dog-eat-dog world of commerce, and reminded me that other values could live alongside financial ones. As I came to know Frank, I looked for ways to follow his example at the *Santa Fe Reporter.* Our company was the better for it, a place that looked after its own and recognized that there were higher values than making money—which was also important.

I realized that the exchange between Frank and me was one-way, with all the benefits flowing in my direction. But considering that the *Reporter* was only about one-twentieth the size of Brown County Publishing Company and fifteen years less experienced, there did not seem much that we might give in return. And Frank, generously, asked for nothing. So I just accepted, and appreciated, his help.

Thus I was thrilled for my friend when, in 1984, he attained the goal that had seemed so impossible: a year-end profit for his struggling *News-Chronicle*. It was just a tiny profit, but it was followed the next year by a larger one. The newspaper seemed at last to have turned the corner.

This achievement did not go unnoticed. Under the headline "A Strike Paper That Has Survived," an article in *Editor & Publisher* proclaimed the *News-Chronicle*'s success historic. According to *E&P*, Frank's paper was "the first successfully established competing city daily in the U.S. since World War II." The article traced the *News-Chronicle*'s full chronology, from its origins to its current status as flagship of the Brown County Publishing Company group. And the turning point, the article made clear, was the day in 1976 when Frank Wood stepped in.

By covering its losses with profits from other operations, Frank refused to let the *News-Chronicle* die. He worked day and night to build a sustaining base of advertising revenue, and slowly he progressed. Along the way, the paper amassed "a remarkable collection of journalistic awards." Yet the *News-Chronicle*'s small circulation was a severe handicap. At just eleven thousand copies, it was dwarfed by the Gannett-owned *Press-Gazette,* whose figures were five times larger.

Even so, the *News-Chronicle* was filling the classic role of a second newspaper. "Its size," said *Editor & Publisher,* "hasn't deterred the *N-C* from providing an alternative voice to the people of Green Bay. For example, the writing of the *N-C,* though far from daring, is often critical and sometimes controversial, as it frequently takes opposing stances from the competition. In doing so, the *N-C* stirs debate on issues that otherwise would not exist." And against all the odds, after more than a decade of unceasing hardship, its future finally seemed secure. "The critical thing," observed a University of Wisconsin economics professor, "is that they've carved out a market, and that market has stabilized."

To former staff members quoted in the article, the reason for the *News-Chronicle*'s hard-won stability was summed up in just two words: Frank Wood. "He had this audacious notion that he could somehow pull off a second successful daily in a city this size," said a former reporter. "It seemed like madness." Added another: "He's a great businessman. He has had to be for what he's done." And a third sounded an echo: "I'm not surprised. Frank's a stubborn, tenacious competitor. He found a way to make it work."

The *E&P* article concluded with a flourish: "Today it's doubtful that the citizens of Green Bay dwell on the fact that they have two local daily papers to choose from. But at a time when competing dailies were being swallowed up across the nation, Green Bay became a two-newspaper town."

What Frank had done was indeed remarkable, and this tribute in the leading journal of the newspaper industry was cause for celebration. But the celebration turned out to be premature. Just weeks after the article appeared, the *News-Chronicle*'s fortunes headed south. At first it was a retreat. Soon it was a rout. The advertisers of Green Bay, whose business Frank had cultivated year in and year out, began pulling out of his paper. First it was major accounts—supermarkets, drugstores, general merchandisers. Soon local stores were also vacating. Barely two years after the *News-Chronicle* was hailed as a history-making survivor, its tiny profits had become disastrous losses.

The cause of the nosedive was no mystery to Frank. In his analysis, the story in *E&P* had been a signal to Gannett that the time had come to deal once and for all with this stubborn irritant in Green Bay. The time had come to put the *News-Chronicle* down. As Frank saw it, his alarming loss of business indicated an all-out campaign to deny him every source of advertising in Green Bay, by whatever means necessary. Nothing else could explain why a venture that had been building for years could collapse in months.

I agreed with Frank's analysis. By now I had learned much about Gannett's ways. But I did not know what he could do. For publishers competing against this chain, no alternative was easy: They could get out, they could go under, or they could carry on. For all the years I had known Frank Wood, he had seemed determined to carry on. But now, in a nighttime telephone call in October 1988, after I had opted to let someone else carry on the work I had started in Santa Fe, he was saying what I never expected him to say: *I'm afraid I won't be able to hold the* News-Chronicle *together.*

"It's really that bad?" I said, absorbing his statement.

"It's that bad."

"What are you going to do, Frank?"

"I know what I want to do," he said. Then silence.

"Well, what is it?"

"I want you to come to Green Bay and help me."

The words surprised me. I was not sure what they meant, but I did know one thing: They were not words I wanted to hear.

"I don't get it, Frank. What could I do in Green Bay?"

"What I want you to do in Green Bay," he said, "is what you did in Oregon. I want you to come here and do what you did in Salem."

2

Wind from the North

AH, YES, SALEM . . . SALEM, OREGON, in the winter of 1981.

Albuquerque and Los Angeles were sunny and warm on that Tuesday in February when I made my way by plane to the Pacific Northwest. But over Oregon the skies turned leaden, and as the plane approached Portland, rain obliterated the view from my window. The windows were no better on the creaky bus that took frugal travelers from the airport into downtown Portland. After years in New Mexico's brilliant sunshine, I had almost forgotten what a socked-in rainstorm was like. Packing for the trip, I discovered I no longer seemed to own an umbrella. I did find a raincoat.

From the bus station a taxi took me to the cut-rate motel I had called from the airport. Trips like this were not a regular part of the *Santa Fe Reporter*'s budget, after all, and I needed to save every dollar I could. The one-story motel, tucked between much taller buildings, was modest but presentable. My room was clean and cozy, and the phone and the television worked fine. I called the lawyers to confirm our dinner that evening. Then, with the assistance of mindless daytime TV, I tried to relax. But my thoughts kept running through the swift chain of events that had brought me here, to learn what had doomed a defunct weekly newspaper I had never heard of until a few days before my trip.

"Are you aware of this?" asked the *Reporter*'s advertising director, Didier Raven, handing me an *Editor & Publisher* article headlined "Oregon Weekly Files Antitrust Suit against Gannett."

I skimmed the story. It related that a Salem, Oregon, weekly newspaper called the *Community Press* had sued the chain in federal court, claiming Gannett had intentionally driven it out of business through unspecified "anti-competitive" actions. I noted that the *Community Press* had ceased publication more than two years earlier, late in 1978, and that the *Editor & Publisher* was an old one, from that time. Didier must have pulled it from our stacks.

"So Gannett is hard to get along with," I said. "And sometimes the neighbors complain. This isn't exactly news." Didier stared back at me in a way that made me realize I was missing his point. "OK," I said, "I don't get it."

"Salem," he said, "is where Wayne Vann just came from."

Wayne Vann was the newly appointed president and general manager of Gannett's Santa Fe daily, the *New Mexican*. No stranger to the city, he had been the *New Mexican*'s advertising director in the early 1970s, before the paper was sold in 1975 to Gannett by its owner, an imperious former ambassador to Switzerland named Robert McKinney. Less than a year later Vann was gone, transferred to some other paper in the chain's vast network. But now he had come back, and come back in style: as top man at the bitter crosstown rival of my newspaper.

I knew Wayne Vann. For a short time during his tenure at the *New Mexican* I had worked there, as a writer and editor. I remembered him as a ferocious competitor, seeking always to set new sales records in his department. Unlike many advertising types in the newspaper business, he also had an appreciation of good journalism. He understood that hard-hitting news and commentary could get a town talking about a newspaper, which could lead in turn to even higher sales.

I was hired by the *New Mexican* not long after arriving in Santa Fe in 1971, fresh from four years at one of the nation's best and biggest papers, *Newsday*, on Long Island, New York. Though I had grown tired of big-city life, I was not at all tired of big-city standards of journalism, and was determined to practice them at the Santa Fe paper. Yet my efforts to dig beneath the placid exterior of the news were not welcomed at the *New Mexican*, which was run by a cautious accountant who did not like to make waves.

During our brief association Vann and I had become, if not close friends, at least allies on the job. For his own purposes he supported my tough stories, and I was grateful for his help. When I grew discouraged enough to talk about quitting, he urged me to stay. But the frustration was too much. A year after joining the *New Mexican* I resigned, with dreams of starting what I envisioned as a real newspaper for Santa Fe. And somehow, less than two years later, in June 1974, the *Santa Fe Reporter* was launched on seventy thousand dollars of hard-won investment.

Many times in the first perilous months we just about went under. Terribly undercapitalized, monumentally naive, we barely survived from issue to issue. Helping to make life miserable was Wayne Vann, who seemed obsessed with denying the *Reporter* even a few leftover crumbs of advertising business. Still we managed to squeeze out enough to hang on. And then, mercifully, Vann was promoted out of town when Gannett bought the *New Mexican.*

His successor, a transferred newcomer to Santa Fe, was not nearly as adept at laying claim to the sources of revenue in town. Slowly the *Reporter* made inroads into the *New Mexican,* in advertising sales and particularly in readership. Led by inspired editorial staff members willing to work twelve-hour days for one hundred dollars a week, our free weekly paper was at last bringing Santa Fe the kind of journalism I had dreamed of. We dug deep, hit hard, wrote tough but gracefully—and broke story after story that the daily either ignored or did not know about.

Soon the town was waiting each Wednesday to see what we would stir up that week. And steadily, advertising dollars followed where readers had rushed in. By 1981, when Wayne Vann came back, the *Santa Fe Reporter* was seven years old, firmly grounded, and even making a little money. Yet every bit of it had come hard.

Despite all the growth and progress, the *Reporter* brought in less than a sixth of the *New Mexican*'s $5 million in annual revenues. The daily paper remained highly profitable for its parent chain, while we struggled always to pay down our debt, improve our quality, and inch toward a long-awaited prosperity. And Gannett fought us each step of the way. Apparently even our small share of the market was an affront to the chain. Relentlessly it sought to undermine us, by ridiculing our free circulation, by pressuring advertisers to drop us, by spreading the idea that nobody was reading us—which was laughably untrue.

Lately the *New Mexican* had escalated its game of hardball by starting its own free weekly supplement, delivered to Santa Fe homes on the same day that the *Reporter* came. The move was a curious one, for as long as we had been in existence, the paid daily had sneered at the fact that our paper was free of charge. But the town had responded so well to the content of our pages, and advertisers were getting such good results from our saturation delivery to all their customers, that the Gannett paper was finally forced to offer its own free product. None of it, however, was working. And then Gannett sent Wayne Vann back to town.

His emergence atop the *New Mexican* was cause for concern. Remembering how passionately he played the game of business and how much he wanted to win, I was sure he would prove a rougher opponent than the inept general manager he was replacing. As a precaution, I called a meeting to warn our staff to brace itself. "The return of Wayne Vann is not good news," I said. "He's smart and tough. He knows his way around Santa Fe. And unlike the folks who *have* been running the *New Mexican,* he knows the value of good journalism. Things are going to get harder for us."

"What should we do?" asked a typesetter. "Are you afraid he'll run us out of business?" As I looked over the worried faces in the quiet room, I felt I had overstated the problem. "No, not at all," I replied confidently. "The *Reporter* will be eight years old in June, and we're in for the long haul. If you all just keep doing your jobs as well as you possibly can, I'm sure we'll continue to do fine. But maybe the message I want to leave with you today is that everybody needs to give it an extra push, now that Wayne Vann is back in town."

An amusing memory flitted through my mind. Back when Vann was selling against us years ago, one of his advertising representatives had told me, laughing, that Vann often fired up his sales staff by reading them locker-room speeches of the legendary Green Bay Packer football coach Vince Lombardi, who gained some measure of immortality by saying: "Winning isn't everything—it's the only thing." Well, different strokes for different folks. That was not the *Reporter*'s philosophy, but if it was what drove Wayne, I figured we could hold our own against it. We had when he was trying to nip us in the bud, and now we would have to do so again. It would be hard enough, but it might also be fun.

"No, just work hard—maybe a little harder than ever—and things will be fine," I repeated to the staff. "It's not easy being the second newspaper—but it never has been, and we've done OK so far. I respect Wayne Vann. He plays rough, but he plays by the rules. That's all we ask or need. Now let's get back to work."

In the days after the pep talk I kept meaning to call Vann at the *New Mexican.* Though I did not expect us to become pals, I preferred a cordial footing between his newspaper and mine. Lunch seemed like a good idea, if only to clear the decks. But before I found time for the call, our advertising director confronted me with the story of the defunct weekly in Oregon.

Didier Raven had been with us about two years. A French-born Jew, he had fled France as an infant with his family, to escape the Nazis. In his thirties he moved to Albuquerque and there sold real estate. Tiring of that work, he began thinking about the newspaper business. He became advertising director of a tiny, cantankerous weekly in Albuquerque. Soon it was carrying more ads than ever before. Then he took a similar post with the city's largest shopper. It also swelled to unprecedented size. In newspaper advertising, it seemed that Didier had found his domain. He was a born salesman, with an insistent yet polite manner that made prospects feel they really should do what he suggested. He was a cultured man as well, with an appreciation of good writing, layout, artwork, headlines—the elements of the news craft. Journalism's ability to influence events excited him.

Didier reveled in the ferocious competition for advertisers in a market with more than one paper. He had an affinity for the underdog, and nothing gave him more pleasure than convincing a client to use the little guy in addition to the dominant newspaper. Didier joined the staff in March 1979. Things happened quickly after that. He increased the number of sales reps from three to four. He taught them sophisticated selling techniques. He imposed a dress code on his crew, while writers and typesetters were showing up in blue jeans. When hiring he almost invariably chose attractive young women, who soon were being called "Didier's Angels." And he made sure they knew how to sell advertising—which they did in greater volume than anyone had before.

Prior to Didier's arrival, the *Reporter* had built a solid base of local advertising. First he expanded that base. Then he went hunting for bigger game: giant chain stores, such as Kmart, Sears, J. C. Penney, Montgomery Ward. And slowly he was getting them to test us—with a four-week trial, a preprinted circular, a big ad for a special sale, coupons for items also advertised in the *New Mexican*. In these tests we held our own, and the stores came back for more.

None of the chains abandoned the *New Mexican*. After decades of using it, they had no intention of dropping it. They needed its daily frequency, for promotions at times when the weekly *Reporter* was not published. They also still had reservations about unpaid circulation. The chains were merely splitting their advertising budgets between Santa Fe's two papers, giving a little bit to the *Reporter* but leaving the lion's share with the *New Mexican*.

For us, this was cause for rejoicing. Even a small slice of the chains' business meant a dramatic leap in revenue. But for Gannett, accustomed to 100 percent of everything, it was cause for retaliation. Both Didier and I were certain that Wayne Vann had been sent to put a halt to our growth. But where I was apprehensive, Didier seemed paranoid. While I expected things to get tougher, he was expecting sabotage. Knowing Wayne, I feared him as a competitor. Didier, who had never met him, apparently felt he was an assassin.

The first weeks after Wayne's return brought no discernible change in the advertising volume of the *Reporter* or the *New Mexican*. The same could not be said, however, of the tension level in the old brick building that housed our offices. Didier was frustrated by my confidence that if we just worked harder than ever, we could withstand whatever Vann had in mind for us. I in turn was annoyed by Didier's melodramatic insistence that my former colleague, whom I remembered as a good old boy at heart, was an agent straight from hell.

"We've already taken their best shot, that free weekly supplement, and laughed it off," I pointed out to Didier. "What could they possibly throw at us worse than that?"

"That's just what I expect to find out," he shot back.

I wanted to be aware of our competition and to respond intelligently. But I did not want to invest too much energy in trying to beat the *New Mexican* in the game of business. My fulfillment came from using words, exposing corruption, shaping raw talent, putting out an exemplary newspaper. Didier, however, needed an adversary, against which to measure his own success. Vann's arrival had underlined this difference between us, and there seemed no easy way to resolve it. We continued to work together, but each felt the other was mistaken. The impasse was not broken until Didier hit me with the *Editor & Publisher* article.

This was a gauntlet thrown at my feet. I had to respond. Instinctively, I responded as a journalist, by seeking more information. The same day that Didier showed me the story, I was on the phone to the publisher of the defunct weekly. What I got from him, however, was not what I expected. I expected a bitter, seething man, full of indignation for what Gannett had done to him and eager to share the details with anyone who asked—particularly a fellow publisher facing a similar threat. Instead, Richard Dickey was tight-lipped.

He was courteous, and he understood my reason for calling. But he provided almost no information beyond what was in the article. Yes, he was president of a company called Community Publications Inc., based in Portland, Oregon. Yes, from 1976 to 1978 CPI had published a free weekly newspaper called the *Community Press* in Salem, sixty miles away. Yes, it had competed with a Gannett daily. Yes, the *Community Press* had prospered briefly, then gone out of business. Yes, CPI had filed an antitrust suit against Gannett, seeking from $12 million to $18 million in damages, claiming that the chain had "systematically set out to destroy" the weekly and did so through "extremely callous" means. Yes, he expected to win.

Yet when I asked how Gannett had killed his paper, Dickey clammed up. The judge in the case had imposed a gag order, he said. If he disobeyed it, he could face contempt-of-court charges. I tried to get more out of him, by rephrasing questions, by asking for generalizations or hints, by promising confidentiality. But no matter how I reapproached the subject, he evaded it. As a newspaperman himself he knew all my tricks, and was not going to fall for them. Finally he suggested I call his lawyers. Beyond that, he was sorry but he simply could not give me any details.

Grasping for something, anything, that would help, I asked in closing if Wayne Vann had played a key role in the "systematic destruction" of the *Community Press*. Dickey paused a long time before answering. "Let's just say he was Gannett's advertising director at that time," he finally said. "That's on the record."

"Then off the record and strictly in your own opinion," I concluded the frustrating conversation, "do you think we have reason to be concerned now that he's been sent to Santa Fe?"

Again Dickey paused. "In my opinion," he then said, stressing the words, "yes. You definitely have reason to be concerned."

Before calling Dickey's attorneys I collected my wits. It was imperative to get more information from the lawyers than I had from their client. But I was not hopeful. In my experience, lawyers rarely made comments they did not intend to make. When I did call the case's lead attorney, Al Malanca, an hour or so later, Dickey had already told him to expect to hear from me. But this advance warning proved a blessing in disguise. Instead of automatically refusing to talk, Malanca had had time to consider. Apparently Dickey did sympathize with my plight, and had asked Malanca to assist in any way he could, short of violating the gag order. But that was the obstacle.

My reception from the lawyer was cordial and helpful, up to a point. I learned some useful procedural details about the case, its predicted timetable, the laws on which it was based. I got more background on CPI and Dickey. Malanca said his firm had taken the case on a contingency basis, a sign that he was hopeful of winning. But each time I asked just what had Gannett done to cause the lawsuit, I was politely stonewalled.

"Look, I understand your need, and I'm not offended by your questions," Malanca said. "But I can't give you that information. We expect to win this case when it goes to trial, and I'm not going to jeopardize our position by compromising the gag order."

Just as he understood my persistence, I appreciated Malanca's caution. It would be reckless of him—not to mention unlawful—to divulge sealed information, over the telephone, to a stranger, who happened to be a newspaper editor, with a clear motivation to reveal what Gannett had done to destroy the *Community Press*. No, I did not expect this obviously prudent attorney to come across with embargoed evidence. But I still had an urgent need to get that information, even if I did not know how.

My calls, first to Dickey and now to Malanca, had stirred fear inside me, all the more frightening because it was so vague. I had to find out what Gannett was planning for the *Santa Fe Reporter*. There was no point in holding Malanca on the phone, but I wanted to give him the question I had put to Dickey. "Do you feel," I asked the lawyer, "that we have reason to be worried about Wayne Vann coming to Santa Fe?"

"That much I can tell you, because it's just my opinion," he said, deliberately. "And in my opinion, you have every reason in the world to be worried."

Something clammy moved in my stomach. At that instant I knew I had to go to Oregon. What I would do after getting there I was not sure. But clearly there was no more I could learn by telephone from either Dickey or Malanca, and I did not know who else to call. Maybe if I went there I would make some contacts. It was the only straw I saw, and I grasped at it. "Look, I've got to know more," I blurted to Malanca. "I'll be coming to Portland next Tuesday. Can you meet with me then?"

"Well, sure," he replied. "But you realize I can't tell you anything more then than I've already told you."

"Yes, I know, but I need something more to go on—a clue, a hint, anything I can follow up myself. You know what you can and can't say. Just meet with me, and I'll take it from there."

"OK, then how about dinner Tuesday night? I'll bring along my associate on the case. But don't get your hopes up."

Within the hour, I had my plane reservations.

Into the Storm

3

THE STORM IN PORTLAND KEPT getting worse. In ten years in New Mexico, I had not seen anything like it. Hour after hour the rain came down, and the wind grew ever fiercer. As I dashed from the motel to the taxi, my head got drenched. Below the raincoat, my pants were soaked. The streets flowed like rivers, over the curbs, and my feet too were soaked. Another dash through the tempest took me windblown and dripping into the restaurant. Upon my entrance, two earlier arrivals broke out in grins. They turned out to be Al Malanca and his colleague on the *Community Press* case, John Guadnola.

As soon as the waiter took our orders, things got testy. Both parties were braced for a friendly/adversarial encounter. I was determined to come away with something I could use. I hoped that the mellowness of drinks and dinner might make the lawyers more forthcoming. For their part, they wanted to help, but were ever mindful of the restrictions of the gag order.

They had no problem with giving me a quick history of the *Community Press*'s rise and fall. It was started as a Wednesday weekly in March 1976. Seven months later it added a Sunday edition. It was delivered free to the seventy thousand homes in Salem. Most of Salem's retailers, including the chains, had supported the *Community Press*. The newspaper had in fact been started at the request of advertisers. In 1975 a delegation of major merchandisers visited Dickey at CPI, to beg him to establish some competition in Salem, where the market was controlled by two Gannett dailies, the *Oregon Statesman* and the *Capital Journal*. The two papers were run as one financial unit.

Flaunting its monopoly status, Gannett had in 1975 imposed a staggering 43 percent rate increase, accompanied by new lows of arrogance and shoddiness. Ads were full of errors. When mistakes were caught on proofs, no second proof was provided. Deadlines were early and rigid, and late ads were not run on the desired day. In place of trained sales representatives, "dispatch runners" were the only contact with many accounts. The papers charged an unusual "make-ready fee" above the normal cost for distributing preprinted inserts, though no extra work was involved. Nor did Gannett observe the practice, common to newspapers throughout the country, of giving credit to reduce the per-inch rate of advertisers who exceeded the volume of an annual contract.

Gannett's attitude toward its clients in Salem was simple: Take it or leave it. With no other place to turn, the clients were taking it—until they talked Dickey into starting the *Community Press*. Two months after its debut the new paper had almost a fifth of the advertising market, and its future seemed unbounded.

In mid-1976, Gannett placed a new publisher in charge of the Salem operation. His name was N. S. "Buddy" Hayden, and he previously had headed the Gannett newspaper in Huntington, West Virginia. Hayden chose Wayne Vann from the chain's Santa Fe paper as his advertising director. Two years later, the *Community Press* was out of business.

This was scary. "What did they do?" I asked nervously. "Sweetheart deals? Price-slashing? What?"

"Some of that might have been involved, but we can't be more specific," was Malanca's answer. "Now you're getting into the area covered by the gag order."

"That damn thing again. Just what does it cover, anyway?"

"A lot," said Guadnola. "All the evidence gathered for the lawsuit, subpoenaed or voluntary: the documents, the depositions, the testimony of Hayden, Vann, Gannett's president Al Neuharth, all the people representing CPI. Anybody who even talks about it could be held in contempt. And that includes the lawyers."

"But why? I thought that was what a lawsuit was supposed to do—get stuff like this on the public record."

"That's the theory, all right," Malanca said with a crooked smile. "As far as we're concerned, we'd like to see everything in the file out in the open. It would help us if it all came out. But Gannett got it sealed. It contained 'trade secrets,' their lawyers said. Revealing them might damage Gannett's 'competitive position' in the marketplace."

"Yeah, but those trade secrets are what I've got to find out," I said. "Will they come out at the trial?"

"Yes, they will—if the case goes to trial," Malanca said. "There's always the chance that Gannett will settle instead. That would be too bad, in a way, because what they did ought to be told. But if Gannett offered enough money, it would be up to our client to decide."

"Well, what should I do in the meantime? How can I find out what they did, before they do it to us?"

"You might go to Salem and see who'll talk to you there," Guadnola suggested. "That's out of our hands. You never know."

"All right. Who should I talk to?"

"We can't tell you that."

"But unless I have names or leads to people with something to say, it will just be a fishing expedition," I groaned. "It could take a long time. And I have to be back home on Monday."

"Sorry. We just can't give you any names."

I was getting nowhere. "Have other newspapers written about what happened in Salem?" I asked.

"Well, the *Community Press* announced the lawsuit in its final issue," Malanca said. "But it didn't say anything you don't already know. The Gannett papers dutifully reported the suit, as briefly as possible. Not much help there."

Guadnola was more helpful. "Come to think of it, there was a pretty good story in an alternative weekly here in Portland, the *Willamette Week*. You could probably get that."

It was something, but not much. Dinner was winding down, and I had little more to work with than when it started. "Is there anything else at all you can tell me?" I asked over coffee. "I can't do much with what I've got so far." I tried to keep my voice firm, but I heard a pleading note in it. "You do understand that I'm trying to save my own newspaper, don't you?"

The lawyers exchanged glances. Finally Malanca spoke, deliberately. "Do you know about the Dobermans?"

"The what?"

"I can't tell you any more than that. But you might want to ask about them in Salem. The Dobermans."

"And while you're at it," Guadnola added, "you might also ask about Operation Demolition."

"You mean ask the advertisers, or city officials, or the police, or who?"

"That's all we're going to say," Malanca replied. "It may be over the line already, but I don't think so. As far as I'm concerned, everything in the goddamn file should be revealed to the public. That would answer all your questions. But the judge doesn't agree, and she has sealed it up. I wish she hadn't. But I'm not going to fool around with the gag order. That's just the way it is—and I think it's time to call it a night."

Suddenly I realized I had been overlooking the obvious. "The file at the federal courthouse," I asked, slipping into my damp raincoat, "is it totally sealed, or is at least some of the evidence available to look at?"

"I couldn't say," Malanca shrugged. "We have our own file, so we don't keep up with the one in the courthouse. There might be something left in it. Why not take a look? Couldn't hurt anything. The name of the case is *Community Publications Inc. vs. Gannett Co.,* the docket number is Civil Action 78–865, and the name of the presiding judge is Helen Frye. Happy hunting, my friend."

As we left the restaurant, the rain was coming down even harder than before.

4

The Secret File

NEXT MORNING, THE MOTEL TELEVISION confirmed that the storm had been ferocious even by Portland standards. Much of the city was flooded, and the winds had toppled a radio tower. But now it was over, and the sun was shining through scattered clouds. The city map showed that both the federal court and *Willamette Week* were within walking distance. I called the weekly newspaper and got the writer of the Salem story. He was friendly but of course was on deadline, and could not talk. He agreed to leave a copy of his article at the paper's front desk. "That's a hell of a story and I only got part of it," he said in closing. "Good luck."

I called Richard Dickey at Community Publications. He could see me only briefly, on Friday afternoon, but had asked a subordinate named Larry Miller to give me more time. He reminded me, however, that everyone at CPI was bound by the gag order. Each useful tidbit I gathered came with a warning that it would remain just that—a tidbit.

I walked to the offices of *Willamette Week,* where the promised article was waiting. It was a big page-one story, and its headlines were not comforting: "A Death in the Family: One Paper Left in Salem—Did Gannett Kill All the Rest?" Over three cups of coffee in a restaurant, I read the long report.

Published almost two years after the demise of *Community Press,* the article was not really about the failed weekly. It focused instead on the recent shutdown of one of Gannett's two dailies in Salem. To economize, the chain was now publishing only one paper in Oregon's capital city. Though called a merger, the move essentially terminated the ninety-two-year-old *Capital Journal.* Many observers were cynical. "Insiders and former insiders at the two dailies see a pattern in Gannett's action," the article stated. "All over the country the big chain has been buying up newspapers in small-to-medium-sized towns. The objective, the insiders allege, is to monopolize the smaller markets, cut costs at the expense of news coverage, and drive out any competition.

" 'This is just another example of an out-of-state chain, whose primary objective is to make a profit, refusing to give news coverage first priority,' charges Robin Olsen, former publisher of the Salem-based *Oregon Observer*, an alternative weekly that was also forced to close its doors in May. Adds Alfred Jones, a 27-year news veteran with the *Capital Journal* and one of 31 employees laid off in the merger, 'Despite all the protests when Gannett bought the papers that they weren't planning to kill the *Capital Journal*, we knew they were lying.' "

Pretty strong stuff. But I needed to learn exactly how Gannett had eliminated the weekly competition. Unfortunately, the *Community Press* was mentioned only briefly, and in terms that seemed familiar. The defunct weekly was seeking damages for "unfair and illegal anti-competitive and monopolistic practices by Gannett in Salem that drove it out of business there."

But the next paragraph did add something new: "While the case has not yet come to trial, *Willamette Week* has discovered a memorandum filed in federal court on June 27 by Community Publications that lays out much of its case against Gannett in Salem. The memorandum makes two basic charges: first, that Gannett's Salem operation was the beneficiary of a discriminatory newsprint contract from Boise Cascade Corp., giving it a 10 percent price break over market prices; and second, that Gannett brought in N. S. 'Buddy' Hayden as publisher, who, 'pursuant to instructions from Gannett,' set up what was called 'Operation Demolition,' in short, 'an intensive campaign to destroy CPI in Salem.' In this campaign, the operatives were labeled 'Dobermans' in internal Gannett correspondence."

Operation Demolition! The Dobermans! Plus a sweetheart deal with a supplier that played footsie with Gannett for an unspecified payback. But maddeningly, the article did not elaborate, moving on into a lengthy discussion of Salem's new status as a one-newspaper city. Gannett's lawyer, reported *Willamette Week*, "wasn't in town to comment." My need to know was mounting. Yet more than anything so far, this article encouraged me. It provided a first peek into the secret court file. And where *Willamette Week* had discovered this memorandum, there was no telling what else might be lying around. I walked the few blocks to the federal courthouse.

The clerk in the records room, a young black woman, took my written request for the file on Civil Action 78–865. She said she would bring it as soon as she got a chance. When she did, my heart sank. It was only a quarter of an inch thick, and held nothing but procedural papers: notice that the lawsuit had been filed, announcements of the time and place of hearings, a statement of the nature of the case, from the initial filing.

The most telling document was the gag order itself, which spelled out in detail just how much evidence Gannett did not want anyone to see. "The term confidential material shall include," the protective order stated, "(a) all documents, interrogatory answers, deposition testimony and other information or material produced or otherwise made available to the parties to this litigation; (b) all copies, extracts, reports, studies, complete or partial summaries and other documents or materials made or prepared from confidential material; and (c) all transcripts, briefs, memoranda, exhibits, and other pleadings or writings which include, summarize or otherwise disclose any confidential material." It was as bad as I had feared, and worse. Another dry well.

So that my trip to the courthouse would not be a total waste, I wanted to copy the protective order and a few other papers. I found I could not do it myself. When I asked where the copier was, the clerk told me to show her what I needed. She would make the copies as soon as she got a chance, at twenty cents a page. When she brought them back my business at the courthouse seemed finished, with almost nothing to show for it. From old habit, I made a last feeble attempt to get more. "Are you sure this is the complete file?" I asked the clerk. "This is a big case, and evidence has been coming in for more than two years. This can't be all of it. Is there anywhere else to look?"

"Let me see," she replied, and went to a card catalog. I was sure she would say the reason the file was so thin was that the case had been sealed—at which point I would thank her and be on my way. Instead she returned with a three-by-five-inch index card and said, "According to this, the main file has been taken to the chambers of Judge Frye. You could ask for it there, if you want to."

I knew why the file was in the judge's chambers, and I knew there was no point in seeking it there. But what the hell, I figured, I might as well get rebuffed one more time. At least then I could say I made every effort. I rode the slow elevator to the fifth floor, where Judge Frye's chambers were located. Outside the door I took a deep breath. Then clutching my briefcase, I entered. Judge Frye's chambers seemed more like a sitting room than a legal office. A sofa and a couple of stuffed chairs, plus two smaller wooden ones, surrounded a long coffee table. Three people were seated, reading magazines. The judge's receptionist was busy with someone else, so I waited politely for my turn.

"May I help you?" asked a brisk, dressed-for-success blond woman who suddenly entered the room from a side door.

Here goes nothing, I thought. "Yes, please. I need to see this file." I handed her the case number. "The records room clerk said it was in Judge Frye's chambers." I had anticipated this moment, and I knew what would follow. This woman, whoever she was, would either tell me that the file was not available or would ask why I wanted it, then send me packing. I had decided to identify myself merely as a reporter rather than the publisher of a paper competing with Gannett. Such a statement would be truthful. But I had no illusions that the judge would give any sort of journalist access to the file.

"The receptionist is really backed up. Let me see if I can find it," the woman said, disappearing through the door that had brought her in. I wondered if she might be the judge, but she seemed too young to have enough experience for the federal bench. More likely she was a recent law school graduate, clerking for the judge.

"Here it is, or at least part of it. It was on Judge Frye's desk, so I guess she's been going over it. There may be more, but I couldn't find it. See if what you need is in here. If not, we'll look some more. But one thing—you can't take it out of this office. If the judge wants it, we'll need it right away."

She handed me a stack of documents more than a foot thick. I hoped my astonishment did not show. As calmly as possible I asked, "I may need to take some notes. Where should I work?"

"I'm afraid we don't have a good place for that. Right here in the sitting room is the best we can do. Sorry." What I wanted was a closet—but you don't always get what you want. Thanking her, I placed the stack on the coffee table. Suddenly she had an afterthought. "What case is this, anyway?" she asked, picking up the top document.

That's it, I thought. The end of the road. Right now. "Oh, yes. Community Publications vs. Gannett. That's an interesting one." Then she was gone. There could be only two explanations. Either they took me for a lawyer on the case or the file was not flagged as sealed, and the clerk was not aware of the gag order. Whatever, it was not my problem—and my need was to see what the file held.

Earlier arrivals had claimed all the chairs, so I settled onto the couch.

I picked up the inch-thick top document, and almost gasped. In bright red ink, its first page was stamped:

CONFIDENTIAL
SUBJECT TO PROTECTIVE ORDER IN
CIVIL ACTION NO. 78–865
UNITED STATES DISTRICT COURT FOR THE
DISTRICT OF OREGON
DO NOT DUPLICATE

I flipped the document over, so the red letters would not show, and caught my breath. How had the clerk overlooked that? And how long would it be before she or some other member of the judge's staff noticed it as they passed my painfully public working place? It seemed that my project could be nipped as soon as anyone asked what I was doing. Therefore, my course was clear: to proceed as rapidly and as casually as possible while I had the chance.

Hiding the CONFIDENTIAL stamp whenever it appeared, I flipped through the file. Some documents were legal briefs, seeking to establish or discredit the jurisdiction of U.S. District Court as the proper venue. Much of the material was obscure, lists of alleged violations of numbered sections of the Sherman, Clayton, and Robinson-Patman antitrust acts. Everything was in legalese.

The first hour brought more questions than answers. Many documents awaited, but my enthusiasm was sagging. I was sure we were in trouble, but was no closer to a plan for coping with it.

Several long depositions from potential witnesses were next in the stack. I scanned the first, by someone named Vernon Daniel. My eye was caught by a familiar name: Wayne Vann. In his deposition, Daniel testified that he had sold ads for the Salem newspapers for almost twenty years, but had resigned shortly after Vann became advertising director. Then he explained why:

> **Question:** As a member of the sales staff, were you given any specific instructions as to practices you should engage in to combat the *Community Press*?
>
> **Daniel:** I remember one sales meeting where Wayne Vann had instructed us to go out and create rumors about the *Community Press,* specifically that they were going broke and going out of business very soon. He and Buddy Hayden had another meeting immediately following that, a sales meeting, and on the way out I remarked to Wayne, I

said, "Well, you know, we shouldn't be doing this. If we rephrase the intent of what we're saying, what we're saying is, we should create lies about the *Community Press,* and I don't think we should be a party to that."

I don't remember his remarks, but he really didn't agree with what I was trying to tell him. The following week at the sales meeting, he gave a $5 spiff to a salesman by the name of Green, because he had started the rumor and it had filtered back through an advertiser that the *Community Press* was going broke.

Q. What is a spiff?

A. It is a word for achieving certain goals. If a person sold a large section or something like that, they might give you a $5 or $10 spiff.

Q. It was just a form of bonus?

A. Yes.

Q. Was it your understanding, at the time that Mr. Vann gave the instructions to spread rumors, that he had any knowledge at all as to whether or not there was any basis for believing the *Community Press* was going broke?

A. They were constantly monitoring on a weekly basis who was advertising in the *Community Press,* the size of the ad, and so on. But to my knowledge, they certainly wouldn't know how much money the *Community Press* had behind it, or the intent, how much they were going to spend, anything of that nature.

Q. Did you understand Mr. Vann to be telling you and the other sales-men that you should spread these rumors without regard to whether they were true?

A. In essence, yes.

I opened another folder. It held photocopies of what appeared to be internal correspondence within the Gannett Company. One letter was ad-dressed to the chain's president, Allen Neuharth, and signed by Gannett's Salem publisher, Buddy Hayden. "Now that I feel containment has been accomplished," Hayden wrote, "our goal is to fatally cripple the *Community Press,* and to accomplish this we have instituted 'operation demolition.'" In the same folder was a long memo from Vann to Gannett's Salem sales staff. It began: "OPERATION DEMOLITION/13-Week Display Sales Program With a BANG!!! It is important in any aggressive sales organization to have a positive sales program to actively attack other media, namely the *Community Press.*"

There was no mistaking what I had struck at last: pay dirt, an excruci-atingly explicit lode of information on how the nation's biggest newspaper chain operates when it goes in for the kill. Included in the rich vein was testimony from staff members, advertisers, and people in Salem, plus dozens of items from Gannett's files: memos, billing statements, internal letters, many tracing all the way from headquarters. Almost every document showed that Gannett had deliberately destroyed a small competitor.

Like the contents, the extent of the file overwhelmed me. There was far too little time to deal with it. I did not even know how much time I had, for at any moment someone might ask me to explain what I was doing, and then the game would be over. But even if I were left alone, the clock was ticking rapidly. Lunchtime was approaching. Already it was Wednesday. On Friday afternoon I had an appointment at CPI. My return flight was booked for the weekend, and I wanted to visit Salem in the meantime. But now I had an even greater need: to read and absorb, and somehow take with me, the information in this thick file.

There was one easy way to get it all done: make photocopies of everything in the file, then flee the courthouse. I gladly would have paid the cost, but this alternative was not available. Almost every document was stamped CONFIDENTIAL—DO NOT DUPLICATE. Asking to get around that command would be inviting disaster. Even if my workplace were not such a fishbowl, even if I could take the file outside the judge's chambers, I remembered that the courthouse had no self-serve copiers. If I asked the clerk downstairs to reproduce the sealed items, she would have to get authorization—which would also be the end of the road.

No, my only choice was clear—and nerve-racking and tedious at the same time. I must sit in Judge Frye's reception area, in view of staff and visitors, and copy every essential document by hand. Nor could I rush through them in my usual crazy shorthand. In this matter I would not have the luxury of recalling the gist of the moment and filling in the details from memory. Each item must be taken down verbatim, in handwriting that could be precisely deciphered later. There would be no second chance.

I pulled a yellow legal pad from my briefcase, and began.

5 |

Dobermans and Demolition

I FORCED MY HAND TO write as fast as it could, while I maintained a calm demeanor. Considering the information I was transcribing, this was no small achievement. There before me was everything the lawyers had hinted about. And more. I began with Operation Demolition, launched in the Christmas season of 1977. It was explained in Vann's memo to his staff:

OPERATION DEMOLITION
13-Week Display Sales Program
With a BANG!!!

It is important in any aggressive sales organization to have a positive sales program to actively attack other media, namely the *Community Press* . . .

You will be given a list of accounts which have published ads in the *Community Press* during the past four weeks. This is your BASE LIST.

When an advertiser is *demolished* from the *Community Press,* you receive a code C for credit of $10.00 per account each week the account stays demolished. (But the $10 credit is lost for each week the ad goes back into the *CP*—that is, it is taken away.)

The whole idea of the program is to reduce or eliminate each of the advertisers on your base list, while at the same time you keep additional advertisers from advertising in the *Community Press*. The more successful you are in this effort, the more money you will accumulate during the program, and earn extra Christmas cash.

Example: If you have 10 advertisers on your base list, and you eliminate five and keep them out of the *Community Press* for 13 weeks, you could earn $650. Let's see how the program works. [An example is given.]

Your Base List accounts do not have any value until you demolish (remove) the account from the *Community Press* the first time. Until that occurs, the account will carry the code I, for inactive.

On and on the long memo went. Beyond individual incentives for the Dobermans, Operation Demolition also provided bonuses for collective

2

performance, to heighten group motivation. Under the plan, every sales-person's final cash bonus would depend on the total number of accounts "demolished" during the thirteen-week period. Near the end of the memo, its main point was reiterated:

> REMEMBER—We are talking about the *numbers* of accounts, NOT LINAGE—So the large advertisers running a lot of space are still only one advertiser. It is quite possible for you to reduce the total numbers of advertisers by 75% OR MORE.

Before it was implemented, Operation Demolition was submitted to Gannett headquarters. There it met with warm approval. A congratulatory memo was sent to Vann by Paul B. Flynn, corporate director of marketing services:

> I like this. It's a tough contest, but gives the salesperson a big, budgetable incentive, and pays off before Christmas.
> Best of all, it targets in on *Community Press.*

The file showed a relentless attempt to drive even the smallest advertisers out of the weekly. Numerous documents demonstrated it, including a memo sent to Gannett's sales staff shortly before the *Community Press* folded. It was signed by retail advertising manager Jody Carson, who worked under Vann:

> March 22, 1978
> The *Community Press* knows how important "meat and potatoes" accounts are to them. Especially in light of the fact that they are losing more and more major accounts.
> Once we start eliminating the small "meat and potatoes" accounts out of the *CP,* they will have a very difficult time surviving.
> Let's make a real effort to keep the small accounts out of the CP.

As I took down the evidence, I felt a fear of being caught. For all I knew, copying the secret files was contempt of court. But I would worry about that later. Right now I had to get as much material as possible, while the getting was good. "What's that you're so interested in?" the blond clerk was sure to ask, sooner or later. "Oh my God, that's a sealed case! I never should have given it to you." She would seize my pad and briefcase. Then she would tell me to wait, while she called security.

I could not determine whether my fears were reasonable under the circumstances or ludicrous. But I was sure my work would be halted immediately if anyone got curious and questioned me. Thus every half-hour or forty-five minutes I went to the men's room, tore the notes from my pad, and hid them in my pockets. The authorities might take my pad, but unless they frisked me too, I might get out with something. Each time I returned, I was relieved to see that the file had not been whisked away. And back to work I went.

Another Gannett tactic, according to the file, was providing free advertising to keep business out of the weekly. One folder showed that more than six thousand dollars' worth was given to a supermarket, on condition that it stop using the *Community Press*. Gathered as evidence were a letter and a memo from the Gannett publisher:

Mr. Bill Armintrout (Private)
Owner/Manager
Quality Food Market/Thriftway
625 Marion Street
Salem, Oregon 97301

Dear Bill:
    In accordance with our discussion in January concerning Thrift-way's participation in our FOOD WEEK promotion, applicable charges for February were $6290.90 (copy of statement enclosed).
    A credit of $629.09 will appear for the next 10 consecutive months—March through December—which will provide the total credit as we discussed.
                                        —Buddy
                                        (N. S. Hayden)

To: Mike Hertz [Gannett's Salem business manager]
From: N. S. Hayden
    Please arrange to have a $629.09 credit issued once each month for the next 10 consecutive months to account 1578035—Thriftway Stores.
    This should not be charged back against revenue, but should instead be charged to account 22–0630, department promotion in advertising.

There was more, and I took it all down. Hours passed. Lunchtime came and went, but I was too wired to feel hunger. When earlier visitors left, I claimed the coffee table as my desk. Between the file and the legal pad, my work spread out over almost all its space. Other business swirled around me. Though immersed in my task, I tried to be aware of the general hubbub, if only to be ready for the inevitable moment of apprehension. A stream of attorneys, each looking far more lawyerly than I, flowed through. Some just dropped off items at the reception desk. Some were shown into the judge's private chamber. Whenever one took a seat near me, I was certain he or she would be working on the Gannett case and would demand to know what I was doing with the file. But none of them said anything at all to me.

From time to time Judge Frye emerged from her inner sanctum. A pleasant-looking, graying woman, she had an air of friendliness. She chatted easily with her staff and visitors, and laughed often. But each time she passed I ducked my head, fearful she would make a courteous inquiry that would blow my cover. Even more, I expected her to send for the file. But she, too, did not interrupt me.

Finally the court's quitting time, 4:30, arrived. Sure that I would never get the file again if it went back onto the judge's desk, I had devised a strategy. Now to see if it worked. At two minutes past the designated time, I approached the receptionist, who was pointedly covering her typewriter. "I didn't get finished with my work," I said apologetically. "But I hate to ask you to lug that big file back and forth. How about if I just left it there in the corner, and came back first thing in the morning, before it gets in anybody's way?"

"That would be all right," she said, relieved that this all-day visitor was not creating after-hours work for her.

"What time does the office open?" I asked. "Nine o'clock?"

"No, this is a federal agency. We open at eight-thirty."

"Fine. I'll be here at eight-thirty sharp," I smiled. "Thanks so much for your help."

Out on the street, with my briefcase and pockets laden with "trade secrets" that the nation's biggest newspaper chain had suppressed, I felt almost frenzied. Then I felt weak. I realized that all I had eaten that day was three cups of coffee, before heading for the courthouse. I had dinner at a Chinese restaurant, then walked the streets of Portland to calm myself. I slipped into a movie theater. I kept thinking that my briefcase, on the seat beside me, might be snatched at any second. I knew such thoughts were crazy, but they would not subside.

Back at the motel, lying in bed trying to sleep, I felt in my bones that the *Santa Fe Reporter* was next on Gannett's list. Once they unleashed their Dobermans and their Operation Demolition against us, we would not have a chance. Even with all the resources of a multimillion-dollar parent company behind it, the *Community Press* had died. And we had no such resources.

In the black Oregon night, I knew as a certainty that my newspaper and its small proud band of believers had been marked for elimination by cold-eyed men two thousand miles from Santa Fe, at Gannett headquarters in Rochester, New York—not because we had really hurt them, but because we were holding their Santa Fe profits below the margin they desired. I could not see how we would survive. A profound sadness settled upon me.

I knew I needed sleep, to fortify me for the long day's work ahead in the secret file. But as the hours crept by I got no sleep. Instead there came a cascade of memories—of where the *Santa Fe Reporter* had come from, what it had endured, and the life that beat inside it.

6

"Not a Bad Job"

THE TIME WAS JANUARY 1971, *the air was cold and clear, the road ahead dry and fast, and my wife Laurie Knowles and I were leaving behind the life of New York City journalists. She had worked at* Women's Wear Daily, *I had worked at* Newsday. *Both of us had done well, and our prospects were bright. We still loved the news business, but we were weary of life in the big city. We also were disillusioned with the New York mentality, which measured someone's worth only in terms of income and job status. So with two thousand dollars in the bank, out we set, for far-off New Mexico, where we knew no one, to taste adventure and make a new life. I was twenty-nine, Laurie twenty-five, and we had been married one year.*

Leaving Newsday *had not been easy. As far back as I could remember, I had always wanted to be a journalist. Where this desire came from, I could not say. Growing up in rural Georgia, I had not known anyone in that line of work. But while the boyhood heroes of my chums were cowboys, firemen, or bold Confederate raiders, I could imagine nothing more romantic than a tough-talking reporter. While a cowboy might save the ranch, and a fireman might save the pretty girl from a burning building, a newsman would save the whole town from evil politicians or racketeers, with nothing on his side but the truth—and the power of the press.*

Beginning in the fifth grade in a little rural school, I got my first newspaper job. Or rather, I created it. Every Friday afternoon I thumb-tacked onto the class bulletin board a hand-penciled, loose-leaf-sheet journal called The Torch. *It had the weather, sports, comic strips, and that week's news of the classroom. No teacher assigned me the task, I got no grade for it, and often it kept me long after school. But it was far more important than my class work.*

Throughout my school years I never lost sight of the dream. I read every book about journalism I could find. I thrilled to its legends and legendary figures: John Peter Zenger, Thomas Paine, Benjamin Franklin, Horace Greeley, Joseph Pulitzer, Ernie Pyle, William Allen White, the brave Ralph McGill sounding the call for racial justice in my own Deep South state.

At Vanderbilt University I was editor of the campus newspaper. Three years later I was hired by Newsday. *Named by* Time *magazine as one of the nation's ten best newspapers,* Newsday *was by any measure outstanding. Under the leadership of publisher Bill Moyers, it was principled, bold, innovative, creative, and superbly professional, and its pay scale was among the highest anywhere. My first year there,* Newsday *won the Pulitzer Prize for public service. Other Pulitzers followed.*

My first two years at Newsday *were wonderful. But then something began to gnaw at me, and I knew what it was. Though I lived in Manhattan, one of the most exciting places on Earth, my work was on Long Island,* Newsday's *home base. And Long Island was a sad place, terrified of the perceived horrors of the very thing that defined its suburban identity: New York City. The residents of Long Island were afraid of many things: blacks, Puerto Ricans, high-rise buildings, low-rent housing, drugs, the Mob, overcrowding—anything that might shatter the illusion that they had made good their escape from The City. Though miles away, the skyscrapers of Manhattan cast a long shadow, which ran the full 118-mile length of Long Island.*

I understood these fears. Indeed, I wrote many stories about them. But after a while, they got me down. There was something negative about Long Island. Instead of being itself, it consumed its energy not being something else, namely New York City. And there was no hope that things would ever be different. The spaces had all been filled, the pieces were all in place. No matter how brave the work of the reporter, this was a town that could not be saved. It was already lost, in its own mentality. "This is not the place for me," I concluded regretfully. "Even if it means leaving a great newspaper, I cannot pour my life's juices into a place such as this."

By the fourth year, even Manhattan's seductions had worn thin. The noise, rudeness, strikes, smog, which once had been accepted as parts of the whole, had become unceasing irritants. I longed for open spaces, clean air, surprise glimpses of beauty, room to move around: the things I had known at other times in my life. On a long western vacation Laurie and I agreed we both were ready to go seeking such things. And so we left.

In May of 1971 we arrived in Santa Fe, with five hundred dollars left. We meant to stay only a few days, before pushing on to a bigger city such as Albuquerque, or maybe Denver, where we could find work. We pitched a tent in the Black Rock Canyon campground of the Santa Fe National Forest. Then instead of moving on, we left it standing. We took jobs at the local racetrack, Laurie making sandwiches, I tending bar. We had fallen under Santa Fe's spell.

Butt-up against a magnificent range of twelve-thousand-foot mountains, Santa Fe was high, cool, old, green, brown, pretty, lively, rustic, and sophisticated at the same time. Best of all, it was splendidly laid-back, largely unconcerned with the values we were fleeing. The first dozen people we met in Santa Fe, it seemed, had no visible means of support, and no visible worries about it. Dropouts from the rat race like us, they drove school buses, waited tables, hired on as laborers or handymen, tended art galleries when the owners were away, and otherwise made ends meet. All of us lived hand-to-mouth, and no one complained.

All through a crystalline summer at our eighty-five-hundred-foot campsite in the mountains, week followed week in this world-outside-the-world. It was a life without rent, electricity, or plumbing. Its address was "General Delivery, Santa Fe, N.M. 87501." It provided enough money to eat and play and make car payments, but was not burdened by thoughts of career. And it was full of wonders: Canyons and mountains and deserts. Indian ruins and dances, and Indians shopping in the supermarket. Cowboys. The Spanish language overheard in the street. Arroyos, acequias, portales, canales, burritos, plazas, santeros, curanderas, and brujas. Museums. Dirt roads. Clear, clear air, and room enough. Strangers who smiled in passing and said hello. All in a place that treasured its uniqueness, unconcerned that the rest of America marched to a different beat.

Hiking in the sunshine, we watched fierce thunderstorms assault dark mesas miles away. Waking up in our sleeping bags, we heard squirrels and blue jays quarreling furiously overhead, and wondered

who came away with the pine nuts. The weeks passed as in a dream,
a dream that must end someday soon. From May until October the
tent remained our home. Then one morning we awoke to find our little
home white with snow and the air too frigid for making breakfast. The
time had come to end our Santa Fe idyll and return to reality. But we
didn't want to.

We drove to a hill above the city and gazed at a mountain eighty
miles to the north. "The whole rest of the country busts its butt fifty
weeks a year for the chance to spend the other two weeks here," I said
to Laurie. "Yet we have it every day, free for the taking. We've got to
figure out a way to stay."

I took the job at the New Mexican *not so much for the income as*
for the chance to write about Santa Fe. There was so much going on
that I knew about but which the daily paper was ignoring. I longed to
sink my teeth into stories about Chicano militancy, infighting at the
city's only hospital, a revolt within the school system, skulduggery at
City Hall and the State Capitol, strident protest murals erupting on
adobe walls on the chic east side, to the equal distress of historical
purists and the moneyed set.

But while I had some success and surprising impact in airing
such turmoil, I had to fight the New Mexican's *timid, complacent*
Establishment all the way. As the only journalistic show in town,
the paper led a smug existence, raking in profits from advertisers
who had no other place to turn. Under the circumstances, it saw
no need to make waves or look for trouble. My feelings were just
the opposite; so quickly I became the resident malcontent. Certain
that my concept of journalism was superior to the prevailing one at
the New Mexican, *I did not even try to curb my indignation—or my*
temper. Soon I was quarreling openly with the accountant who ran
the paper for its absentee owner, Robert McKinney, a former U.S.
ambassador to Switzerland, who spent most of the year on his estate
in Virginia.

One of the few allies I had at the New Mexican *was Wayne Vann*
in advertising. Alone among the paper's top management, he was
seeing on the street that my controversial stories were not driving out
business but stirring up interest, which he was converting into sales.
Repeatedly he advised me to calm down, cool off, hang in there, and

work slowly toward my goals. But I was too hot and righteous to heed his counsel.

The end came when the accountant killed a story just an hour or two before it was to go to press. The subject was the hazardous waste being pumped into area streams by a major mining company. Rather than bow to his authority, I accosted him in the city room, demanding that the story be reinstated. "Do you know how many people that company employs in northern New Mexico?" he said angrily. "Do you know what it means to the economy? That story is not going in."

I boiled over. Months of suppressed anger poured out. "The only thing this newspaper cares about is the economy—its own!" I shouted back, with no regard for the workers all around us. "It has no standards, no guts, and no integrity!"

"In that case, Dick," replied the accountant with an icy calm far more devastating than my fury, "you might want to think about whether this is the right place for you to be working."

When I had cooled off, I realized that my time at the New Mexican *was over. I had stepped out of line, had been insubordinate in public to a superior with legitimate authority over me. It was immature and unprofessional, and unacceptable behavior in the workplace. The next day I gave my notice, which was accepted with obvious relief. Two weeks later I cleared out my desk and departed the premises of the* New Mexican, *certain that my journalistic career in Santa Fe had ended. I did not even suspect that it had just begun.*

A few weeks later Laurie and I moved to Albuquerque, where she took a job as a reporter for the afternoon daily. I, meanwhile, drifted—and sank into depression. Only after leaving did I realize just how much the work at the New Mexican *had meant to me. Having a direct influence on events in a town I truly loved was the richest experience I had ever had as a newspaperman. The intimate scale of small-city journalism was far more compatible to me than the huge, impersonal scale of* Newsday, *even though the standards there were so much higher. Moping around our apartment, I came to understand that I had finally found what I really wanted to do. And now I had burned my bridges in the only place where I wanted to do it.*

To make things worse, Laurie and I could barely stand Albuquerque. Hot, flat, and dusty, it was a boomtown of strip malls and subdivisions. And it was dominated by a booster mentality, in love with development, money, and growth. It bore no resemblance to our beloved Santa Fe.

While Laurie's paycheck made ends meet, I took feeble stabs at freelance stories, but abandoned most before they got started. I found myself staying in bed until noon, staring bleakly into the future and seeing no hope. Then a surprise diversion broke me out of my funk. Through a friend's connections I was hired by the Ford Foundation for a temporary project. The work lasted only a few months, but when it ended I had saved five thousand dollars. More important, the project's deadlines had shown that I was still capable of doing work.

In the autumn of 1973 Laurie and I went to a dinner party in Santa Fe at the home of wealthy friends. The table talk turned to the New Mexican, *and soon everyone was agreeing: "What Santa Fe needs is another newspaper." The conversation moved on, but after dinner the host drew me aside.*

"Do you think a second newspaper could make it here?"

"I really couldn't say," I replied. "I know a lot about writing and editing, but very little about business."

"Would you be willing to look into it?" he persisted. "If it looks good, I would invest in it. I think my parents would too, and I know some friends who would probably be interested. What do you think?"

"Sure, why not? I'm not doing anything else just now."

Back in Albuquerque, Laurie and I made a decision. We would put the notion of a second newspaper in Santa Fe to the test. Until the savings ran out, I would work full-time to pull the pieces together, while she supported us. And if in the end it came to nothing, at least we could say we had tried.

I did not expect the project to succeed. We had so little money, such narrow experience, such ignorance of the task. I expected to learn that a newspaper could not get off the ground for less than five hundred thousand dollars, or a million. I expected technical matters to swamp me. I expected financial prospects to be hopeless. I was braced for advertisers and investors to scoff the idea to death or, just as bad, to politely dismiss it to death. I learned that I had a lot to learn.

I did know enough to know that starting a daily would be impossible, so I concentrated on learning about weeklies. Editors in nearby towns showed me that a small weekly could be produced with a minimum of equipment: a typesetting machine or two, a photostat camera, a basic darkroom. Commercial printers gave me price lists that were surprisingly low. I found people to ask about advertising rates, circulation, billing, supplies, utilities, taxes, insurance, bookkeeping, interest, and investment—none of which I had dealt with before.

With a hand-held calculator I added up what I thought it would cost to publish a weekly newspaper in Santa Fe. The sum was far less than I had assumed. Keeping it down was the basic salary that the newspaper would pay: just one hundred dollars a week. When the costs were totaled, I determined how much advertising must be sold to cover them. It was not a huge amount. I felt the first faint suspicion that this thing might fly.

Laurie and I chose the name Santa Fe Reporter, *as a simple statement of what our paper meant to do. I designed an eight-page "dummy" issue to show what we had in mind, and got five hundred copies printed. Then I began visiting advertisers, to ask if they might support such a paper. The response floored me. One after another, merchants promised to try the* Reporter. *Their reason was always the same: Because of its monopoly position, the* New Mexican *had grown arrogant and unresponsive to its advertisers. "It's high time that outfit had some competition!" became a refrain in my ears. After some fifty calls I stopped. The business community's message was emphatic.*

By now I was convinced that if we got the Reporter *going, it would have strong advertising support. What still was needed, however, was what we did not have: money. I calculated that an initial investment of one hundred thousand dollars was needed. But we were starting from zero. And if the money could be raised at all, it would have to come from strangers.*

A discouraging time followed. I made a list of every wealthy person I had heard of in Santa Fe. One by one I called them cold, briefly explained my purpose, and asked to meet to discuss it. Most declined, a few agreed. After hearing me out they wished me well, but reserved decision on investing. Soon my list was exhausted. I pumped friends for more names, and contacted them. Yet each call from Albuquerque to Santa Fe was long-distance. Our start-up fund was vanishing fast. For the few prospects who gave me an appointment, I drove to Santa Fe, spending yet more money on gas.

*But slowly an investor list formed. All those on it were convinced
that Santa Fe needed a second newspaper, and all could easily afford
the five-thousand-dollar minimum stake I asked. When their pledges
reached thirty-five thousand dollars, Laurie and I used cosigners to
throw another fifteen thousand dollars from us into the pot, though
we had no money of our own. Investment in the* Reporter *now totaled
fifty thousand dollars. I re-ran the numbers, and decided we could
start with only seventy thousand dollars. But week after week the fund
stayed at fifty thousand, despite all my efforts to attract more. Gloom
settled over the project, and me. Sometimes after a fruitless morning
in Santa Fe I canceled my afternoon appointments and dozed fitfully
in the car, saving strength for the next day. But it would be no better.*

*On the last day of March 1974, I told Laurie the project was dying.
There was nowhere left to turn, no more resources for going on. We
must be braced for the collapse of our dream. She flared at me, called
me a quitter, tried to goad me back into action. But she could suggest
nothing else to try. We went to bed in a black mood, resentful, tearful,
and defeated. When it had passed, I returned to the job. And somehow,
by the first of May we had our seventy thousand dollars—and not a
dollar more. The* Santa Fe Reporter *was in business.*

*The newspaper made its debut on June 26, 1974, heralded by a
radio advertising campaign boasting that the* Reporter *had assembled
the finest collection of talent in the history of New Mexico journalism.
Perhaps it was true: Our sports editor came from* Sports Illustrated,
our managing editor from the (pre-Murdoch) New York Post. *Our featured columnist was a national award winner from* Newsday. *Laurie
brought experience from* Women's Wear Daily, *I from* Newsday, *other
reporters from the* Pittsburgh Press *and the* Arizona Republic. *The*
Omaha World-Herald's *retired Washington bureau chief was a con-
tributor.*

*Most members of this cast were old friends. They signed on not for
the money—the standard salary was one hundred dollars a week, and
as general manager I drew an additional twenty-five—but for the once-
in-a-lifetime thrill of starting a newspaper. All told, some fifteen eager
people assembled to launch the* Santa Fe Reporter. *Rolling up our
sleeves, we swept and vacuumed our dingy rented offices. We mopped
the basement where the paper would be pasted up. We converted a*

windowless storeroom at the top of a rickety wooden stairway into the newsroom. We furnished the place with army surplus desks and chairs bought from a junkyard. Then we were ready to start putting out a newspaper.

The first issue was thirty-six tabloid pages, filled with good writing, snappy headlines, provocative commentary, and ads from businesses wishing us well. The front page featured an old Hispanic man who still kept oxen, as well as our first scoop: the return of commercial airline service to Santa Fe after a hiatus of three years. But the biggest headline told our own story: "New Santa Fe Newspaper, the Reporter, Starts Today."

Then week after week, we tore into the news of Santa Fe. On the day after our debut, the New Mexican ran its own belated front-page story about airline service coming back to town. It was just the first of many occasions in which the embarrassed daily was forced to follow our lead. The Reporter broke the story that nurses at the hospital were organizing a union. We disclosed that a nearby ghost town was coming back to life, repopulated by hippies. We were the first to report on the new police SWAT team, the first to warn about packs of savage dogs running loose at night, the first to announce the planned renovation of Santa Fe's seedy old red-light district. We were the paper that alerted the city that harsh minerals in the water supply were destroying household plumbing systems all over town.

Those salad days were a constant rush, at least on the surface. Barely submerged in the bustling operation, however, were profound troubles known only to me, Laurie, and our business manager. Despite my efforts to anticipate every detail, I had miscalculated badly on the most essential financial element. I had been too trusting of the words of advertisers. Dozens had said they were fed up with the daily, and had promised to support a competitor. Yet after a quick flurry of "Good luck, Reporter" ads, most of them decided to wait and see. Until they were satisfied that the new paper was for real, they refused to put their money where their mouths had been.

By August we were broke. Only after it was too late did I learn that we were horribly undercapitalized. By any sound financial equation, the Reporter never should have started. Our naïveté was greater even than our idealism. And although we were doing fine journalism, we were just playing at running a business. Barely three months into a *venture meant to stand the test of time, we faced the clammy likelihood of ceasing publication, before our newspaper had even become a decent footnote in the journalistic annals of New Mexico. It was only then that the* Santa Fe Reporter *was really born.*

Refusing to accept the grim message of the numbers, which spelled out sure obliteration, we dug in. We cut costs everywhere. The page count was reduced, to lower production and printing bills. All non-essential purchases were forbidden. Reporters wrote their stories on the backs of press releases. Everyone shared duties such as mopping the basement and taking garbage to the dump. Our veteran writers, photographers, and editors delivered the Reporter *to stores and homes.*

At an emergency meeting of our shareholders I appealed for more funding. All we needed was time for our new austerity to catch up with our journalism, I said. Apprehensive, they responded not with new investment but a loan. It threw the Reporter *deep into debt, but it enabled us to keep publishing.*

Quickly the thrill of starting a newspaper dimmed. When disenchanted employees quit, we did not replace them. For those who stayed, wages got no better. Our business manager knew just how bad things were, so he asked his wife to work as our receptionist without pay. On some paydays Laurie and I got no checks, for there were no funds to cover them. But somehow we never missed a payroll for anyone else. Because there was so little money in the bank, we delayed paying bills. The printer told me that never before had a customer been so far in arrears. Though sympathetic, he warned that soon he must refuse to print us—a step considered the last resort in the newspaper business. Our tax payments fell months behind, and I was shaken by a visit from a rough IRS agent who threatened to padlock our doors.

Fear moved in to live with me, through fourteen-hour workdays and largely sleepless nights. Every month promised to be our last. Sometimes the next issue was as far ahead as I could see. Temporary relief came just once a week, on Tuesdays, our deadline day. Only then did the cold knot in my stomach dissolve for a few blessed hours, as the intoxicating crush of getting the paper out displaced everything else. Though production night lasted until 4 A.M., I welcomed it, for nothing but the deadline took my mind off our troubles, and nothing but exhaustion gave me sleep.

Yet no matter how heavy the burdens, the alternative was too horrible to contemplate. Physical and mental punishment could be endured—but the collapse of the Santa Fe Reporter *was simply unacceptable. Unthinkable. That way lay sure disaster for me, and the betrayal of all those who had bought into my dream. The need to preserve the paper was so absolute within me that I never doubted its ultimate survival. When I could not even see the way, I still knew we would get through. No matter how deep our hole, no matter how grim our prospects, it never occurred to me that the* Reporter *would perish in the end.*

Our fortitude got us through, and better times came for the Santa Fe Reporter. *By 1978, four years into the game, we were operating almost at breakeven. In 1979 we made our first profit, a respectable thirty-two thousand dollars. Our revenues were climbing, and our salaries were creeping toward a living wage. Progress was slowed by the debt we had taken on, but the important thing was movement: Slowly but surely we were getting ahead.*

The draconian cost controls remained in place. Meanwhile, advertisers began to follow readers into the newspaper. But it was slow going. Most advertisers found it difficult to break old habits, and the New Mexican *lost no opportunity to assure them our young weekly was a waste of money. Timidly the city's merchants took their cues from what their competitors were doing. Few wanted to run the risk of trying something new.*

Readers, however, had a different dynamic. The number of them responding to the energy and imagination on our pages grew every week. People were talking about the Reporter—*and in time, the shopkeepers could no longer ignore us. One by one they placed trial ads, and where one retailer's message appeared, a competitor's followed. "They're like sheep," muttered one of our sales reps, in a tone that blended gratitude and disgust.*

The Reporter *displayed a spirit that attracted exceptional talent, from surprising quarters. Once the paper was established, most members of the founding staff moved on, pulled by career and monetary needs. But behind them came a steady stream of splendid journalists eager to take their turn. Some came from big and famous daily newspapers, to taste again the idealism that first drew them into the business. Others were raw recruits, with rare journalistic gifts we were lucky enough to spot. After their apprenticeship with us, they graduated to major publications all across the country.*

Aided by such talent, the Santa Fe Reporter *became a distinguished newspaper. The honors came slowly at first, then more and more rapidly. A 1975 series on property taxes was judged the best real-estate reporting in the nation, by any paper of any size. The same story also won a prestigious Scripps Howard public service award, the first by a New Mexico newspaper. In 1977, our first year in the New Mexico Press Association, we won seven awards. Subsequent years brought dozens more, in all categories: news, features, sports, photography, design, columns, advertising, community service, general excellence. One year we won twenty plaques, the most ever by a single paper. The emcee joked that we would need a U-Haul to take them home.*

We kept earning national recognition as well. Probes into New Mexico's state prison and mental hospital both were honored by the country's foremost investigative journalism society, Investigative Reporters and Editors, and the hospital report won IRE's highest honor, the Bronze Medal. In 1979 the Reporter *was the only double winner in the National Press Club consumer journalism competition. One prize was for a series on Santa Fe's life-threatening ambulance service, the other for an exposé of a huge land scam. That report also won journalism's biggest cash prize for economic reporting, five thousand dollars—just a little less than the yearly salary of the staff member who wrote it.*

We fared particularly well in the annual competition of the National Newspaper Association. Through the years the NNA judged our efforts the nation's best in editorials, criticism, special supplements, investigations. But the greatest tribute came when the young, poor, free Santa Fe Reporter *was named the second-best weekly newspaper in the country. And our editorials almost won the biggest prize of all, the Pulitzer. We ultimately became the runner-up, when the Pulitzer board overruled the recommendation of its national panel of jurors that year and gave the prize instead to the* New York Times.

Somewhere past two hundred, we lost count of our awards. More than forty were national, many in open competition with the best and biggest dailies. And we did it all without money.

We pretty much did it without technology as well. While the rest of the newspaper world was installing video terminals at every desk, wired into a computerized system that could produce full pages without the touch of a human hand, our equipment remained primitive. We punched out stories on manual typewriters and edited them with pencils. For years our only electronic typesetting machine was a pre-used model from the first generation ever sold, subject to all manner of breakdowns. Eventually we were able to afford more sophisticated machines, still primitive by most standards, and still secondhand. Yet we never let mechanical limitations prevent us from putting out a paper as handsome as any other, anywhere.

In the midst of poverty, we were having fun. Our dogs came to work with us. Except for the ad reps, employees dressed any way they chose. We stocked beer in the Coke machine and booze in desk drawers. We partied down, cared about each other, and once a week, on production night, all got crazy together. On many a Wednesday morning, after shipping that week's Reporter *on a 4 A.M. bus to the printer in Albuquerque, we toasted the rising sun with vodka, scotch, and bourbon. The word "family" was frequently heard.*

Often I marveled that we could draw and hold such an extraordinary cast of characters, in defiance of every notion of what is acceptable in the business world. I had to wonder why. The answer seemed to lie in a few key principles. The first was that we were all in it together. Everyone knew that his or her contribution was indispensable for the Reporter *to appear each week. We could no more get by without a receptionist or a typesetter than we could without an editor or sales manager. And everybody realized that from the publishers on down, we all were just squeezing by from paycheck to paycheck.*

Another was the attitude that Laurie and I developed as copublishers. We felt that everyone on the staff was doing us a personal favor by putting her or his life force into our venture, and we wanted their lives to be enriched in return. We never got comfortable with the idea of being bosses, and certainly not with the power that came with it. Rather, we accepted that role in order to make the organization work. We never asked anyone to do more than we did, and we never stopped working for the Reporter. *After staggering home at midnight for a can of soup, we kept pecking at its problems till we dropped into bed.*

Of course the Reporter *needed money to exist, but money was not at the heart of anything we did. It boiled down to a simple distinction, which we formulated early and which held up through all the years that followed. "Some people put out a newspaper in order to sell ads," we would explain. "At the* Santa Fe Reporter, *we sell ads in order to put out a newspaper."*

One day a writer friend who had left Life *magazine to move to Santa Fe summed things up. "You know," he mused, "what most people want is to sign on with a big company, the bigger the better. And once they do, they spend their lives manufacturing what that company tells them to: 'IBMs,' 'Time Inc.s,' 'General Motors,' 'AT&Ts,' like they were on an assembly line. Yet here you are, out in the godforsaken desert, broke all the time, always busting your ass, just so you can manufacture 'McCords'—which nobody outside Santa Fe ever heard of. It must be harder than shit, but I say keep it up. It's not a bad job."*

He was right. Putting out the Santa Fe Reporter *was not a bad job. And it was harder than shit.*

As we held on through the early years, a major source of assistance was a peculiar one: our rival, the New Mexican. *In the struggle for advertising we got no slack, for under Wayne Vann the daily's sales staff made us fight for every inch. But in terms of news, the town was handed to us on a platter. We were winning the readers of Santa Fe, and that was the key to our future. But I was sure the* New Mexican *would fight back.*

Every week, every month, I expected Robert McKinney, the New Mexican's *owner, to swat us hard, with a major upgrading. Yet strangely he did not. Then in December 1975, eighteen months after the* Reporter's *birth, the* New Mexican's *front page told why he had ignored us. He had been too busy negotiating to sell his newspaper to the nation's largest chain.*

News of the New Mexican's *acquisition by the Gannett Company rattled us at the* Reporter. *The rivalry in Santa Fe had ceased to be a hometown one. It was now a whole new game, and we were not sure what the rules would be. A call from the owner of the daily in nearby Los Alamos did nothing to ease my mind. The* New Mexican *competed with him as well as with us, and he was upset. "This is not*

*good news for you or for me," he said. "Gannett is one tough outfit.
They didn't get where they are by pussyfooting around."*

"What do you think they'll do?" I asked.

*"I don't know, but I imagine we'll find out," he replied. "And I
imagine you'll find out more than I will. Good luck."*

Gannett was the country's fastest-growing chain. The New Mexican *was its fourth announced takeover in 1975 alone. It published
fifty-three daily papers in eighteen states, from Hawaii to company
headquarters in Rochester, New York. In geographical distribution as
well as numbers, Gannett was unsurpassed. Most of its papers were
in small or medium-size cities, so its yearly revenues ranked only
fourth among American chains. Knight-Ridder, Scripps Howard, and
Cox Newspapers, with many of the nation's premier mastheads, all
generated more income. But Gannett liked monopoly markets, where
even small towns produced enormous profits.*

The New Mexican *was a typical acquisition. Its circulation of
eighteen thousand, small by big-city standards, fit the chain's norm.
It had no daily competition. And it was a prized state-capital paper.
With few nationally known mastheads, Gannett sought regional prestige. Already it operated in six capitals: Honolulu, Hawaii; Lansing,
Michigan; Olympia, Washington; Boise, Idaho; Nashville, Tennessee;
and Salem, Oregon. Santa Fe was now the seventh.*

*The official statements accompanying the sale underlined what
we were up against. Clearly we faced a new attitude, spelled out by
Gannett's president, Allen Neuharth, who said: "We regard Santa Fe,
and New Mexico in general, as among the most promising growth
areas in the country." Now* there *was a businesslike motivation.
Simple-minded by comparison was our own reason for publishing
a newspaper in Santa Fe: because we loved the place.*

*Gannett's chairman, Paul Miller, added some disquieting specifics:
"The* New Mexican *will have access to corporate personnel with
expertise in equipment research, development, procurement and newspaper production, and to our capital resources." It was enough to
make me tremble.*

*The coming of Gannett was something I had not anticipated and did
not want. If Gannett had been in place all along, no investors would
have been foolhardy enough to sink money into the* Reporter—*and,*

moreover, I would not have been reckless enough to launch it. Taking on a cranky old ambassador was one thing. Going up against the nation's largest chain was something else.

The dread I felt was largely formless, which only made it worse. I felt certain of only one thing: The New Mexican*'s quality would quickly improve. The* Reporter*'s time as Santa Fe's only hard-charging newspaper would end, and when we lost that edge I did not know what we would have left. But surprisingly, Gannett came on slowly. By contractual agreement, McKinney remained the* New Mexican*'s publisher, and his accountant remained general manager. Wayne Vann was sent to another Gannett paper, but this made things easier for us, not harder. And there was no editorial renaissance. Instead of getting bigger the news hole dwindled, and contained more distant wire copy than local coverage. Santa Feans ridiculed it.*

The Reporter, *meanwhile, continued to grow. As time passed, I realized that we were competing better against the chain than we had against the independent* New Mexican. *Instead of vanishing within months of Gannett's arrival, we survived 1976, then 1977, then 1978, 1979, and 1980. Revenues climbed from $245,000 in 1976 to almost $800,000 in 1980. Salaries too were rising. As general manager I drew almost $17,000 in 1980, more than twice what I made at the start. Everyone else's pay had at least doubled.*

As we got stronger, the daily weakened. Its circulation dropped steadily. Two years after buying the paper, Gannett fired McKinney's general manager and replaced him with a circulation expert. The decline continued. A short while later McKinney himself was stripped of all authority. Furious, he responded by suing Gannett for fraud and breach of contract.

At the Reporter, *we were enjoying the fireworks immensely. Yet I also was mystified. All our gains against the* New Mexican *were the result of journalistic fervor. All along, the obvious way for the daily to curb us was to upgrade its own effort. But five years after Gannett and its limitless riches hit town, the paper was worse than ever. I did not understand. The question that hung in the air was: "Why don't they just improve it?"*

The answer came when McKinney's lawsuit went to trial in 1980. It was delivered by the accountant, who testified that he was fired as general manager because of Gannett's "impossible" profit demands.

Although annual revenues at the New Mexican *had soared past $5 million under him, and profits had doubled to 24 percent of income, McKinney's accountant said he was told the chain expected a return of from 36 to 38 percent. Making such "big gobs" of money would be "impossible on a short-term basis," he testified, "short of the destruction of the newspaper." When he balked, Gannett fired him and got someone else to pursue its goal.*

At last I understood why the nation's richest chain could not put out a better newspaper than the struggling Santa Fe Reporter: *There was not enough money in it. In a supreme irony, it was the* Reporter's *lack of emphasis on profits that had freed us to push ourselves to the limits of our ability. And it was Gannett's monetary obsession that had given us room to fly.*

The more I thought about it, the more I was reassured by the situation. At the end of 1980, after five years of prickly coexistence, both newspapers in Santa Fe were achieving what they had set out to do. The Reporter *was producing journalism that made us proud. Gannett was making big gobs of money.*

By each doing our own thing, we posed no real threat to one another. As long as Gannett placed money above quality, the Reporter *would have room in which to flourish. And as long as we came out only once a week, and generated only one-seventh of the daily's sales, we would pose no threat to the profits that had drawn Gannett to New Mexico's "growth area."*

Of course we would continue to compete for advertisers and readers. From time to time the New Mexican *would throw a free weekly spinoff at us, and we would throw a big new supplement at them. Each of us would be forced to respond to the other's maneuvers. But that was good. Competition was the heart of the economic system. It would prevent either paper from getting lazy. It would guard Santa Fe against the excesses of a monopoly. Both the* Reporter *and the* New Mexican *were now positioned securely, to the benefit of all concerned.*

Never before had I felt so confident about the future of the young newspaper we had created out of thin air. There was a wonderful balance to the equation that encompassed both the daily and the weekly in Santa Fe. And as long as the balance held, I figured we would do just fine.

But that was before I went to Oregon, and before I learned what Gannett was capable of.

Lying awake in my cheap motel bed in Portland, I recalled an incident from a year or two earlier. I was in the archives of the New Mexico State Library, poking through stacks of old newspapers, researching a story. By accident I picked up a yellowed, crumbling bundle and pulled out an issue. It was a tabloid newspaper I had never heard of, the *Santa Fe Tribune.* It was dated 1910.

I interrupted my work to peruse it. Its stories, though archaic in style, were energetic. Its editorials were spirited. Its editor was named on the masthead. I wondered if he had loved this long-forgotten little journal with the same fire I felt for the *Reporter,* and I knew that he had.

Suddenly I could see into the future, to a day when the *Santa Fe Reporter* in turn was no longer remembered. *Everything passes,* a voice whispered, *and you and yours will pass too.* My vision was not sad, just absolute. It was not something to lament, only a message to make the most of the time we had.

This memory was strangely reassuring in the sleepless night. Before morning came to Portland, I made a vow. What Gannett had in mind for us was unacceptable. Like every living thing, the *Santa Fe Reporter* would someday die. But it would not be this year, or the next, or the next. And it would not be at the hands of these bastards.

7

"I Guess That's What It's All About"

IN THE MORNING I WAS READY. To tide me through lunch, I put down a big breakfast. I was at Judge Frye's chambers in the federal courthouse at 8:28. Only the receptionist was there before me. She smiled and nodded at the file, which was where I had left it. I set it on the coffee table and resumed.

I knew what I had to do. If ever there was a mismatched fight, the one shaping up was it. Compared to the nation's biggest chain, the *Santa Fe Reporter*'s strength was minuscule. But we had one advantage. Unlike the people running Gannett, we were journalists. And we knew what journalism was for. We would reveal how the *Community Press* had been killed, and leave it up to Gannett's hit men to explain why. Once the story was told, they might have a hard time doing the same thing again.

Each folder I opened revealed a new weapon they had used. One of them, according to the deposition of Vann's retail advertising manager, Jody Carson, was coercing firms doing business with Gannett's daily papers to drop out of the weekly.

> **Question:** Did you ever offer any services or rate concessions or any special arrangement to any customer which was contingent upon that customer agreeing not to use the *Community Press*?
> **Carson:** Yes.
> **Q.** And to whom?
> **A.** Rowen Typewriter.
> **Q.** What was the offer to Rowen Typewriter?
> **A.** Basically, it was we like to do business with those businesses that do business with us, and we would use their services for repairs if they advertised with us.
> **Q.** Did you tell them you would not use their services if they advertised in the *Community Press*?
> **A.** "Not" is a bit strong. Consideration.

Q. Did you intend to imply to them that you would not use their services if they advertised with the *Community Press*?

A. I intended to imply to them we wanted to do business with those that did business with us.

Q. And did Rowen Typewriter thereafter stop doing business with the *Community Press*?

A. Yes.

Q. Were you directed by Mr. Hayden or Mr. Vann to approach Rowen Typewriter on this?

A. Yes.

Q. By whom?

A. Both of them.

Another tactic used to drive business out of the *Community Press* was the creation of questionable "associations" to give advertisers special rates on the understanding that they would stop using the weekly. Memos from Hayden to Vann spelled it out.

April 7, 1977

I had lunch today with Bruce Philippi to discuss with him the promotion which begins next week by Philippi Ford and John Lucas Chevrolet in Stayton.

First Bruce agreed to register the name "Stayton New Car Dealers Association," which I suggested would provide a vehicle for using a combined rate based on the fact that the two were an association. . . .

November 16, 1977

. . . I would also like you to check with MAB Enterprises about the *Community Press* buy for the Reed Opera House promotion. My understanding was that the association rate that we gave them was a quid pro quo expecting loyalty. . . .

Please be careful of the confidentiality of this information.

Advertisers behind in their payments to Gannett were particularly vulnerable to pressure to stop using the weekly. How to apply it was made clear in a memo from Hayden to Vann.

November 16, 1977

. . . On another note, I was astonished to see another full page for Stereo Wizard in the Tuesday *Community Press*. My understanding is that they have not met the commitment of paying us $2,000 a week for the past two weeks. I think we have no alternative but to stop their advertising with us, but I would hope that you, or Jody, would make it plain that we consider their practice highly unethical and unbusinesslike.

Unethical and unbusinesslike! The secret workings of Gannett were truly amazing. Recording them, I felt a sharp excitement, the kind a journalist experiences only rarely in the course of a career. I recognized the sensation, for it had come to me three times before, twice at *Newsday* and once at the *Santa Fe Reporter*. The first time was at Newark, New Jersey, in 1967, when I was my newspaper's first reporter on the scene of the race riot that touched off the longest, hottest summer in American history. The second was at Kent State University in Ohio, where I arrived just hours after National Guardsmen killed four Vietnam War protesters in 1970. The third was outside the penitentiary of New Mexico in 1980, watching black smoke rise, while behind the wall rioting inmates were butchering thirty-three of their fellows.

Each of these events was the country's biggest news story at the time. Now the same journalistic fervor was upon me again. This time, however, I was not comfortable with my "scoop." It was impure. I was gathering this story not merely for its news value, which was substantial, but even more for self-interest, to preserve the existence of the *Santa Fe Reporter*. Nevertheless, I would tell this tale. If Gannett felt it had the right to exterminate us, then we had the right to defend ourselves.

The second day proceeded like the first. Writing furiously, I continued to record word by word how Gannett had destroyed its Salem rival. By now I had decided not to visit that city, not on this trip. I could always go to Salem, but I would not get another crack at the evidence. I had to make the most of this one.

I picked my way through dozens of letters, memos, internal communications from one Gannett official to another. They left no doubt about the corporate attitude toward the Salem campaign. The execution of the *Community Press* was not the result of a local publisher and advertising manager running amok, taking liberties that would have horrified higher executives if they had known about them. Rather, the campaign was applauded all through Gannett's hierarchy, from president Allen Neuharth down.

Just weeks after arriving in Salem, N. S. Hayden declared his intentions in a letter to John E. Heselden, Gannett's senior vice president for staff and services at headquarters in Rochester:

August 3, 1976
Dear Jack:
    . . . I am forced to take the position that we must get the business back at any cost. That's not a very businesslike decision, but seems necessary and prudent under the circumstances.
                                        Buddy

Within a few months, Hayden had both launched his assault upon the *Community Press* and set a timetable for its ultimate destruction, as he proudly reported in a letter to Neuharth:

> October 11, 1976
> Dear Al (Private)
> Having used my first three reports from Salem to describe the gravity of the situation, I think it is about time I turned my attention and reports to revealing the positive aspects of what we are doing.
> The situation with the *Community Press,* in my view, can be summed up as follows: I think that in the first three months after my arrival we worked exclusively on "containment." I think that we have won that battle, in spite of the fact that they have started the weekend edition. In my view, it has been a dismal flop. . . .
> Now that I feel containment has been accomplished, our goal is to fatally cripple the *Community Press,* and to accomplish this we have instituted "operation demolition," which is a program of bonuses for the ad sales staff for moving advertising accounts completely out of the *Community Press* on a 13-week basis. . . .
> I am very optimistic, and we are literally pulling out every stop, from normal selling to endless (and tiring) entertaining.
> There are, to be sure, tough days ahead, with reduced revenues and higher expenses. Each detail is planned with your admonition to me in mind: protect the franchise. My timetable remains a normal operation, free of outside influence and unnecessary extra expense, by January 1, 1978.
> That's the way it is in Salem, Oregon, September 1976.
>   Buddy

Nor did the efforts of Wayne Vann go uncelebrated at headquarters. Among other pats on the back came one from the highest advertising executive in the chain:

> November 22, 1976
> To: Wayne Vann (Private/Confidential)
> From: Paul B. Flynn, Director of Marketing Services
> Congratulations on the November 14 efforts. The impact of your "demolition derby" is very evident, and deeply appreciated here. You are a superb ad director!

But although my old colleague was a key figure in the drive to kill the weekly, the boss at all times was Hayden—who did not hesitate to rebuke Vann when things were not going as planned:

March 15, 1978
To: Wayne Vann (PRIVATE)
From: N. S. Hayden

A glance at the *Community Press* this week, as for the past several weeks, indicates that we may indeed be dropping the ball.

The most disheartening aspect of the current issue is the Self Service Furniture ad. What's the story there? Whose account?

Our linage looks strong, but are we running the risk of becoming too complacent? There are many, many small accounts in the *Community Press.*

More importantly, Wayne, what happened to the program I asked to be instituted in January? My gut feelings at that time were that advertising *management* needed to follow up on those accounts appearing in the *Community Press.*

As far as I know, the instructions I laid down were followed twice. At least those are the only reports I got. What happened to that program? If it was abandoned, under whose authority was it abandoned, when it was a direct request from me to discuss the detail with you?

I'd like to have some answers on the *Community Press* advertising on a weekly basis. I'd like a report from you indicating the status of every *Community Press* advertiser, and what feedback the sales people provide and which member of advertising management has made contact to verify the situation.

I think if we allow *Community Press* sales people to get smaller accounts and build their ad count, we're looking for continued trouble.

Dobermans don't sleep.

As he watched his campaign "fatally cripple" the *Community Press,* Hayden expressed his self-satisfaction in a letter to Rollan Melton, the head of one of Gannett's newspaper groups, a member of the chain's board of directors, and a personal friend:

February 3, 1978
Dear Rollie:

Twenty months ago I began an intensive three-month fact-finding mission upon my arrival in Salem. I reported most of my fact-finding in Rochester in early September 1976. Al Neuharth's admonition was simple: "protect the franchise."

Following that visit, Gannett all but gave me carte blanche for the capital items we deemed necessary. At no time since my arrival in Salem has any corporate officer exerted any bottom-line pressure on me while we dangled in the lower part of the bottom fourth in profitability. All of us, apparently, had the same visions and the same patience and the same understanding of investment. . . .

This announcement [of the Sunday *Community Press* folding], coupled with the steadily eroding linage of the *Community Press* during the past six months, is a source of inspiration and pride to all of us here. We are doing the job the way it ought to be done. We are getting results. We have protected the franchise.

Rather than rest and smirk, we will move forward with an eye towards eliminating the *Community Press* from the market all together. That may not be a practical objective, but at the current levels of operation, the *Community Press* is no more than any other shopper in any other market, and we can live and prosper and co-exist without any material adverse impact.

All of us are naturally pleased. My praise and my warm professional respect goes to my associates and colleagues. My thanks go to the Gannett Company and its executives for giving me the latitude to do what needed to be done, and having the confidence to let me do some very, very unusual things in what was a very, very unusual situation.

It's been one hell of an experience. . . .

Buddy

Carbon Copy: Al Neuharth

When the *Community Press* announced it was considering an antitrust lawsuit against Gannett, the news was taken as a compliment by the chain's western region president, who chuckled about it in a memo to Hayden:

July 13, 1978
Dear Buddy:

That's unique praise indeed to be recognized publicly for "unusual and severe competitive reactions." My lexicon says that's a Wall Street euphemism for "they're beating our ass off."

Congratulations again.

Make a liar of their prediction of "short-term adverse effect on . . . profitability" and send them back to the pickle works.

Robert B. Whittington
Gannett West

Hayden was clearly a man who concentrated on getting the job done. But as I discovered in a passage from a March 3, 1978, letter to his friend Rollie Melton at headquarters, he was not without his poetic—and even rhapsodic—moments:

Sunday *Community Press* is no longer . . . the Dobermans are now working on mid-week. We feel confident that we are moving in the right direction, and although we intend to take a sniff of the rose from time to time, fear not that we will rest on any laurels.

It's been an interesting 18 months or so, and I think all of us have grown professionally. As a matter of fact, Rollie, it's been a ball, and when I look around to see what we have accomplished, both physically, mechanically, philosophically, attitudinally and tangibly, I get a little touch of managerial pride. I guess that's what it's all about.

Buddy

Whew. It was really incredible stuff.

Though less acute than the previous day, the fear of being discovered never left me. My guess was that looking through the file was probably not illegal, since I had gained access to it without subterfuge. But if someone told me outright that nothing in it could be published, I would be in a terrible predicament. If I acquiesced, this exercise would be futile. Worse, I would now know what we faced at the *Reporter* but would have no effective means of combating it. Publicity was really our best and only shot. We had to get this information out in the open, to prevent a repeat performance in Santa Fe.

But I was unsure of our legal footing. I did not know how the broad press freedom of the First Amendment applied to sealed court files. If I refused to agree to keep the information secret, could an injunction forbid us to print it? And if we published knowing it was sealed, could I and my paper be held in contempt? Any way the matter unfolded, I would be needing legal counsel. My immediate objective, however, remained the same: to get through this file and out of this courthouse without revealing what I was doing or lying about it.

Again I took frequent breaks to pocket my notes, and to rest my hand, which was developing writer's cramp. As morning moved into afternoon, with me almost a fixture in the reception area, my apprehension diminished. No one seemed to be paying any attention to me. No one, that is, except Judge Frye. She was in and out of her chambers often, and sometimes I could not avoid meeting her eyes as she passed. She nodded and smiled, and each time I feared the end was just a curious inquiry away. But wordless courtesy was the extent of her involvement.

When closing time came I still was not finished. But the end was in sight. With luck and a writing hand that did not seize up on me the next day, I might be through in time to get to CPI for my afternoon appointment. Again I asked to tuck the file away and return first thing in the morning.

The receptionist agreed, but with a roll of her eyes that said my welcome was wearing thin.

That evening I considered not returning the next day. There were more documents I needed to copy, but the ones I already had were potent. No one had even asked my name, so if I faded away now, there would be no way to contact me with a belated demand not to use the material. If I went back to my bizarre workstation, however, any moment could be the last. Yet I felt compelled to exhaust the file before abandoning it. I had gotten it only by a fluke, and no other reporter was ever likely to see what it held. Mine was the best and perhaps only chance to reveal its contents. I must squeeze this opportunity dry. Returning one last time to the U.S. District Court was a calculated risk, but one I had to take.

8

The Third Day

ON FRIDAY MORNING I WAS weary. Another night of troubled sleep had done nothing to settle my fears. But at 8:30 sharp I was back to finish the job. I plunked the thick file down upon the coffee table and was reaching for a legal pad, when suddenly the receptionist stood before me. "Pardon me," she said.

You imbecile! You jerk! I berated myself silently. *You knew better than to come back, but you did it anyway! This is where the shit hits the fan, for sure. You blew it!*

"Pardon me, but you're sort of in the way here in the middle of the office," she was saying, in an apologetic tone. "We had no idea you needed so much time. Would you mind moving into the law library across the hall? The judge is expecting several visitors this morning, and we need this area for them."

Would I mind? Would I mind! A secluded corner had been my prayer for the past two days—and now, just when I thought the jig was up, my prayer was being answered. I scooped up the stack and followed the receptionist to a small desk in the silent library. "I'm sorry we had to make you move," she said as she left.

I felt like I had been paroled from prison. In the library I had an actual desk, complete with reading light and chair. I could sit upright, which soothed the backache caused by two days of hunching over the low coffee table. Most blessedly, I was at last out of the path of the judge, her staff, and curious passersby, any one of whom might bring instant disaster.

My task on this final day was to learn how Gannett had driven every chain store out of the *Community Press*. The chains, after all, had implored CPI to break Gannett's monopoly in Salem. All the majors placed huge ads in the weekly's first issue. But slowly, inexorably, they had fallen away, until not one was left. As the nation's largest newspaper company, Gannett was not intimidated by the merchandising giants supporting the weekly.

Systematically, Gannett went after Montgomery Ward, Sears, Fred Meyer, and the other chain stores. And one by one, they buckled.

Most gripping to me was the story of Kmart. The huge discounter was an original backer of the *Community Press,* and remained steadfast when things got rough. But in the end, when it was the only major advertiser left in the weekly, Kmart too caved in. When it pulled out, *Community Press* closed down. A detailed account of Gannett's tactics was provided in the long deposition of Kmart's western regional advertising manager, Michael W. Moors.

I had a personal interest in his testimony, for I knew Mike Moors. We had met through Didier Raven, who was wooing Kmart for the *Santa Fe Reporter.* A few months earlier, the big merchandiser had begun using us as well as the *New Mexican* for its weekly circular. Moors struck me as a straight-talking, no-nonsense kind of guy. I was eager to see what he said. In his deposition, he said plenty.

> **Question:** Did anyone employed by the *Statesman-Journal* company ever offer you or to your knowledge anyone else at Kmart any sort of preferential treatment as an inducement for abandoning the *Community Press* in Salem?
>
> **Moors:** Yes.
>
> **Q.** What kind of inducements were offered?
>
> **A.** There were rates that were considerably less than had been in the market with the *Statesman-Journal* for several years. We were aware of parties that were given, inviting our people to attend. We were aware of all-expense-paid trips to Reno and Lake Tahoe offered to our management.
>
> **Q.** Did the *Statesman-Journal* company ever offer a two-year contract with a guarantee of no rate increase in exchange for a commitment by Kmart to stop using the *Community Press?*
>
> **A.** Yes.
>
> **Q.** Do you recall who made that offer?
>
> **A.** It was made by their publisher, Mr. Buddy Hayden, and their advertising manager, Mr. Wayne Vann.
>
> **Q.** Did either Mr. Hayden or Mr. Vann indicate to you that similar offers of two-year contracts had been made to other advertisers?
>
> **A.** No.

Beyond the promise of no rate increase, Gannett was prepared to up the ante considerably, Moors testified. He expanded as he discussed a letter sent to him by Wayne Vann on February 4, 1977.

> **Question:** Let me direct your attention to the first paragraph on the second page, which says, and I quote: "It is my understanding that

Kmart missed out on two rebates because the newspaper did not have a rebate system at the time. In 1973 you would have earned a rebate of $9,000 and in 1975 a rebate of $3,797.28, or a total of $12,797.28. Although it can be said that our newspapers do not owe Kmart these rebates, I feel that our two companies should get together and discuss a plan that would be mutually beneficial. I am led to believe your contract with *Community Press* expires on March 1, 1977, so February would be an opportune time for our two companies to get together."

. . . Was Mr. Vann proposing that the *Statesman-Journal* would pay Kmart the nearly $13,000 in missed rebates if Kmart would agree to stop using the *Community Press*? . . .

Moors: That's the way—that was our impression of this particular situation, yes. . . .

Q. Did you consider that offer unusual at the time you received this letter?

A. Yes. . . .

Q. What was there other than this letter, if anything, that left you with the impression that that was the nature of his proposal?

A. Well, the telephone conversations that we had. Again, it was our impression that that was the intent, and if I can clarify why it was our feeling that this was the intent, was that this offer has never been made to us by any advertising medium that we deal with. No one ever goes back and says, "Here's money for something that, you know, we just kind of forgot about two years ago." That is just not done in this business.

If rebates are in existence and it's a policy of a newspaper or a television or a radio operation to return to the advertiser X amounts of dollars based on over-performance of a contract, it is stipulated in the contractual arrangements, the contract itself, the rate-card data that are given to the customer at the time he purchases the agreed-upon space. So this was an unusual situation, and therefore our assumption of the proposal was that we would get the money should we go back into the *Statesman-Journal.* There was no reason for us to believe otherwise. . . .

Q. Did you or Mr. Kreitz [Ed Kreitz, Kmart's corporate director of advertising at headquarters in Troy, Michigan] or anyone else that you discussed this with at Kmart characterize this proposal as an attempt to bribe Kmart?

A. No.

Q. Did you feel that it was?

A. Personally, yes.

Despite such temptations, Kmart stayed in the *Community Press*. Then, Moors said, Gannett began to play rougher.

Question: Did you ever hear, either directly from representatives of the *Statesman-Journal* or indirectly from people in Troy that the Community publications division of Early California Industries, the company putting out the *Community Press,* was in financial difficulty or was on the verge of bankruptcy?

Moors: Yes. . . .

Q. Do you remember who told you?

A. It came back to us from our corporate offices.

Q. Was it your understanding that it originated with the *Statesman-Journal?*

A. It was our assumption, quite frankly, that that's where it was coming from. It was—we had never had any of that type of activity before, and after our meeting with Mr. Vann and Mr. Hayden in Salem, where we discussed a test program, we did not commit our total advertising to them. It was after that time that all of those—all of this rumor activity and all the negative comments about *Community Press* started coming back to us from our international headquarters.

None of this had ever occurred prior to our not committing our total—you know, giving—making the decision and informing Mr. Hayden and Mr. Vann that we were not going to place the bulk of our advertising with them. None of this occurred prior to that. So therefore, that's why we have assumed, if you will, it was because of our not placing the advertising that all of this campaign to discredit everyone involved in the situation was ever started in the first place.

As Kmart kept using the weekly, Moors and his colleagues felt mounting attacks from Gannett—not only upon their standing within their company, but upon their personal integrity as well.

Question: Do you recall telling Mr. Pounds [a corporate-level Kmart executive] that you were unhappy or concerned about an exchange of correspondence between the *Statesman-Journal* company and the corporate headquarters in Troy?

Moors: Yes.

Q. What was the nature of your concern there?

A. Each of our regions operates fairly autonomously in judgment decisions on media that we're to use. There was an extremely high amount of communication going from Gannett in Detroit into our corporate offices: specifically, to our advertising director, Mr. Ed Kreitz.

We had received several phone calls from Mr. Kreitz concerning conversations that he had with Gannett representatives indicating that they couldn't understand why Kmart would allow one of their people to make poor media judgments as in respect to the Salem situation, where we were running in a community newspaper versus a daily paid-circulation newspaper. . . .

There were conversations concerning our advertising manager in Portland who had purchased a car from Mr. Dickey [publisher of the *Community Press*], had paid a sale price for it. However, it was turned around when it got in our corporate headquarters as to that Mr. Dickey had given this individual this car free. We received a phone call concerning that situation.

There were other rumors that our people were being given trips and what-have-you from the *Community Press*. There was an unusually high amount of rumors floating around that were coming to us from our international headquarters, along with negative comments about the *Community Press* as it was being compared to daily paid circulation in the *Statesman-Journal*. There was talk, again, as I say, that this office was incompetent in its judgment factors in the marketplace, that our local management did not really know what they were doing when it came to advertising, that no one could understand why Kmart would waste their dollars, and so forth.

We received quite a few calls concerning this type of a situation, and it was always just after a visit by a Gannett representative in our corporate headquarters, or a phone call from a Gannett representative.

Q. Let me make sure I understand the rumor about the free car. As I understand it, Mr. Dickey sold his car to a Kmart employee in Portland.

A. In Portland.

Q. And then somebody at the *Statesman-Journal* reported to Troy that Mr. Dickey had given the car to the Kmart person?

A. Yes.

Q. Did anybody at Kmart make an attempt to verify whether or not the car had been sold?

A. Yes. I did.

Q. What did you do to verify it?

A. Well, basically, we called and talked to both Mr. Dickey and the employee that was involved, and on our next trip to the Portland market, which was very shortly thereafter, we determined that the car had been purchased and not given to him, as had been inferred.

It was our feeling that everything possible was being done to make us look absurd from all standpoints, from our decision-making to taking graft and being involved in graft and corruption. It was very disturbing that Mr. Hayden, Mr. Vann, those at the *Statesman-Journal* that were trying to get us back into the *Statesman-Journal,* would go over our heads on a regional basis, and directly to our corporate advertising manager in an attempt to get business from Kmart. We're not used to that type of a situation, and quite frankly, it was the first time it had happened since I've been in this capacity.

Q. Has anything like it happened to you since?

A. No.

After the campaign against *Community Press* had driven out all the chains except Kmart, Moors and his local manager knew that the Salem store must resume advertising in the daily papers to compete. It was then that Gannett played its final card.

> **Question:** Turning for one moment to the rumor that the *Statesman-Journal* would boycott Kmart if the *Community Press* went out of business, did [store manager] Mr. L'Esperance tell you directly that he had heard the comment from Mr. Hayden?
> **Moors:** Yes.
> **Q.** Can you tell me, as best you can, precisely what Mr. L'Esperance told you Mr. Hayden had said?
> **A.** Well, basically, that all the major advertisers were back with the *Statesman-Journal;* that because of this fact the *Community Press* could not stay in business much longer from the loss of revenue; and that if we didn't return our advertising to the *Statesman-Journal,* that there would be nothing for us to advertise in should the *Community Press* go out of business. . . .
> It seemed rather sour-grapes type of thinking on their part that, you know, "We have everybody in Salem back now except Kmart, and by God," you know, "we know the *Community Press* is going to go out of business, so we're going to screw Kmart over real well."

So these were the tricks that Wayne Vann had learned as Buddy Hayden's right-hand man. And fresh from this triumph, Vann had been sent to Santa Fe. There was not a doubt in my mind that his orders were to apply his newfound expertise to the *Reporter.* A final piece of testimony from Moors underlined my fears.

> **Question:** Are there other Gannett markets that you're aware of where the Gannett paper faces competition such as the *Community Press* posed in Salem?
> **Moors:** Yes.
> **Q.** Which market?
> **A.** Santa Fe, New Mexico, San Bernardino, California, just to name two I can think of specifically, where there are weekly media that have penetrated the market to an extent that it is fragmenting the circulation of the daily newspaper, which, of course, is owned by Gannett.

In the privacy and comfort of the library, the work fairly flew. By early afternoon I had copied everything I felt I needed. I also had read the remainder, much of which corroborated the evidence in my notes. My work in the courthouse was completed. Yet it was not complete. As extensive as the file was, it was obviously not the full record on *Community Publications*

Inc. vs. Gannett Company. Missing were the depositions of Dickey and other CPI executives. Missing was any evidence regarding the alleged sweetheart contract with Boise Cascade Paper Company. Distressingly absent was any defense of Gannett. There was nothing from Buddy Hayden, nothing from Wayne Vann. Most disappointing, the file did not hold the testimony of Gannett's president, Allen Neuharth. I longed to know his interpretation of Hayden's message that "our goal is to fatally cripple the *Community Press.*" But his deposition was not there.

Returning to Judge Frye's office with the file, I felt one last temptation to ask for the rest of it. But already my luck had held past all reasonable expectation. I would push it no further. What I needed now was a clean getaway. The receptionist was talking with someone at her desk. I placed the file, facedown, on an adjacent table. I waved, and mouthed the words "Thank you." Then I walked out the door and across the big hallway to the elevator. As its sliding doors moved to seal me in, I exulted. My mission had succeeded. But I began the celebration too soon.

"Elevator! Elevator!" a woman called out. "Down, please."

Instinctively I reached out and blocked the closing of the doors. And then Judge Frye scurried into the elevator with me. She smiled and said hello, but I could scarcely hear her above the pounding in my chest. The doors slid shut. Five floors in the air, I was trapped in a tiny cubicle with the judge who had watched me work nonstop in her office for three days. She recognized me, undoubtedly she was curious, and she had a friendly nature. It was a certainty that during the course of our descent she would ask what I had been working on.

I saw just one chance. "That's a very attractive dress," I blurted out. And in fact, her dress was striking. Dark blue and properly decorous for a woman of her position, it also had a nautical flair, with white sailor stripes and splashes of red.

"Why, thank you," she replied automatically.

"It's kind of like a navy uniform, isn't it?" I rushed on, as the elevator crept downward. "I mean, not really like a uniform, but like a uniform that's been redesigned for a woman. Actually, it's very graceful and feminine, not military-looking at all." I realized I was babbling, but I could not pause long enough for her to change the subject. I could think of no other way to fill the endless seconds. The light above the elevator door showed we were passing through the third floor.

"Would you mind telling me where you bought it? I have a friend who would look terrific in that outfit. But maybe you'd rather not say. I know you ladies like to keep these things to yourselves sometimes." Stupid, sexist bullshit. I was embarrassing myself—but no other words would come.

"Oh, I have no problem with that," she said. "It was sent by a friend in Florida, but I don't know where she got it."

"Oh, from Florida. But I guess that makes sense, down there by the ocean and all. Well, that's too bad. I sure would like to get one just like it. I'll be on the lookout for something similar. That sailor design is really nice, and quite unusual."

I had no idea whether it was unusual. I was sure, however, that the judge felt she was enclosed with a blithering idiot. By now, she was probably as eager as I for the ride to end. And then, mercifully, it did. The second the doors opened onto the big stone lobby, I looked at my watch. "Oops, I'm late," I said, feeling a strange compulsion to take an official farewell from this person I had never met. "Nice talking with you. So long."

As I walked rapidly away, I sensed Judge Frye's eyes on my retreating back. But whether she really was staring at me or going about her business I did not know, for my paranoia had returned. The elevator ride had rattled me badly. *Just a moment, please,* I seemed to hear the judge calling after me. *Could I have a word with you?* But those sounds were only in my mind. I was flipping out.

Looming ahead was an obstacle I had barely noticed until this moment: a security guard's station, with a tall, uniformed black man on duty. He had ignored my previous comings and goings, but this time was sure to be different. At any second his beeper would sound, with my description and instructions to bar my exit. Even after I pushed through the revolving doors and onto the street, I did not feel I had eluded the authorities. I wanted to break and run. Of course, that would just draw the attention of anyone following me. Not that anyone was.

What was real? My intellect told me I had accomplished my purpose in Portland's federal court and was free to proceed with what I had gotten there. My imagination insisted that a hand was about to fall on my shoulder and a voice was about to say: *Please come with us, if you don't mind. We'd like to see what's in your briefcase.* At the first corner I took a turn. I did the same at the next. With each twist of my path I felt more confident of giving my pursuers the slip. I did not breathe easily until I was driving my rented car to the headquarters of CPI.

9

Victim and Villain

AFTER THREE DAYS IN THE secret file, my visit to Community Publications Inc. was an anticlimax—but an essential one. CPI's president, Richard Dickey, was polite but guarded, nervous about overstepping the gag order. He preferred to talk about his company in general, rather than its experience in Salem.

For ten years CPI had published a free weekly in Portland. The results its advertisers were getting had caused the Salem delegation to ask Dickey to start a paper there. A CPI-owned weekly also competed with Gannett in Honolulu, Dickey said, and part of his motivation for the lawsuit was to prevent a similar campaign in Hawaii. CPI's annual sales were about $21 million. For years CPI had been a division of a larger firm, Early California Industries. Dickey had headed that division, before buying CPI in 1981. With the purchase he acquired the lawsuit, filed when the *Community Press* failed in 1978. But he really couldn't talk about that. Dickey did not give me much I could use. But Larry Miller, the Salem weekly's former marketing director, did.

A thin, neat man whose appearance was still boyish despite the gray creeping into his black hair, Miller understood exactly why I had come to Oregon, and he wanted to help. Like other CPI officials he was bound by the court. But unlike the lawyers and Dickey, he was a frontline survivor of Gannett's attack upon the *Community Press*. His involvement was emotional as well as professional. In him I found what I had been seeking: someone willing to stretch the limits of the gag order in my direction.

We established rules for the interview. Miller would talk freely about the competitive situation in Salem, the *Community Press*'s brief history, his own feelings about watching the paper being killed before his eyes. But he would not disclose the specific tactics Gannett had used. From his point of view, he was staying on safe ground. From my perspective, I no longer needed to pry out those secrets. I did not tell him what I knew.

"We started out like gangbusters," Miller said, handing me a copy of the first issue of the *Community Press*. "People around here said they had never seen anything like it." Nor had I. That March 3, 1976, issue had seven sections, in eighty-eight broadsheet pages. I recalled the *Santa Fe Reporter*'s first effort: thirty-six tabloid pages. This paper was five times larger. A full-color photograph held the center of the front page, and color was sprinkled liberally throughout. The news content was abundant and decidedly local, with staff articles on people, politics, social issues like interracial adoption. Readers found out who got married, which bands were in town, who had starred in high school games, what was on television all week. There were sections for commentary, entertainment, and sports, plus numerous syndicated features: crosswords, horoscopes, comic strips.

For my taste, the content was a little "soft." There were no tough investigations, no bold opinion columns. But for the first issue of a newspaper created to bring relief to suffering advertisers, the *Community Press* was indeed a remarkable piece of journalism. And the paper's greatest glory was its advertising volume. It was massive. Local merchants by the dozen featured their goods and services in the brand-new weekly, and every chain store in Salem was also there, with page after page of paid advertising. Flipping past the ads of Sears, J. C. Penney, Montgomery Ward, food and drug chains that were just beginning to talk to us at the *Reporter* six years after our emergence, I could only marvel at what support like this would do for our bottom line.

"We made a profit in our very first month," Miller said proudly. "And for the next ten months after that." The debut was one of the most spectacular in publishing history. But as Gannett tightened the screws, things began to slip. Advertisers began dropping out. Many refused to say why. Some of the reasons were evident. Responding to competition, the dailies rescinded rate increases, upgraded services, and dropped the extra charges that had infuriated advertisers when Gannett had a monopoly. But other things were happening in secret. "We couldn't see the forest for the trees," Miller said. "We would be dealing with a raft of rumors two weeks old, while they would already be doing something else against us."

Yet the cruelest blow of all, Miller said, came not from Gannett but from the advertisers of Salem, among whom he lived and worked and did business. One after another, once they got their special deal and saved a few bucks at the dailies, they abandoned the struggling weekly that had made it all happen. "The thing about it was: People knew what was going on," he said. "It was like we were being beat up and stabbed in front of a guy's store, and he wouldn't come out and help us."

Even so, Miller was now convinced that the best defense would have been to expose Gannett's tactics as soon as they were implemented. He blamed himself and his superiors at CPI for waiting too long, for being too gentlemanly, for not blowing the whistle on their own behalf, long and loud and in public. "You don't want to seem like a crybaby," he said. "But if anything like this ever happened to me again, I would broaden the base of people I had conversations with. I would inform my own people sooner. I would tell the community what was happening, so the community could say, 'We aren't going to let that happen here.' Your customers need to know what Gannett is going to do, so when they're sitting across the desk the customer will be saying to himself, 'Yep, that's just what we were told they would do.' "

Miller said he would also stress every advertiser's stake in not getting trapped in a monopoly situation. "You've got to tell them: 'If we don't succeed here, no one else will ever come to this town.' Like any other businessman, Gannett must be put in the position of saying, 'Oops, this isn't working. It's actually costing us business. We've got to try something else.' " But Miller's paper had not done those things, I pointed out, at least not in time. "Yes, we waited much too long," he said. "But you've got to understand something. We couldn't believe it was happening to us. We simply didn't believe it was happening."

As the campaign against the *Community Press* unfolded, Miller said, his company did not adopt the tactics being used by Gannett. "You can't get in that game and play with them," he said, "because their resources are so much more than yours. They can play that game forever. They can give their space away. But you've got to play straight, or you'll go broke." And there was an additional reason why CPI had watched its moves very carefully. "Even if we had not been honest, we were smart enough to see that this thing could end up in court," Miller said. "So we were sure not to do anything to compromise ourselves there. But the truth is, we're honest people."

It was CPI's integrity, Miller said, that caused it to undertake the expense of a years-long legal battle. "Somebody had to show Gannett that they would take them to the wall," he said. "We have the resources, so why the hell let it happen? We just weren't going to let them kick us in the butt. The industry as a whole will benefit if Gannett changes its ways."

Miller's injured decency added a personal element, a flesh-and-blood victim, to the evidence I had smuggled out of the courthouse. For my purposes, for what I was planning to do in Santa Fe, this session with him was going very well.

I had one more question. If Gannett gets caught this time, I asked, and is forced to pay millions of dollars for what it did to the *Community Press,* what do you think it will learn? Noting that his company's case rested upon evidence seized under subpoena after the lawsuit was filed, Miller replied: "I suspect that what Gannett learned from Salem is this: Do what you did before, but don't document it the next time."

On the first leg of the return flight I felt crushed by weariness—and no wonder, for I had barely slept since leaving home. A quick post-Portland visit with a sister near Seattle had done nothing to slow my racing emotions. I downed an airline cocktail, then dozed. During a layover in Denver I stayed on the plane, for it was going on to Albuquerque. I dozed again on that final leg. But when we landed, I was jolted awake.

To avoid the crush, I remained seated while the other passengers exited. As I idly watched them pass, I recognized Wayne Vann! There was no mistake. I remembered him vividly from our time together years ago. Except for perhaps a few more pounds, he had not changed. Our eyes met, and he knew me, too. "Dick—Dick McCord!" Vann said, in a mixture of surprise and bonhomie. "What are you doing here?" In the press of deplaning passengers, however, this was no time to chat. "I'll wait for you in the airport," he said. A woman I did not know was with him.

A rush of panic, similar to the paranoia I had felt in the Portland courthouse, welled. Wayne Vann on the same plane? Too strange to be true! Had he been in Salem last week, too? Would he now deduce what I had been doing? No, no, that was unlikely. The flight had originated in Seattle and stopped in Denver on its way to New Mexico. In that mix of geography, the purpose of my trip surely was hidden. I pulled my briefcase with its hot cargo from beneath the seat, and headed for the terminal and a reunion with Wayne Vann.

"Been meaning to call you, Dick!" he said, pumping my hand with all the heartiness I remembered. "Say, this is Carol, my wife. Uh, you knew my first marriage broke up, didn't you?" I shook hands with Carol, an attractive, black-haired woman. "I've told you about Dick, Honey," Wayne said. "He puts out the *Santa Fe Reporter*. He and I used to work together at the paper. Good to see you!"

As we stood face to face, I felt something akin to revulsion for this affable blond man, with his gold necklace and receding hairline. The name Wayne Vann had run throughout the courthouse file in Portland, second only to Buddy Hayden's as an instrument of death for the *Community Press*. Now he had been sent to do the same thing to my newspaper. Even as he smiled and smiled, he knew what he was planning for me. But he did not know that I knew too. "Been meaning to call you for lunch, Dick. Even if we're competitors, no reason why we can't get along. Never expected to run into you here, though. Where you coming in from?"

"All the way from Seattle. I spent the weekend with a sister up there," I said. "Is that where you got on?"

"No, we just flew down from Denver. Had a conference there this weekend. You know how it goes. But I know Seattle quite well. My last assignment was up that way, in Oregon."

"Yes, I read about that when you came back to town," I said. "How does it feel to be in Santa Fe again? Did you miss it?"

"Yeah, Dick, I've missed it a lot. I missed the sunshine. Santa Fe feels like home to me. I'm glad to be back—and this time I'm here to stay."

Well, we'll see about that, I thought, clutching the briefcase almost close enough to brush my enemy's leg. Maybe your homecoming won't be quite as enjoyable as you expected it to be.

10

"The Newspaper That Was Murdered"

"EXTREMELY HOT BUT PRINTABLE—AND definitely newsworthy. We'd have no trouble establishing that point." That was my lawyer's assessment after reading the material from Oregon.

"It's evidence for a trial, so technically it's on the public record even though it's temporarily sealed," he went on. "Sooner or later, evidence like this is meant to become public knowledge. You just want to go public with it sooner rather than later." This was definitely the advice I wanted. "You broke no law getting this information. You didn't misrepresent yourself in any way. You told no lies. You didn't break into a locked file. Sure, it'll probably stir up trouble if you publish it—but most likely the trouble will be for the judge and her staff and Gannett, not you or the *Reporter*.

"There is, of course, some chance that you'll be charged with contempt. You did know the file was sealed. But if that happens, I think I can defend you successfully. You're not a party to the lawsuit, and you're just using what you were given voluntarily. An injunction forbidding you to publish it is unlikely. That would be prior restraint, and there's not much precedent for that. But you never know what a judge will do, and if there *is* an injunction, it would be a real problem. My advice is not to tip your hand until it's too late for them to try to stop you.

"This is a tricky situation, not at all black-and-white. Some guesswork is involved. But my guess is that if you go with it, you'll get away with it. It's your decision."

My decision was easy. To preserve the *Santa Fe Reporter*, I was determined to tell what Gannett did in Salem. It was our only hope for avoiding the fate of the *Community Press*. And to succeed in this goal, I must use the pages of my newspaper to accomplish a difficult task: educating all of Santa Fe in the complex realm of federal antitrust law. Fortunately, living with Gannett had taught me much about it.

Designed to encourage competition and prevent monopolistic practices, antitrust laws are weighted in favor of small companies and against large ones. As demonstrated by Standard Oil, U.S. Steel, American Tobacco Company, du Pont, United Fruit Company, the railroads, and other gargantuan organizations in the decades before crusading "trust-busters" broke them up, huge companies and cartels of huge companies have the means, the power, and the will to crush small competitors standing between them and absolute control of a market. The laws were enacted to stop this from happening.

With their limitless resources, the trusts frequently lowered the price of goods and services to a level below the cost of providing them. This brought short-term benefits for customers, and short-term losses for the trusts, easily covered by their wealth. It also caused the collapse of competitors who had to make enough on their sales to cover the cost of doing business. With the competition gone, the trusts recovered their losses and accumulated even greater riches by charging exorbitant prices and delivering inferior goods to the now choiceless public.

America's legendary fortunes were built in the era of the trusts, at the bitter expense of ordinary citizens. Eventually Congress heeded the cries of the populace. Over strident protest from the monopolies it passed reform legislation. First came the Sherman Antitrust Act in 1890, followed by the Clayton Antitrust Act in 1914 and other laws. Violations are considered so serious that damages awarded in civil suits are tripled by the court.

The antitrust laws were not meant to prevent large companies from competing fiercely—just to ensure that they did so fairly. The tenets of the free-enterprise system called for an atmosphere in which small businesses had a chance to emerge, somewhat protected from anticompetitive practices that could stamp them out. If small companies failed, it should be because of inferior goods or services, not the unrestricted might of a giant adversary. Thus the laws had a double standard, one for big guys and one for little guys. While small companies were generally free to cut prices, make unusual offers, and essentially try anything that might get them a foothold in the market, big companies had to tread carefully. If their actions took unfair advantage of a dominant market position, they could land afoul of the law.

Antitrust was a gray legal realm, open to interpretation and argument. Determining just where the proper line had been crossed posed a Solomon-like challenge to judges and juries, for their duty was not to block hard-nosed competition, merely to police it. Moreover, antitrust enforcement was subject to shifting political winds. "Populist" prosecutors and officials might be quick to take on the cause of the little man, while "pro-business" authorities might see nothing wrong in anything a huge corporation wanted to do. So despite the noble purpose behind antitrust, how it applied to the real world of business was often anybody's guess.

After consulting the *Santa Fe Reporter*'s lawyer, I pulled from my files a booklet titled *The Applicability of Federal and State Antitrust Laws as Related to the Publishing of Newspapers and Shoppers.* Written by a lawyer specializing in such matters, it had a checklist of practices that would be either questionable or illegal for a dominant paper to use against a smaller company. The checklist was a blueprint of Gannett's Salem campaign:

  • Offering special discounts to advertisers that do not normally advertise in the newspaper.
  • Maintaining advertising rates at an unreasonably low level during the period when the most serious competition existed.
  • Granting premiums or special rates to new advertisers.
  • Threatening to cut off advertisers' credit where such advertisers use competitive publications.
  • Offering discounts to certain selected advertisers.
  • Selling advertising only on the condition that the buyer not purchase advertising from another publication.
  • Threats against advertisers to discontinue their ads.
  • Refusing ads from clients using competitive publications.
  • Monopolization or attempt to monopolize.

Included on the list of predatory practices was one I was familiar with in Santa Fe: "Blanketing a competitive geographic area with free copies of the newspaper or shopper. This may be particularly anti-competitive where the circulation is made on the same date as the publication of the smaller competitor." Maybe the *Reporter* had grounds for a lawsuit of its own.

The Salem lawsuit charged Gannett with "extremely callous" disregard of the antitrust laws, and the term was accurate. It was inconceivable that the chain's legal department had not signed off on a campaign as blatant as this one was. Gannett obviously had no regard for the law, if the law got in the way. Soon we would find out if it had a regard for the truth.

It troubled me that I did not have the whole story. I wanted to know how Vann, Hayden, and Neuharth had defended themselves. I also wondered how many additional tactics were described in parts of the file I had not seen. But I saw no way to find out. The lawyer emphasized that our plans would be jeopardized if the court ordered us not to publish the sealed record. I would not run that risk. We would go with what we had.

For a week I holed up in my office, writing a report on the Salem story. Each segment was passed on to the lawyer. Normally I trusted my own feel for what could and could not go into print, but I remained uneasy about this story's dual motivation: news value and self-interest. The lawyer suggested few changes, however, because the material from the file spoke for itself.

The volume of information I brought back from Oregon posed a difficulty. Printing all or most of it would overload readers, causing many to turn away. Also, much of the evidence was redundant. This could be useful in court, but it was not effective journalism. Finally, printing all the material would require a vast amount of space. A law of diminishing returns was at work, and I heeded it. I trimmed the report to the most telling pieces of evidence from my notes. I was confident they would be sufficient to make the point.

At first Laurie and Didier were the only people at the *Reporter* who knew what I was doing. Both were sworn to silence. But as publication day drew near, others were brought in. Each new initiate posed a risk. Any careless remark could fly across town to a friend of a friend at the *New Mexican*— and Gannett headquarters was just a phone call away. But that could not be helped. Demanding secrecy, we expanded the circle.

Because there was no way to get photographs from Salem, I hired an artist, Betsy James, to illustrate the report. Betsy loved aggressive journalism, and worked fast. In two days she turned in a stunning set of symbols. For the even more delicate task of getting the report into type, I took aside the *Reporter*'s only compositor, a woman in her sixties, and asked her help. Many extra hours would be needed to punch this, I said, and its content must not be revealed to anyone. Would she be willing to work all weekend? Of course she would—and as for her leaking even a word of it, I did not have to worry.

I called our printer. We would need an overrun of several thousand for the first six pages of this week's newspaper, and he should schedule for it. "No problem," he replied. "What's the deal?" I hedged: "It's a special report, but I can't tell you any more than that. You'll understand when you see it."

On Tuesday morning, closing day, all the pieces were in place—except the most difficult one: contacting the key Gannett officials named in the report and asking them for comment. I dreaded this task, but it had to be done. The principles of journalism dictated that we give them a chance to respond. With a deep breath I dialed the *New Mexican* and asked to speak with Wayne Vann. "I'm sorry, he's away from the office today," his secretary said. I had not expected this.

"It's extremely urgent that I reach him today," I said. "Will he be calling in for messages? Or would it be possible for you to contact him directly for me?"

"I do expect him to call in," she said. "I'll be glad to give him the message. What is the nature of your business?"

"Just say I need his comment for an extremely important news article concerning him," I replied, not wanting to spell out what we were doing. "He knows me. I think he'll understand. But please emphasize that it's urgent I get in touch with him *today.*"

A frustrating beginning. Once I explained the nature of my call, I expected—and even hoped—that Vann's reply would be: "No comment. I can't talk about these things, because the matter is in litigation." And then I expected him to burn up the telephone lines to his superiors in the chain. But for him to be unavailable . . . I hadn't counted on that.

I dialed Gannett headquarters and asked for Allen Neuharth. He too was out of his office. I stressed that I urgently needed to reach him. "Could I ask what this is about?" his secretary asked coolly.

This time I was direct. "I'm the editor of a newspaper in Santa Fe, New Mexico, and we're planning to publish a highly critical story about how the Gannett papers in Salem, Oregon, drove a weekly competitor out of business. Mr. Neuharth is mentioned in the story, and I'm calling to get his comments." Though I tried to make my request sound imperative, the Gannett president's secretary was unimpressed. "When he calls in I'll give him the message," she said, in a tone implying that her boss had more important affairs than this breathless call from a small-time journalist.

In the comment-from-the-accused department, I was not doing well. This was cause for concern. Experience made me expect a refusal to comment on pending litigation. But the story must show that Gannett had been given an opportunity to respond. I toyed with the idea of holding the report, but it was not a real option. A full week would pass before our next publishing date, and during that time all sorts of things might happen. I had told Neuharth's secretary my purpose. Was his office now alerting its Salem operatives to refuse my calls? It would be a passive but effective way to buy time. But if I held the story, that would give Gannett time for an injunction, a preemptive denial, or other action. I had to keep trying to reach the accused.

On the next call, I scored. I reached Buddy Hayden. After eliminating the *Community Press,* he became publisher of Gannett's paper in Camden, New Jersey. Then he crossed the Delaware River, to be publisher of a huge non-Gannett daily, the *Philadelphia Bulletin.* My call there went straight through to him. When I stated my purpose he was surprised. When I started asking about things that had happened in Salem he was more so. But he remained composed. He refused to discuss any particulars, citing the lawsuit. To my central question of whether he had deliberately run the *Community Press* out of business, he replied: "Of course not. Absolutely not. Emphatically not. My business out there was to publish a newspaper and do the best job I could." He would say nothing more. But that sounded like a response to me. He courteously took his leave, and as our talk ended I could not help thinking that Buddy Hayden seemed an engaging chap.

I then called the Oregon law firm representing Gannett in Salem. With Hayden and Vann both gone, and their successors not present when the *Community Press* was driven under, the lawyers were the best source of comment from Oregon. But this would be the most dangerous call. The lawyers were in Portland. They surely knew Judge Frye. If anybody could get a quick injunction, they could. But things could not have turned out better. When I told Susan Hammer, a Gannett attorney, why I was calling, she clammed up. The matter is under litigation, she sniffed. Therefore, it cannot be discussed. Her client has denied all wrongdoing. That was all she was going to say.

I hung up feeling much better than I had an hour earlier. Now we had two direct responses, indicating a genuine effort to reach the accused. Messages had been left for Vann and Neuharth. Already it was lunchtime in Santa Fe, and two hours later in the East, where Neuharth and Hayden were based. And way out West, the lawyers in the same city as the sealed court file seemed unconcerned that a paper in New Mexico was writing about the case. Press time was just hours away. Now nothing was going to stop us from running the story, with all the elements it needed.

I did follow up on my calls to Neuharth and Vann. The Gannett president's secretary confirmed that she had given him my message, and told him I considered it urgent. But whether he would respond was up to him. For me, that was the end of that. But I kept trying to reach Wayne Vann. Because he lived in Santa Fe, he would be hardest hit by our report. Until the last minute,

I felt an obligation to alert him to what was coming. He could comment or not, as he chose. But he had to have a chance. Repeated calls to his office confirmed he had gotten my message. When the business day ended with no reply, I called his home.

I reminded his wife of our meeting in the airport. I emphasized it was crucial for me to reach him tonight, before the *Reporter* went to press with a story extremely critical of his job in Salem. She would not say where he was staying, but promised to call him for me. I phoned back as we were locking down the last pages. She had relayed my message, she said. If he had not called, he probably did not plan to do so tonight. I could think of nothing else to do. The *Santa Fe Reporter* for March 5, 1981, went to the printer without comment from Wayne Vann, and I went home to bed.

In the next day's *Reporter,* a startling page-one graphic by Betsy James showed a newspaper labeled the *Community Press* caught in the crosshairs of a high-powered rifle. Above it was a huge black headline that gave the special report its title: "The Newspaper That Was Murdered." In the next ten thousand words, we told what Gannett had done in Salem.

11

No Decency

"THE NEWSPAPER THAT WAS MURDERED" was a major production by the standards of the *Santa Fe Reporter*—or of any newspaper. Six full pages were devoted to it, the first six pages of that week's issue. The riveting illustrations by Betsy James anchored the pages, and the text told the story. The lead article gave the history of the rise and untimely fall of the *Community Press*. Accompanying stories drawn from the court file provided details. "How to Break the Little Guys" told how Gannett had squeezed local advertisers out. "How to Break the Big Guys" told how the chains were driven away. Gannett's internal correspondence was quoted extensively. Operation Demolition and the Dobermans were described in the words of Vann's memo. Larry Miller of the dead weekly was profiled. The responses from Hayden and Gannett's lawyers, and our efforts to reach Neuharth and Vann, were featured in boldface type.

And lest any reader not understand why a weekly newspaper in New Mexico was devoting so much space to events that took place years earlier and thirteen hundred miles away, I spelled out the reason in a signed commentary headlined "What Gannett Must Learn."

> During three days in U.S. District Court in Portland, Oregon, this writer could not help but be reminded of the McCarthy Hearings of the 1950s, and of their electrifying climax, one of the great moral moments of the last half of the 20th century. After days of probing the wanton human destruction caused by the fanatical anti-communist U.S. Sen. Joseph McCarthy, Army counsel Joseph Welch confronted the zealot from Wisconsin and wrote the epitaph for that evil era with these words: "At long last, sir, have you no decency?"
>
> In Oregon's capital city, Salem, a few years ago, all the terrible might of the huge Gannett newspaper empire was brought to bear on a young weekly that tried to meet the needs of a town suffering under the arrogance of a Gannett monopoly. And once the *Community Press* was targeted, Gannett and its hired guns stopped just this side of arson in their efforts to eliminate it.

The campaign worked, and the *Community Press* folded in 1978. But for once, Gannett had bullied the wrong victim. The parent company of the defunct weekly fought back with a federal lawsuit, charging the giant chain with blatant violations of the antitrust laws.

Evidence in the case has been gathering for the past two and a half years; and although Gannett wants to seal the court file from public inspection, a glimpse into it tells a sordid tale. According to sworn testimony, documents, letters, memos and other evidence, Gannett was not concerned with scruples or legalities once it decided to exterminate the *Community Press.*

The court record indicates that deliberate lies about the financial condition of the *Community Press* were launched by Gannett; that numerous secret deals, including thousands of dollars' worth of free advertising, were made to keep business out of the weekly; that multi-thousand-dollar bribes, termed "rebates," were offered for the same reason; that trips to Reno and Lake Tahoe were held out as lures to advertisers; that high Gannett officials visited chain store corporate headquarters far distant from Salem, to suggest that local managers using the *Community Press* were incompetent, and to smear them with false allegations of graft; and finally, that once the *Community Press* was on the run, advertisers faced the threat of not being accepted back into the Gannett paper unless they stopped using the weekly immediately.

Decency, indeed. In a world where most matters are colored various shades of gray, seldom does a record so rotten come to light.

Now the advertising manager who directed his Salem staff in the methods that destroyed the *Community Press* has been sent to Santa Fe, with a promotion, to become president and general manager of this city's Gannett-owned daily, the *New Mexican.*

At the *Santa Fe Reporter,* we are concerned that Wayne Vann comes with instructions to make us the newest target on Gannett's hit list, using the techniques that worked for him in Salem. We have been advised by antitrust experts that we have every reason to be concerned—and that to sit quietly and let it happen to us is the best way to invite extinction. We have been advised by the victims in Salem that the most important thing we can do is to let this community know what Gannett is capable of.

On our behalf, we make these statements to our readers, our advertisers and our friends:

• If you hear that the *Santa Fe Reporter* is in bad financial shape and going broke, it will be a lie. Last year was by far the best in our brief history, with the highest revenues and profits we have ever had. Moreover, except for our mortgage, we are free of debt. We started out very modestly and we still have a long way to go, but we are stronger now than ever before.

• If you hear that the *Santa Fe Reporter* is making deals with advertisers, coming off the rate card, giving away free color, etc., it will be a lie. We print our rates, and we stick by them. We always have, and we will continue to do so now.

• Finally, we would like to state that we do not fear competition, as long as it is clean. We have been competing with the *New Mexican* ever since we started in 1974, and we've done OK so far. If the new regime keeps it clean, there will be no complaints from us.

But based on the record in Salem, when Gannett decides to kill something, it turns readily to a number of weapons that clean competition abhors: greed, lies, deceit, fraud, intimidation, bribery, fear, pressure, illegality. These are powerful weapons, fully capable of causing death, as the *Community Press* sadly learned. Yet when companies and individuals have no decency of their own, they do not realize that decency itself can be a weapon far more potent than anything in their tawdry arsenal.

What Gannett will learn in Santa Fe, if it tries any of that stuff here, is that the aroused decency of this fine city—that the decent men and women here, on guard against the tactics that destroyed a good, community-oriented newspaper in Salem—constitutes a force against which not even the billion-dollar muscle of the largest and dirtiest newspaper chain in the land can prevail.

My primary purpose in publishing "The Newspaper That Was Murdered" was to make it impossible for Gannett to launch a Salem-type campaign in Santa Fe. I wanted advertisers to be on guard against unusual offers from the *New Mexican,* and to suspect that any deal too good to be true was probably crooked. I wanted the daily's sales staff to be forewarned about sleazy tactics it might be assigned, and to refuse to do them. I wanted to shame Wayne Vann and his masters into playing fair, or at least make them fear they could not get away with what they had done before. And I wanted to send a clear signal to Gannett that we were onto their game—and that where one lawsuit had been filed, others could follow.

In other words, I wanted the *Santa Fe Reporter* to live. Our best hope was to strike a swift preemptive blow. Our strongest weapons were surprise and publicity. So those were the ones we used. There was, however, another motivation for getting the Salem story out of the sealed court file and into the open. For the good of journalism, the ethics of its largest chain had to be exposed.

Though it was fading fast, I wanted to cling to my belief that the press was a noble institution. I saw little difference between the turn-of-the-century railroad and oil trusts that crushed everything in their path, and a giant newspaper company that did the same. If anything, the newspaper company was worse, because of the moralistic cloak in which it wrapped itself.

I did not consider myself totally naive. I was aware that the journalistic landscape of America was dotted with kingdoms that had brutalized all rivals. I knew that many legendary press lords were bloodthirsty businessmen as well as brilliant publishers. Even so, I was disturbed by my discoveries about Gannett. There was something particularly sinister about the biggest chain of all systematically perfecting lethal tactics for rubbing out the competition, then exporting them throughout its constantly expanding empire. While the old barons dominated one city or at most a few, Gannett's appetite seemed insatiable.

In just the five years since Gannett had entered my life by buying the *New Mexican,* its holdings had grown from fifty-three daily papers to more than eighty, with a combined circulation of some 3.5 million. Almost every month brought news of more acquisitions, and every year the chain was casting its eyes on larger papers. What had once been an inconsequential regional group, concentrated in upstate New York and distinguished neither for its journalism nor its size, had grown into a juggernaut, driven only by money. And every dollar that poured into headquarters merely fueled the ambition to get even more. Because monopoly was essential to the enormous profits it craved, Gannett had decided to do whatever was necessary to eliminate the competition. Moreover, Gannett was getting away with it. Scarcely a voice in print had been raised in protest.

By publishing "The Newspaper That Was Murdered," I wanted to get voices protesting. I thought what Gannett had done in Salem was too flagrant to be ignored once it got into the spotlight. I wanted our report to be the start of something big. I felt sure that other elements of the press would follow the *Reporter*'s lead. I was confident that major newspapers and the electronic media would be sufficiently outraged to tell the Salem story on a national level. If anything could change Gannett's ways, I thought with delicious irony, it was the power of the press—the widespread disclosure of the truth.

I was in for some surprises.

12

Aftershocks

IN JULY 1981, FOUR MONTHS after our report, two of the country's foremost
media trade journals, *Columbia Journalism Review* and *Advertising Age,*
published lengthy accounts of what had happened in Salem. Both stories
referred frequently to our report, and both quoted extensively from the
evidence I found in the Portland courthouse. The file was shut tight after
our disclosures. No other reporter ever gained access to it.

"How Gannett Took Oregon" was the title of *Advertising Age*'s front-
page article. It was basically a retelling of the campaign to kill the *Community Press.* But writer Joseph Winski dug up new details. The best one was
in his first paragraph:

> SALEM, ORE.—Shortly after he became publisher of Gannett
> Co.'s daily newspapers here in May 1976, N. S. (Buddy) Hayden
> stood atop a desk in the Oregon Statesman newsroom and made a
> little speech. He told about 100 assembled employees, according to
> several who were there, "The *Community Press* will be out of business
> by Christmas."

Winski also quoted William Mainwaring, who sold the Salem papers to
Gannett in 1974 and stayed on as publisher. He was told, Mainwaring said,
"that I would have almost total local autonomy." But he soon learned that
autonomy was impossible under Gannett. After two unhappy years in his
post, Mainwaring resigned. "The job had ceased to be fun," he said. "I wrote
that I had concluded that I wasn't cut out to be a Gannett-type publisher
and that I would like to be replaced, the sooner the better." Another non-
Gannett-type was Robert Pritchard, the Salem papers' longtime advertising
director, who quit shortly after the arrival of Hayden and Vann. "Wayne
and Buddy were just not my kind of people," he said. "The job became
unbearable to me."

The article noted that after the *Community Press* failed, Gannett's two
newspapers in Salem were combined into one. With the merger, thirty-
one employees were laid off, news content was reduced by some ninety

columns a day, and Salem became a one-newspaper town. The service given to advertisers, however, did not sink back to the depths reached in the days before the *Community Press*.

Hayden, Vann, and Gannett headquarters refused to discuss the case in any depth. But they denied all wrongdoing, as did a Gannett lawyer. Again Hayden was the most talkative. "To my knowledge, we didn't do anything illegal in Salem," he said, dismissing his campaign as mere "hype to get our people moving." Hayden acknowledged his desktop vow to run the *Community Press* out of business "by Christmas." But that, he said, was just "more hype." When Winski noted that the weekly survived the holidays of both 1976 and 1977 before folding in September 1978, Hayden replied: "I didn't say which Christmas."

Columbia Journalism Review was more pointed. "A tireless champion of the public's right to know, the nation's largest chain thinks Operation Demolition is nobody's business but its own," said the introduction. The story then contrasted Gannett's public policy on openness with its private one:

> The Gannett Co. has made freedom its business. As a conspicuous defender of the First Amendment, it has filed dozens of lawsuits challenging courtroom secrecy. It has instituted more cases to open public records and meetings than any other media organization, with the possible exception of Knight-Ridder. Allen H. Neuharth, president and chairman of the board, has hopscotched around the country to speak on behalf of freedom of information. The public has been apprised of these activities through a million-dollar advertising campaign that identifies Gannett as "A World of Different Voices, Where Freedom Speaks." Full-page ads in leading newspapers and magazines have followed such themes as: "At Gannett we believe that today, more than ever, journalists must be prepared to move quickly and effectively to defend the public's right to know—the cornerstone of our rights as a free people in a free society."
>
> This dedication to the public's right to know, however, does not extend to the right to know about how Gannett does business.

Across five pages, the magazine described how Gannett had achieved its ends in Oregon. It concluded:

> "There's no room for secrecy in a courtroom, during the trial or pretrial proceedings," says Neuharth flatly, at the outset of a brief telephone interview. "Courts are supposed to be public." Neuharth has consistently argued that the right to gather information is inherent in the

right to report it. Does he think there are any circumstances under which court records ought to be closed? "Only in cases involving minors or family matters." Does he see any inconsistency in that position and Gannett's insistence that most of the file in Salem be closed and people connected with the case be ordered not to discuss it? He bristles with annoyance at what he clearly considers a dim-witted question. "No, I don't think it's inconsistent at all. That's a civil case involving a controversy between one business and another. The records of a corporation hardly seem to me to fall under the First Amendment. That's *business*! I don't think it has anything at all to do with the First Amendment."

Publisher's Auxiliary, the weekly journal of the National Newspaper Association, also recognized the Salem case as one of great significance to the industry. After our report, *Pub Aux* followed each new development, often with front-page articles. Yet the "bible" of the industry, *Editor & Publisher,* barely touched the story. Only one item appeared after our report, and that one, on page 89, was just a nine-paragraph notice of the upcoming trial. This lack of interest mystified me, until someone pointed out that Gannett was *E&P*'s biggest advertiser.

Even less concerned were the major media. I sent our report to the *New York Times.* No response. The nation's leading business paper, the *Wall Street Journal,* also was uninterested. *Inside Story,* the Public Broadcasting System's weekly television report about the press, hosted by former independent newspaper publisher Hodding Carter III, seemed excited. A camera crew came to Santa Fe to interview me about Salem. But nothing was aired. The commercial networks showed no interest. Nor did papers operated by the other big chains—Knight-Ridder, Scripps Howard, Thomson. Most distressing of all, the daily newspapers of Oregon chose to remain officially unaware of what Gannett had done in the state's capital city. Of Oregon's nineteen daily newspapers, fourteen were chain-owned, and none faced head-to-head competition. They all found it possible to ignore the downfall of the *Community Press.*

In the town of Canyonville, 160 miles south of Salem, a perplexed reader showed the editor of the weekly *Canyon Creek Current* a copy of "The Newspaper That Was Murdered," sent to her by a sister in Santa Fe. Why, she asked, had there not been a word about this in the four Oregon dailies she subscribed to? Why had she first heard of it in a New Mexico weekly? "Having grown up in Salem," the editor replied, "—and even having had a relative featured once in the *Community Press*—my interest was immediate. And after finishing the exhaustive piece on the *Community Press,* my question proved the same as Mrs. Benedict's: Where has this been written about in the Oregon press? My reaction, as she surely knew it would be, was also the same as hers: indignation." But still the state's major papers refused to cover the Salem story.

Those articles that did appear, however, identified the *Santa Fe Reporter* as a foe of Gannett. I learned we were not alone. One by one, until they numbered in the dozens, messages arrived by mail and telephone from all over the country, all expressing outrage about what we had revealed. Several messages, some of them desperate, came from papers trying to survive against Gannett, and facing variations of the Salem campaign. Some came from papers competing against other chains using similar tactics. And many calls and letters came from Salem itself, where copies of "The Newspaper That Was Murdered" apparently began circulating immediately after it was published. The Salem letters came from various places: civic groups, the community college, the sheriff's department, an organization called Small Business Advocates Inc., a human relations company, an Arabian horse ranch, and several individuals. Their messages all were similar: Our report was true, the people of Salem were furious at Gannett, and they wanted the *Community Press* back.

Almost everybody wanted copies of "The Newspaper That Was Murdered." Fortunately, we had printed thousands of extras. Soon they were going all over the country—to Indiana, Colorado, California, Georgia, Virginia, Oregon, Michigan, Vermont, Ohio, New Jersey, Florida, Arkansas—and to Green Bay, Wisconsin. As the story spread, even without the help of major media, I was heartened. Each publisher, elected official, journalist, civic leader, or ordinary citizen who was offended by Gannett's tactics was another obstacle for the chain to contend with the next time it launched a similar campaign.

But distressingly, the rest of the Salem story never came out. Unwilling to have its practices revealed in an open court, Gannett made a private settlement with CPI a week before the trial was to begin. The dollar amount was not revealed. As it had for the pretrial file, Gannett demanded that the terms of the payout be kept secret. Other conditions insisted upon by Gannett were that all evidence be sealed from public view forever, and that all parties be ordered never to discuss the case.

The gag did not quell speculation about how much Gannett had forked over to keep its "trade secrets." In a page-one story, *Publisher's Auxiliary* set the amount at between $3 million and $4 million. The rumors cited by *Advertising Age* were more cautious, putting the payout at between $1 million and $2 million. The five-inch brief that appeared in *Editor & Publisher,* on page 43, made no mention of any amount. "The terms of the settlement were not disclosed," *E&P* reported. Whatever the sum, it brought Community Publications Inc. more money than the company could have made over many years of publishing in Salem. But its newspaper remained dead.

Gannett's decision to offer no defense reassured me that I had not missed any evidence that might have justified the Salem campaign. I also felt certain "The Newspaper That Was Murdered" had helped Gannett conclude that silence was worth purchasing. Even the media that had ignored our report were now alerted to the Salem case, and the trial would have to be covered. To avoid exposure, Gannett bought its way out. A statement from chain headquarters sought to wave away the damage. The payout, the statement emphasized, would have "no material financial impact" on the company.

With the secret settlement, all hope of ever getting the full story died. Though not unexpected, the settlement left me with mixed feelings. I was glad that CPI had gotten some compensation for what it had suffered. I was glad that we had been able to get at least part of the story out. But mainly I was discouraged—that the nation's richest newspaper company could simply weasel out of trouble by writing a check.

Within weeks, however, came a development that raised my spirits: The U.S. Justice Department's antitrust division announced it was investigating Gannett. The feds were looking into the chain's practices in Salem, Santa Fe, and other cities. In one of them, Boise, Idaho, a publisher whose free weekly was forced to close had filed a lawsuit charging Gannett with violations "amazingly similar" to the ones in Salem. The Justice Department attorney in charge, Bruce Pearson, did not mind saying what had touched off the probe. "It's because of guys who write news articles," he explained when I telephoned for a story about the investigation.

The next call for the story brought a pleasant surprise. Richard Dickey, the CPI president who refused to be quoted for the Salem report, was ready at last to talk. He proved a forceful spokesman. "Most businesses," he said, "compete for a share of the market. But many newspapers, particularly those owned by chain operations, think of their share of the market as 100 percent—and if competition springs up, they snuff it out by any means.

"What would I like to see happen? I'd like to see the Justice Department pursue the investigation to its conclusion. I'd like to see them take sanctions against Gannett for the activities that went on in Salem. And I'd like to set a precedent: that the daily newspaper industry has to play by the same antitrust rules that all the rest of us must obey."

In Santa Fe we wanted the same thing: for Gannett to play fair. "The Newspaper That Was Murdered" was meant to inoculate our city against the tactics that had killed the Salem weekly. It was preventive medicine— and more or less, it worked. For two weeks after the report, we kept the issue hot. We warned that unwitting advertisers could become snarled in antitrust litigation if they jumped at too-attractive offers. We printed several letters pledging support if Gannett tried its tricks in Santa Fe. But then we dropped it. Whoever had not gotten the message by now, I felt, would never get it; and belaboring our vulnerability would only alienate readers.

When the furor faded, Wayne Vann and the *New Mexican* did seek to take business from the *Reporter*. Some of the tactics did seem questionable. Advertisers reported offers of free color, special rates, unusual services, even free ads. Some less talkative clients dropped us and refused to say why. We kept a log of each incident, thinking it might someday be used in our own antitrust suit. The list was long. As time passed, however, I realized our evidence fell short of sure victory in court. Most examples were petty affairs, quick deals that might be made on the spot by an overzealous ad rep. Nothing resembling the Salem campaign was launched against us.

I never doubted that Vann had been sent to destroy the *Reporter*. Nothing else could explain why Gannett, knowing what he had done in Salem, chose not to fire, demote, or even rebuke him, but instead promoted him to another town where a weekly was troublesome. What else could explain why Hayden was made publisher of one of the chain's largest newspapers? Yes, we were on the hit list. But we forced Gannett to alter its plans. Instead of presiding over another execution, Vann played close to the line in Santa Fe. Whenever his people crossed over it, they were careful to dash back before they got caught. This did cause difficulties at the *Reporter*, but we could live with them. A Salem-style campaign would have killed us.

I also never doubted that exposing Gannett's tactics against the *Community Press* saved the *Reporter* from a similar death. The publicity embarrassed and frightened Gannett, and raised our city's resistance. I considered it a victory when the *Columbia Journalism Review* got Vann to state that any suggestion he had been sent to destroy the *Reporter* was "absolutely preposterous." Yet looking back over all the reaction to "The Newspaper That Was Murdered," the remark that lodged longest in my mind was the one made by a store owner in Santa Fe. "I don't see what all the fuss is about," he said. "That's just business."

Ah, yes . . . rainy Oregon, in the winter of 1981.

How long ago all of that seemed now—and how much water had flowed downstream since then. I no longer had the *Santa Fe Reporter,* or any newspaper, to run. I was no longer married. I was seven years older, and tired of the struggle. In many ways I was not even the same person. For more than twenty years I had been a journalist. Now was my time to do something else. I had it coming. So why was Frank Wood from Wisconsin on the telephone, saying all the wrong things? *"I want you to come up here and help me,"* he was saying. *"I want you to come to Green Bay."*

"I don't get it, Frank. What could I do in Green Bay?"

"What I want you to do in Green Bay is what you did in Salem."

Part II

Green Bay, Wisconsin

13

Not in the Cards

OF COURSE I SYMPATHIZED WITH Frank. Moreover, I owed him. But there was one thing I knew for sure: I had no intention of taking on his fight. I had plenty of reasons not to.

Until the end of the year at hand, 1988, I was under contract to remain at the *Santa Fe Reporter,* to assist the new owner in the transition. Three months of this obligation remained when Frank's call came. And looking ahead to the new year, when I was finally free and clear, I had other plans. Early in 1989 I wanted to take a two-month driving trip, to my home state of Georgia and many other places, in this country and Canada, to renew contacts too long set aside. I also was chairman of a summer newspaper conference in Atlanta. My hands would be full through July. After that, I simply wanted to be home. Maybe I would start writing the novel I had in mind. Maybe I would just read and take hikes and goof off. Unwinding from the *Santa Fe Reporter* would not be a quick job. But thanks to the sale, my finances were covered for a period of rest and recuperation.

There were also two deeper reasons not to go to Wisconsin: I did not want to, and I did not think it would do any good.

I had not seen the books of Frank's *News-Chronicle,* but I was sure they were grim. The last time he confided in me, its losses exceeded three hundred thousand dollars and its share of the advertising market was just 10 percent. These figures were not life-sustaining. Moreover, history was against him. Cities with competing daily newspapers had all but vanished from the American scene. Fewer than twenty were left, as advertisers everywhere found it easier to deal with only the dominant paper and save their thinking for other aspects of their business. Since the 1950s, more than four hundred papers had succumbed to the single-buy mentality. How could Frank's puny *News-Chronicle* buck the tide? And my friend faced a danger worse than the mere loss of his failing daily. By subsidizing the *News-Chronicle* with his other operations, he was weakening his entire Brown County Publishing Company—his life's work and the employer of hundreds of people.

No, this was not something I wanted to get involved in.

I also had grown disillusioned about fighting Gannett. Sure, we had stung them in Santa Fe, and had thwarted their plan to take us out in a blitz. So they switched to a siege. Year after year the struggle remained brutal. As time passed and the memory of our exposé faded, the business tide slowly flowed back in Gannett's direction. The *Reporter* held its own, paying its way, doing good journalism, improving its conditions. But we could not break through to prosperity.

We did outlast Wayne Vann. Even if his original plans were nipped, he ran Gannett's Santa Fe paper for several years. He did win a larger share of business for the *New Mexican*. But the circulation decline continued, despite his frantic efforts. It was a festering problem, and in time Gannett sent another publisher, then another, to head the Santa Fe franchise. And so our local battle with Gannett went on. On the national level, however, the trouble we caused with the report on Salem petered out quickly. After the initial concern by a few publications, no one seemed interested in how Gannett took Oregon. All the chain had to do was hunker down, refuse comment, wait for the squall to pass, and then get back to business.

Even more discouraging was the U.S. Justice Department investigation of Gannett. Our report triggered it early in 1981, just weeks after Republican Ronald Reagan became president. But as his administration settled in, it left no doubt that the regulation of business was not in favor. Antitrust enforcement faded away, and the case against Gannett sank without a trace. All of this left small independent newspapers twisting slowly in the wind, fighting without assistance against the chains. The *Reporter* did carve out a niche in Santa Fe. But years of battling a relentless foe had given me my fill. Taking on the largest newspaper chain was like taking on Big Oil or the military-industrial complex: A skirmish could be won now and then, embarrassment could be caused—but in the end, the giants kept right on doing what they were doing before.

Thus I had no desire to undertake whatever Frank had in mind for Green Bay. As gently as possible, I told him. "It's not in the cards, Frank. I'm totally strung out until the end of next summer. And you need to act long before then. Sorry."

"I understand," he said. "Well, I'll figure out something."

I felt a little bad about turning him down. But I knew I had done the right thing. Hopeless gestures did not appeal to me, and the sooner Frank faced facts the better off he would be. I just hoped he did not feel betrayed.

If he did, his next call did not show it. Nor the next, nor the next. "So," he would say amiably, "any new thoughts about coming to Green Bay?" Each time he called, I reiterated more firmly that it wasn't going to happen. "I see," he would say calmly. Then a couple of weeks later, the phone would ring again. "Been thinking over my offer?" I took it as a game, but over and over I told myself not to get sucked into this one.

The year ended, and with it my time at the *Reporter*. My long sentimental journey was to begin on January 28, 1989. As that date drew near, Frank invited me to Green Bay, to discuss a possible antitrust lawsuit with him and John Guadnola, a lawyer in the Salem case. I was happy to go. His chances of beating Gannett seemed better in court than in the marketplace.

In the depths of the grim Wisconsin winter, we huddled. The lawyer and I pressed Frank for specific cases of anticompetitive tactics used by Gannett against him. He had lots of accusations, but evidence was scarce. Many of his suspicions were based on hearsay, secondhand reports, off-the-record conversations. He had nothing resembling the file I had found in Portland. I recalled Larry Miller's words: *What Gannett learned was this: Do what you did before, but don't document it next time.*

I asked Guadnola privately if he felt a lawsuit would work in Green Bay. He seemed to be guarding his words with Frank, and I wanted his candid assessment. "There's definitely something here," he said. "But whether it's enough is anybody's guess."

"Would you take this case on contingency, like in Salem?"

"We'd really have to think about it first."

"And if Frank paid the legal costs, how much would that be?"

"Let's just say—a lot."

On the second day our talks shifted to another potential way for Frank to save the *News-Chronicle:* by entering a joint operating agreement with Gannett's *Green Bay Press-Gazette.*

Established by Congress in 1933, a joint operating agreement—or JOA, as it is called—is an exemption from antitrust laws. It lets two papers in the same city merge business functions, such as advertising, printing, and circulation, while keeping separate news staffs, which still compete. Profits from the joint operation are split according to an agreed-upon formula. Under a JOA, newspapers engage in price-fixing, market allocating, and other usually forbidden practices. The rationale for the exemption is that a community is hurt more by the loss of a second editorial voice than by eliminating competition between the papers. Because JOAs openly violate antitrust regulations, each must be approved individually by the Justice Department. In order to gain approval, papers applying for a JOA must establish that one of them would fail without it.

Reaffirmed and made more explicit by Congress in the 1970 Newspaper Preservation Act, the JOA exemption has many critics. They argue that often neither paper is truly failing, and that the agreement between them is nothing but collusion to increase profits enormously. They point out that a JOA is really a dual monopoly, enabling two papers to impose whatever advertising and circulation rates they choose, without fear of daily competition. Even weekly competition often is squeezed out or never emerges, because JOA papers suck up virtually all the advertising in town.

The critics also note that most of the nation's twenty-five or so JOAs exist not between independent papers, struggling to hold on in cities where they have deep roots, but between papers owned by chains, with ample resources to cover deficits with profits made elsewhere. The harshest critics say the title of the Newspaper Preservation Act should be changed to the "Crybaby Billionaire Publishers Act." Not coincidentally, the richest publisher of all, Gannett, was presiding over eight JOAs, the most of any chain.

Even as we plotted strategy in Green Bay, one highly suspect JOA application was stirring up the newspaper industry. It too involved Gannett. The city was Detroit, whose two dailies were owned by Gannett and the second-largest chain, Knight-Ridder. Detroit was the country's fifth-largest newspaper market, and both papers had circulations exceeding six hundred thousand. Yet both were losing money, in reckless slash-and-burn competition. Many observers saw the losses as deliberate, to justify the JOA application. As the country's wealthiest chains, Gannett and Knight-Ridder could cover their dubious losses in Detroit as long as they chose to. What they chose instead was to seek a JOA. The accompanying announcement spoke in pious terms of the importance of preserving in Detroit "two strong and independent news and editorial voices for at least the next century."

Frank learned of the Detroit JOA bid late in 1988, on his return from an ocean cruise celebrating his sixtieth birthday. Its blatant cynicism appalled him. Before Detroit, he had felt that Knight-Ridder, at least, was a principled company. Watching it sell out was hard. Yet now he was contemplating his own JOA with detested Gannett. The prospect did not go down well. To give him further pause, he knew that in most JOAs the stronger newspaper calls the shots. The weaker partner gets enough of the shared business to survive and make some money, but the dominant paper dictates the terms. In any JOA in Green Bay, the *News-Chronicle*'s role would be totally subservient.

"The thought of getting into bed with Gannett is enough to turn my stomach," Frank said grimly. "But if it's the only way I can save the *News-Chronicle,* I'll do it. At least this would be an honest example of a JOA. My newspaper really is failing—and I don't want Green Bay to lose its second voice." Then his eyes glinted with mischief. "But if we can pressure Gannett into doing this instead of driving us under, it would be a real burr under their saddle."

I had my doubts. My own metaphor was a shotgun wedding, and it did not seem likely. "Can a newspaper be forced into a JOA, for the good of the community?" I asked Guadnola. After twenty years in the business I should have known the answer, but I didn't. He raised an eyebrow at my ignorance. "No, you can't force anybody into a JOA. They have to agree to it."

When we broke up, no plan was in place. I returned home and resumed packing. Two days before my departure, Frank called. "John wrote a letter that really puts it to Gannett," he said. "We sent it directly to Al Neuharth, air express."

"A letter, huh? What was it about—a lawsuit or a JOA?"

"A little bit of both. Shall I read it to you?"

The lawyer's letter was a well-crafted blend of threat and appeal, warning and conciliation. It stated that Guadnola's firm had been retained by the *News-Chronicle,* and slyly referred to Salem. It cited possible grounds for an antitrust suit in Green Bay. It acknowledged that Frank's paper would soon fail without some form of relief. But instead of a lawsuit, it suggested, a joint operating agreement would be preferred.

"It is obvious from your statement in Detroit that you share our sentiments regarding the importance of multiple editorial voices," Guadnola wrote. "The opportunity for two voices to be heard is just as important in Green Bay as in Detroit. Consequently, we hope you will be as interested in helping avoid the demise of an alternative voice in Green Bay as you are in Detroit." The letter set a deadline for Gannett to respond.

The points were well made. But I did not expect much to result. All Gannett had to do was sit tight. Then Frank would have to make the next move. Unless a law firm took the case on contingency, I was sure he could not afford a lawsuit. And if he did sue, Gannett could wait until then to take him seriously. No, the letter was largely a bluff—and I was sure Gannett's lawyers were smart enough to figure that out. Without much hope I wished

Frank luck. I was just glad it was out of my hands. Three days later I was on the road.

Dallas, Baton Rouge, New Orleans, Biloxi, Atlanta, Tampa, the Okefenokee Swamp, Chattanooga, Nashville, Washington, Wilmington, New York, Hartford, Providence, Maine, Prince Edward Island in Canada, Quebec, Niagara Falls, Cleveland, Fort Wayne, Kankakee, Davenport, Sioux Falls, Custer National Battlefield in Montana, Casper, Laramie, Denver. And so many points in between. But I did not visit Wisconsin, and I did not call Frank Wood.

For sixty-six days and twelve thousand miles I roamed, mostly on back roads. I saw relatives, college pals, the hometown gang, strangers, old girlfriends, fellow journalists, numerous graduates of the *Santa Fe Reporter.* Some twenty-nine states and four Canadian provinces passed under my wheels. I stopped at a dozen places where I had lived. I felt lonely, happy, nostalgic, thrilled, cold, excited, tired, free, and lost, several times each. Many days I logged six hundred miles or more. In the long solitudes I slipped loose from the ties that had bound me so closely to the *Santa Fe Reporter,* for so many years. It was exactly what I intended to do.

At 6 P.M. on April 3 I pulled into my driveway. The last two hundred miles, through the mountains, canyons, and mesas of New Mexico, had reminded me all over again that this was the best place. At last I was home, and here I would stay. A couple of days later the phone rang. "I thought it was about time for you to be getting back," Frank said.

"So how did it go with the letter to Gannett?" I asked.

"They turned down the JOA. Said it would be 'inappropriate' because of our 'threat.' Their whole reply was four lines long."

"So what's your plan now?"

"I'm still working on it." Pause. "Thought any more about coming up here to help me?"

Our game resumed where it left off. I was as determined as ever to avoid stepping into shit in Wisconsin. I was settling back into Santa Fe. I needed time to be with Bonnie, my lady friend. I wanted to get going on that novel. And I had to pull together the newspaper conference scheduled for July. Frank understood completely. He just kept calling. My refusals got sharper. "Frank, I don't think you can pull it out."

"Well, maybe not."

"Sad as it is, these things happen. Very few little papers can stand up to Gannett. And from what I've seen, the *News-Chronicle* is not one of them."

"But what they're doing is just not right, goddammit!"

"Yeah, Frank, but the good guys don't always win."

The next time, I was blunter still. "Everything dies sooner or later, Frank. It's the way of the world. You've had thirty-five good years in the newspaper business. You're sixty years old. It's time to be thinking about retirement. Can't you just let go of the *News-Chronicle,* and feel good about what you've done? They can't take that away from you. Listen to what I'm saying."

The next time: "Frank, you've got three hundred people depending on your company for jobs. Only forty or fifty of them work for the *News-Chronicle.* If you let it drag down your whole operation, you'll regret it the rest of your life—and a lot of others will, too." The next time: "Frank, let me put it as plainly as I can: I am not coming to Wisconsin. It is not going to happen. I am not coming up there just to help you do something stupid!"

The July newspaper conference in Atlanta came off well. I returned satisfied and relieved, ready to get on with other things. But the phone kept ringing. Frank's persistence puzzled me. Did he not have ears to hear? Did he not know when to quit? Could he not admit he was in a hopeless situation? With all his savvy and experience, could he not see that some foolish last stand would only bleed dry his dwindling resources, with about as much chance of success as the one led by General Custer? I remembered the white tombstones scattered through the hills above the Little Bighorn River.

And oddly, I could tell that Frank had no plan. He just wanted me to "do what you did in Salem"—as though it could be produced on demand, like dropping a quarter in the slot. He knew as well as I that the Salem exposé was a fluke, an accident. And after Salem, Gannett no longer left evidence lying around. Because of this one dramatic episode years ago, Frank seemed to think I could do miracles on request. But I was no miracle worker. Moreover, I was tired of fighting Gannett. Yes, it was disgusting that the nation's biggest newspaper company was guided by contemptible ethics; but that was the way things were in late-twentieth-century America. I had landed a few blows, done my part; but this was no longer my fight. I had no desire to become a full-time Gannett basher. I had other things to do.

So I wished Frank would get off my case. The game he was playing had ceased to be fun. In twenty different ways I had told him I was not coming, yet still he kept calling—to invite me to assist him in his own destruction. What was driving this man? And then one night I got it: Much more than he needed to win, Frank needed to fight.

He knew the odds were against him, that the smart thing to do was shut down the *News-Chronicle,* that a battle would cost money and surely fail.

But he would not roll over and die against an enemy like Gannett. It was not in his nature. He could not live with himself if he did. For his own peace of mind, now and in years to come, my friend had to know that he had not walked away. Even if defeat were certain, he had to fight. This was more important than conserving money, being a prudent businessman, perhaps even saving his company. Only by giving his all could he accept his fate. And somehow, Frank considered me his best ally.

It was sad. The weapons at his command were so few. He could not win this fight, yet he had to take it on. And he needed to know that someone would fight with him. The next time Frank called, late in August, he got a different answer. All right, I said, you wore me down. I will come to Green Bay. I will come to Green Bay and do . . . something.

14

The Green Bay Project

IMMEDIATELY AFTER AGREEING TO GO to Green Bay, I wished I had not. All my old misgivings came back, plus a new one: Now I berated myself for giving in to Frank's persistence. But I had, and there was nothing to do but get on with it.

Whatever I was going to do needed a name. For simplicity I called it the "Green Bay Project," and began a logbook with that title. Somehow it made the job seem more real. As I expected, Frank offered no direction. He said he had complete faith in my instincts. But neither he nor I had a plan. I did feel that the only feasible effort we could mount must be on the pages of Frank's *News-Chronicle*. As in the Salem exposé, publicity and surprise seemed the best tactics. However, I had just the vaguest concept of what we might publicize.

To familiarize myself with the opposing newspapers in the coming struggle, I had Frank send one full week of the *News-Chronicle* and the corresponding week of Gannett's *Green Bay Press-Gazette*. When they arrived, I was dismayed. The *News-Chronicle* was a skinny little thing, just twenty-eight or thirty-two tabloid pages on an average day. It was a competent if lackluster product, with local, national, and international news, sports, business, comics, syndicated features. It had all the ingredients found in a typical newspaper, but in rather short supply. For my taste it was entirely too typical. Just one element was superb: the editorial cartoons. Biting, witty, sarcastic, and devastatingly to the point, all within a four-by-six-inch rectangle, the cartoons were national-class. They were the work of a staff member named Lyle Lahey, of whom Frank was extremely proud— as he had told me many times. But the rest of the *News-Chronicle* did not match their shine.

Alarmingly, only about a fourth of its content was advertising. By industry norms, a financially healthy paper needs from 50 to 60 percent advertising; and to maximize profits, many exceed that ratio. No paper could pay its way with 25 percent. The few advertisers the *News-Chronicle* did

have were not major retailers but small stores placing small ads. There was
no evidence of a hard core of ardent supporters, which had always been the
Reporter's secret of survival. No preprinted circulars, an important source
of revenue, were tucked into the paper's pages. Moreover, it was published
only six days a week—and the missing day was Sunday, by far the heaviest
in advertising volume. At eleven thousand, its circulation was less than a
fifth of its rival's.

By comparison, Gannett's *Press-Gazette* was fat and sassy. It was broadsheet, and its average issue was two to three times larger than the *News-
Chronicle*'s. Advertising flowed across page after page, and it bulged with
preprints. Its Sunday edition had more ads than a full week of Frank's
paper. Editorially, the *Press-Gazette* was the standard Gannett product:
flashy graphics, lots of color, all the usual news sections, with brief stories
of little depth. I saw at a glance, however, that this editorial package was
larger and fuller than most in the chain. And I knew why. The Green Bay
paper was one of the only Gannett franchises that had daily competition.

The *Press-Gazette* did not strike me as a bad newspaper, just an exceedingly familiar one. It certainly was not distinguished—but then, neither was
the *News-Chronicle*. Both Green Bay dailies sought to fit the standard definition of the all-purpose journal, and both were presentable examples. Yet
because it was much bigger, the *Press-Gazette* offered more of everything.
And for the average subscriber, unaware of the bitter underlying struggle,
the Gannett paper would be the logical one to choose.

By any measure, the *News-Chronicle* was dead in the water. How sad
to recall that just three years ago it was steaming ahead confidently. If this
scrawny second paper had any hope of closing the gap on its rival, I felt it
must make some changes. Instead of remaining a smaller "me-too" product,
it needed its own flavor. I had some ideas, but did not know which ones Frank
might like, or which he could afford. Still, the paper must do something to
catch the town's attention.

But I was getting ahead of myself. First and foremost, the *News-Chronicle*
must catch the town's attention by telling its readers about Gannett. We must
demonstrate to the people of Green Bay that the chain was fully capable of
the deliberate destruction of a small competitor. We must stir their moral
outrage. But how to make this point? The Green Bay Project would need
examples, both local and national, of just how Gannett operates. The Salem
file was a strong starting place. But by itself it was not enough. What else
was out there?

From my files I pulled a folder labeled "Gannett." It was a mishmash of clippings from newspapers and trade journals. Since tangling with the chain in 1981 I had saved such stories, but had never had time to study or use them. Now the time had come. Some articles were flattering, some were not. Many were routine: notices of Gannett-sponsored workshops, fellowships, symposiums. A few cited problems Gannett had encountered here and there. Such stories in *Editor & Publisher* tended to be brief.

Three situations especially intrigued me. In Hartford, Connecticut, a judge had ordered Gannett to pay a million dollars in damages for fraud. In Southern California, the Justice Department was prosecuting Gannett on charges of price-fixing. Considering the government's lack of interest in such matters during the late 1980s, it had to be a flagrant violation. And in Little Rock, Arkansas, Gannett was engaged in an all-out newspaper war against a home-owned daily, which claimed the chain was determined to drive it out of business.

Much had been written about Little Rock. Getting that story should not be difficult. But the matters in Connecticut and California had rated only the barest mention in *E&P*, in clippings just three or four inches long. I needed more. So I activated the *"Santa Fe Reporter* Connection"—the network of former staffers now scattered throughout the country. Many times already had I tapped into it. Now I would do so again. A fellow who had started at the *Reporter* now covered courts for the *Hartford Courant*. Sure, he would look for the fraud case decision. A veteran journalist who had thrown in with us for a few midcareer years was now with the *Los Angeles Times*. He would see what he could find on the price-fixing charges.

Perhaps even more important than examples of wrongdoing would be Gannett's economic impact on the communities where it had a monopoly. I was sure the chain was squeezing them for every last dime. But I needed data to back up my suspicions. From the *Editor & Publisher Yearbook,* which lists the circulation and ownership of every daily paper, I identified a dozen or so Gannett cities approximately the size of Green Bay. Now I had to get Gannett's advertising rates in those markets. None of these cities had a competing daily eager to send me this information. But there might be weeklies, with about as much affection for Gannett as we had felt at the *Reporter.* I got a list of the country's weeklies, and pulled out my atlas. After a few days on the phone, I had promises from several weekly publishers to send the local Gannett rate card. What this would reveal was unclear, but it would answer questions.

Early in September I flew to Green Bay for four days, all of which passed in Frank's house. At this point I did not want to go to the *News-Chronicle* or meet anyone there. Premature curiosity would only impede the Green Bay Project, and loose lips could sink it. Secrecy is of the essence, I stressed to Frank. Tell no one what we're hatching, not even your most trusted people. We will draw them in on a need-to-know basis.

I brought along a list of potential tactics, some more likely than others. For hours I pumped Frank for information, to determine which ones might work. Seeking local material for the planned report, I sifted through the records in Frank's big, disorganized office at home. These efforts only discouraged me.

Though determined to put up a fight, Frank had few ideas to contribute to it. Worse, he seemed tired, worn out. In place of spirit, all he showed was stubbornness. Nor did the files help much. They contained no systematic record of provable wrongs perpetrated by Gannett. Scribbled notes, memos open to interpretation, unsubstantiated accusations—these were what I found. Making something out of them would be a long, hard pull.

Just as daunting were Brown County Publishing Company's books. While the entire operation was generating about $14 million a year, many divisions were barely above breakeven. The Green Bay paper's annual losses had increased to five hundred thousand dollars, and were bleeding the company white at a far faster rate than I had suspected. More than ever, I wanted to end this fiasco before it began. "Frank," I said, "you don't have a chance of pulling the *News-Chronicle* out. Are you sure you want to do this?"

"I've got to, Dick."

I implored him to reconsider. Working from a jotted-down list, I grilled him about his reasons. Is it ego? I asked. Is it that you want to leave the company to your children? Is it preserving jobs? Exposing Gannett? Revenge on the *Press-Gazette*? Service to readers? Service to the advertisers who have abandoned you? A monument to yourself? Preserving two voices in Green Bay? Personal income? What is it, Frank? He more or less rejected most of these motivations. The ones that stood were preserving jobs, preserving two voices, and exposing Gannett.

It was time for a break. "One last question, Frank, and this time I want the truth. Is the real reason just that you're a red-headed Irishman, and you love a good fight?"

"Probably."

A pressing item was getting a libel lawyer, to make sure whatever we reported would stand up to legal scrutiny. I had stressed this need by telephone, and now I did so again. But Frank had no good answer. "I'm thinking about Agnes's brother-in-law, a top-notch labor lawyer who just retired here," he said.

"I don't think so, Frank. Labor and libel are different. We'll be printing some hot copy, against an outfit with all the money they need to sue. We need an expert, not a brother-in-law."

"Well, I'll keep looking into it."

Frank, Agnes, and I had dinner at the Union Hotel, near their home. An old-fashioned place, it served hearty midwestern fare in its red-and-white dining room. As we entered, Frank waved at a big, blond, middle-aged man at a corner table, then introduced me to him. As we shook hands, he did not rise. "He was a defensive end for the Packers, back when Vince Lombardi was shaping them into champions," Frank said after we were seated. I looked back at the big fellow with heightened regard. He was my first brush with the mystique of professional football, which permeates Green Bay and defines the city to the rest of the country. But when he got up to leave a few minutes later, I had to look away. Even with a cane, he could barely walk. "It's his knees," Frank whispered as the man limped out.

On Sunday, the last day of my visit, Frank took me to the opening game of the Packers' season. This year they were going to be good, after a long time in the nether regions. The visitors were the Tampa Bay Buccaneers, one of the league's softest teams. The Packers lost. Though the legend of the indomitable Lombardi, whose halftime tirades Wayne Vann had used to exhort his sales staff to defeat the *Santa Fe Reporter,* still hovered over the stadium, only memories remained of the team's glory days.

Packing for my flight, I asked Frank where I would live in Green Bay. "That's easy," he said. "Our spare bedroom is yours." That would never work. I had to have my own space. More and more reclusive as the years went by, I could not undertake a project of this intensity without a place of retreat, where my only obligation would be to the work—and decompression from it. The niceties of being in someone else's home would derail me. "No, I need a place of my own, no matter how basic. Didn't you say there was a little apartment at one of your plants?"

"Well, there is, but I don't think it would do. It's just one room, and there's no kitchen. Also I don't know what shape it's in. The guy who was using it, one of our employees, turned out to have some drinking problems. I haven't seen the room since he left. But this is silly. There's plenty of room here, and we insist—"

"The apartment sounds perfect. I'll take it."

"Sight unseen?"

"Sight unseen."

Not until we were driving to the airport did Frank raise the question that had hung between us for four days. "You haven't said what you're going to charge for your services."

"I've thought about it a lot," I answered. And I had. It had to be worth my while, and it had to be a fee he could afford. But he could not afford much. "How does fifteen dollars an hour sound?"

He waited before responding. "I know that's less than what you ought to be asking," he finally said. "Tell you what: I'll throw in ten shares of stock in the company. They're currently worth about three hundred dollars apiece. Who knows what they'll be worth down the line?" It was my turn to feel gratitude.

I went home to bid Santa Fe good-bye. In the crisp autumn sun, New Mexico had never seemed so lovely. I would miss it terribly. I also was going to miss Bonnie. Already the sale of the *Reporter* had strained things between us. Now, just when I was supposed to be settling down, I was taking off again. The Wisconsin remove would be a hard test. I felt trapped by my pledge.

But momentum was building. My friend in Hartford sent the judge's opinion in the fraud case, along with his assessment of it: "Pay dirt." From Los Angeles came a *Times* story about the price-fixing case. I phoned the *Arkansas Democrat,* the paper fighting Gannett in Little Rock, to make an appointment with its publisher, Walter Hussman. Little Rock was on the road to Green Bay. It was all grist for the mill in Wisconsin.

Packing was a dreary process. Every item I stuffed into the trunk seemed to rebuke me. I really did not want to go. In a closet I found a small, portable tape deck. This and the radio would be my only sources of music. Music was important, one of my greatest pleasures. Carefully I chose the tapes to take—mostly classical, with some country and folk for diversion. As an afterthought I tossed in one more, of Southern gospel songs. In the weeks to come, I would be glad I did.

On the last night of September Bonnie and I had dinner and said our farewells. It was a sad occasion. Watching Santa Fe fade from sight in my rearview mirror early the next morning was even sadder.

15

Whispering Miles

THE FIRST OF OCTOBER, 1989. One year since Frank's first call for help. From the start, his words had not been welcome. This was never anything I wanted to get involved in. Nothing about it was right—not the time, not the place, least of all not its chance of success. I had been so determined to remain detached. How many times had I told Frank to count me out? How many dozens of times? Yet here I was on the road, heading east and then north.

The back-road splendor of New Mexico flew past at seventy miles an hour—the arroyos, the plains, the distant peaks, the fierce and magnificent solitude. How long before it would embrace me again? The autumn sun was brilliant, but the mood in my car was gray. The miles were whispering to me, with the same questions again and again: Why are you doing this thing? Why did you let it happen?

Frank is my friend, I answered. You help out your friends. Look at all the times he helped me—the people he sent to work out problems for the Reporter, *the suggestions and advice, the reckless financial investment he made after the collapse of our Sunday edition.*

I had flown to Chicago to meet him. "It's real bad this time, Frank. That damn Sunday paper crippled us. We're broke again, and morale is shot. We've gone back to once a week, but we're seriously wounded. It will take time to heal, time and money. And we seem to have run out of both. The next wind could blow us away."

From the desk in his apartment on the sixtieth floor of the John Hancock Building he took out a checkbook. "For purchase of stock in The Santa Fe Reporter Inc." was the notation he wrote on the check he handed me. The amount was forty thousand dollars. With the lights of the city reflecting on the waters of Lake Michigan below, I thanked my friend. "Man does not live by bread alone," I said. "You know that, Frank. But man can die by bread alone. This will help us live."

A lone white cross, perhaps placed there by those who loved someone who died in a wreck, perhaps erected by the Penitentes, topped the high hill to the north. Before long I would be in Texas.

The Sunday paper—what a terrible mistake. Laurie and I never really wanted to add this second day to the Reporter's *publishing schedule. We thought we were doing fine coming out just once a week. But Didier Raven told us we were wrong.*

Don't you see what's happening? he asked. Already Wayne Vann and Gannett are undermining us. Sure, we slowed them down with the Salem report, but now they're fighting a war of attrition. They're targeting our customers and going after them one by one. They're getting them, too. Two supermarkets are dropping us next quarter. Want to know why? They need to hit the town twice a week, not just once. Since they use the New Mexican *on Sunday, it's easier for them not to split their budget. At least that's what they're saying. Who knows what else Gannett is giving them? With a Sunday paper we could hold on to the ones we have and go after the others as well. Not to mention all the other Sunday advertising, such as real estate. That's a gold mine waiting to be tapped. We could double or even triple our volume.*

Laurie and I were apprehensive. We reminded Didier that making money had never been the main goal at the Reporter. *Putting out a fine newspaper was. Let's keep our priorities straight.*

But don't you see? he came back more insistent than ever. The only way we can do that is by beating them to the punch. This is Gannett we're up against. We've got to keep surprising them, got to stay ahead of them. We can't let them whittle us down. Any company that is not moving forward is moving backward. After all that we've done, let's not start slipping backward now.

Didier sang a siren song. I heard it, but it scared me. Many members of our board of directors agreed that we should push ahead with a Sunday edition. Still, Laurie and I were not sure. Our feelings were mixed. We did not want to reject the idea merely to assert our own authority. Maybe a Sunday paper would be the best thing after all. Partially persuaded by Didier's arguments, we also feared losing him and his marvelous selling ability if he felt the Reporter *had run out of ambition. In the end, we acquiesced. In April 1982—*

behind the slogan "Once Is Not Enough!"—the Sunday Reporter *was launched.*

At first it was wildly successful. The initial issue had 110 pages and several inserts. It was heavy with advertising from our regular customers, plus Realtors, auto dealers, furniture stores, and other businesses that seldom used us. Revenues in the Sunday paper's first month surpassed one hundred thousand dollars, the most in our history. But the bloom faded fast.

Hard on the heels of the Sunday venture came the nationwide recession of 1982. Unemployment rates soared. Homes, cars, and other costly items stopped selling. Businesses retrenched. Few would try a new, unproven product. Readers too were on edge. Accustomed to a newspaper that could be read all week long, they did not like our new frequency. They also had little use for flashy features such as color comics, a syndicated TV guide, and a food section. I secretly agreed with them. The Reporter's *strength had always been its individuality. Now, on Sundays, we were trying to match a standard formula.*

Then, abruptly, Didier Raven left. He convinced a major publishing company that a twice-weekly newspaper, modeled after the Reporter, *could succeed in Albuquerque. With little warning he headed south to be its publisher, leaving us with his Sunday legacy draped around our necks—and nobody trained to replace him. Six months and seven hundred thousand dollars in losses later, Didier's Albuquerque semi-weekly folded. Meanwhile, we struggled on with ours.*

Each week was harder than the one before. As the Sunday paper dwindled, advertisers—forever like sheep—deserted it, with many cutting back on midweek as well. Our Sunday expenses, however, refused to come down. We used up our reserve funds; then I was at the bank, sadly putting the Reporter *back into debt. After nine months of hell, we did the only thing we could do. We terminated Sunday in the first week of January 1983 and reverted to weekly publishing. We went out with flair. The accompanying announcement admitted: "Twice Was Too Much!"*

For 1982, the year of our Sunday adventure, revenues were $930,000, by far the highest ever. But expenses swept past the million-dollar mark, and our loss was $120,000, a staggering sum. We were publicly embarrassed, momentum was heading in the wrong direction, and our spirit was broken. We also had a staff swollen with people

who had left solid jobs to hire on in good faith, and now were not
prepared to be unemployed in recession times.

I turned to Frank Wood for guidance. From his experience he
suggested ways to cut costs while preserving everyone's job until the
staff reduced itself by attrition. Though it was hard, we did not fire
anyone as a direct result of the Sunday debacle. Frank's check for
forty thousand dollars was crucial in this harrowing time.

The overdrive in my eight-year-old Volvo was kicking in and out on its
own, and I was barely into Texas. A breakdown on the Great Plains was
not part of the plan. If I could just nurse the car to Wisconsin I would get
it fixed there. Luckily, overdrive was not essential. I could always just stay
in fourth gear.

Well, Laurie, I'll miss you while I'm gone. But it's not like we were
still married or anything. I'll just miss seeing you and talking with
you. And working with you. I wish you could help me with the Green
Bay Project. You would be someone I could count on.

Let's run through it one more time. In the end, why did we call it
quits? Was it that the Santa Fe Reporter *devoured everything we had,*
until there was not enough left for the marriage? Or was the real truth
that the Reporter *held us together longer than we would have stayed in*
a more normal life? All those midnight cans of soup, all the invitations
we turned down, and movies that we missed. All those days, nights,
and weekends when we were "down at the paper"—or too tired to do
anything if we were not. The only thing we knew for sure was that if
just one of us had worked at the Reporter *we could not have stayed*
together a year, much less the seven more that we did.

We both cared so much for that little newspaper—which truly was
our only child. We conceived it, gave it birth, nursed it through infancy,
watched it grow, tended it when it got sick, worried about its future,
were amazed by the things it did, enjoyed its weird friends, wanted
it to be strong enough to walk on its own, and were so proud of its
achievements. But we looked after the Reporter *better than we looked*
after ourselves.

Without fighting or bitterness, we just coasted to a halt. When
we finally decided to divorce, you said something fine: "It's very
important not to throw away the good with the bad. We're friends,

we respect each other, we've shared a lot, and we're still going to be copublishers of the Reporter. *All we're changing is the marriage part."*

It worked. Through all that was to come for many more years, we continued to take care of our child. In good times and bad, strain and surplus, celebration and sadness, we did what was needed for the Reporter *and each other. Again and again we learned there was one thing we could count on. Through all that came.*

The days grow so short in autumn, especially heading east. Not yet seven o'clock and already the sun was sinking fast in the Texas Panhandle. But I was good for at least another two or three hours, or more. I would sleep somewhere in Oklahoma.

Across the bank lobby I gazed into the startling green eyes of the blond woman. Was it who I thought it was? Yes, an old acquaintance, a photographer I had not seen in years.

Now I live in Paris, she said. But I still own a house in Santa Fe and I'm in town for a few days. No, my husband and I are no longer together. I heard you had gone ahead and started a newspaper, like you were talking about doing. But I had not seen it until now. It's a terrific paper. Really terrific. "I'd like to tell you about it," I said. "Do you have a telephone? Perhaps lunch later this week? Or dinner?" That would be nice, she said.

Then there was the beautiful dark-haired woman, so good with words, who worked part-time at the Reporter. *Late one night, after everyone else was gone, she stood in my office doorway. She seemed . . . tentative. "I'm going home now," she said. "You should, too. It's so late. I hope you won't be working much longer."*

"No, it'll just be a little while." Maybe another hour or two. I was bone-tired, but tomorrow was deadline day. "Thanks for your concern. And thanks for hanging in so late yourself."

"I wanted to ask you something before I left," she said. Again I felt that her manner was strange.

"Sure," I said. "Have a seat. What is it?"

"I don't want to tell you in your office. Could you just come here into the hallway?"

"All right." This was getting more and more peculiar. Mystified, I covered the few steps to where she waited. "Yes?"

"Long ago I noticed that the Reporter *is really good," she said. "Not just now and then, but every week. When something is good all the time, there is a reason behind it. When I took this job I wanted to find out that reason. Now I think I know." Suddenly she was kissing me, kissing me, kissing me. And after one split second of astonishment, I was responding, responding, responding.*

Later there was the bright-eyed born-again Christian, so passionate in all she did, so determined to bring me to salvation. And later still the teacher, the sweetest, kindest person I had ever known.

Yes, Laurie, I'm going to miss you while working on the Green Bay Project. I sure wish you could help me with it. I hope your long journey with me did not hurt you too badly. Most of all, I hope you got back as much as you gave.

From Stillwater, Oklahoma, to Little Rock was less than 350 miles, an easy drive. With a good night's sleep and a good breakfast under my belt, I pushed on. The overdrive was still acting funny, and the highway was not through talking to me.

That damned Sunday paper. The worst part was knowing we had brought the trouble upon ourselves. We got greedy. We forgot our identity. Instead of trying to become a better weekly, we stepped onto the path of bigness. And on that path we stumbled. It was hubris, nothing else. And the gods have always known how to deal with hubris.

Readers were immediately delighted when we dropped Sunday. Advertisers, as usual, responded more slowly. But expenses plummeted, and in time the staff shrank back to an appropriate size. We reverted to a bare-bones budget and held on. Laurie became advertising director and worked tirelessly. Two more years passed before the Reporter *was profitable again. Even then, we were still in debt. But as always, putting out a good newspaper remained our primary goal. Yet something seemed to have changed. Our journalism still was winning national awards, but at home it was being taken for granted. Santa Fe readers had grown accustomed to our standards. Unless we kept topping previous efforts, each week's* Reporter *was just business as usual. We were victims of our own quality.*

Selling against Gannett became harder than ever. No longer were we the brash newcomer. Now it was Santa Fe's established weekly versus Santa Fe's established daily. And though the New Mexican*'s circulation continued to swoon, the strategists over there found a way to neutralize the damage: They lied. When we pointed out the steady decline, advertisers pulled out signed statements, on* New Mexican *stationery, claiming far higher circulation than was actual. When we produced official audits, in long rows of figures, proving that the daily's claims were false, advertisers would say: "Those audits only confuse me, but the* New Mexican*'s word is good enough for me."*

We kept trying to win over the chain stores, but with scant success. There was a mentality to them that we were unable to penetrate. Usually their managers spent only two or three years in Santa Fe, passing through while trying to surpass the previous manager's profits and thus win a promotion to a bigger store in, say, Lubbock or Salt Lake City. Steeped in chain thinking, they related to the chain approach to business, and to their counterparts at the chain paper. Few saw any percentage in stretching their budgets to try a local, independent journal.

So we built our base on bedrock: home-owned businesses that knew the town. They were enough to live on, and they were dependable. But there were some local merchants who never used us. One day I asked a friend who ran an advertising agency to tell me candidly why two of her clients were not on our pages. "It's like this, Dick," said my thoroughly professional friend. "Everybody knows that Gannett is a sleazy outfit. Everybody knows the New Mexican *is a lousy newspaper. Everybody knows the* Reporter *is excellent and courageous and all that, and that you yourself are noble and honest and a credit to the community. But the other guys are the BIG GUYS! They're the main game, and the* New Mexican *is the paper my clients want to be in. There's nothing personal about it. It's just business."*

I tried not to show it, but her explanation deflated me terribly. It was a harsh reminder that in the big, bad, grown-up world, I was forever the naive outsider. If the difference she spelled out counted for so little, I had to wonder just what it was that my work—and the Reporter*'s—stood for over all the years. Whatever it was, it was not "business."*

After the wreckage of our rash Sunday run had settled, a new, altered balance emerged between Santa Fe's newspapers. With primarily local support, our revenues rose back into the seven-hundred-

thousand-dollar range. We delivered results for our advertisers, and
we appreciated their business. We stabilized, and got on with our
mission. But the flame did not burn as brightly as before.

At last the southern Ozarks. Welcome relief from the vast flatness behind
me. Arkansas can be such a pretty state. Soon I would leave the blue
highways and take Interstate 40 into Little Rock. But not yet. There were
still a few more good miles.

The key was that nothing seemed new anymore. Not the parade
of events, not the city, not the people on the staff or on the streets,
not even next week's issue. I had seen it all before. Another election?
Another land development? Another prison break? Another highway
department scandal? Another union drive at the hospital, or strike at
the supermarkets? Another summer at the Santa Fe Opera? Another
economic slump or surge? Another football season for the Demons
and the Horsemen? It was all so familiar. "The news never changes,"
someone explained. "It just happens to different people."

I realized that neither the city nor the news, nor the work itself,
was less important than before. The town still needed saving, and
journalism still had to do it. The mission was as vital as ever it
had been. The change was in me. The workload had leveled off, but
was eternally hard. As long as Laurie and I could stand the pace,
we could hold the Reporter *together indefinitely, I came to realize.*
We would never grow wealthy, but we could make a decent living,
pursue rewarding work, and live in the place we loved. As long as
we could stand the pace . . . But if we faltered, I did not know what
would happen.

But there was more. Sometimes I would bump into the manager
of Sears or Penney's, and feel resentment that they could not ac-
knowledge what the Reporter *contributed to Santa Fe—among other*
things, holding down their advertising costs in the New Mexican.
When I thought about what even one-tenth of their budgets would
mean to us, I welled with frustration. Don't go down this road, Dick,
I warned myself. Just don't. After all the wonderful gifts the Reporter
has brought, do not let it turn sour.

Before such feelings could fester, most of these managers would
be gone, replaced by successors every bit as myopic. Nor were chain

stores the only places with revolving doors. During my fourteen years as editor of the Reporter, *every bank in Santa Fe, every governmental agency, almost every prominent enterprise changed leadership not once but several times. The* New Mexican *went through five publishers and seven editors. The state had four governors, the city three mayors. Change is the constant, I kept thinking. The variable is timing.*

I peered down the paths that led into the future. All arrived at the same place. One way or another, my time at the Reporter *would end. I could retire in twenty more years, an honored elder. I could be found slumped at my desk, dead of an exhausted heart. Laurie and I could lose our drive, and watch the* Reporter *slide downhill. We could stay strong, through many more good years, and then let go. Or we could sell the paper sooner and move on to other things. Every path led to the day when I would no longer be in charge. There is a time for every purpose under heaven, I mused. Knowing when to leave is essential.*

Dusk already. How did that happen? Today was supposed to be just a quick zip into Little Rock, easily before dark. Yet the day was gone, and there remained another seventy Interstate miles between me and Motel 6. I must have been meandering too slowly through those twisting hills. And through my twisting thoughts.

A wealthy friend was looking to buy a weekly newspaper. She had worked for us years ago, and considered that time the best in her life. Now she wanted a paper of her own. She asked my advice. After a while, we began discussing the Reporter.

It was an opportunity that might never come again. She knew and loved Santa Fe. She was dedicated to telling the news. She wanted the paper she ran to be a credit to its city, and to journalism. She had ample resources to stand behind the paper through thick and thin. Best of all, she would maintain the Santa Fe Reporter *as an independent, home-owned newspaper. After what we had gone through, I could not bear the thought of finally selling to a big, distant chain.*

The negotiations took place swiftly and in secrecy. In February 1988, an agreement to sell the Reporter *was signed. It seemed important to go out with a winner. And we did. Our last issue before the sale was announced included two special supplements. Total revenues topped seventy thousand dollars—the highest single week in our*

fourteen-year history. Producing this issue kept us working until
dawn, as in the old days. Then we broke out the booze.

We got a fair price for the Reporter. *Nothing excessive—the buyer's*
advisers made sure it fell within market norms. Running the numbers,
I determined that some shareholders, those who had invested at the
wrong time in our cycles of boom and bust, stood to lose money if we
divided the proceeds by the usual methods. Frank Wood was one. I
did not want anyone to be damaged for believing in the Reporter. *So I*
proposed that everyone's original investment be repaid in full before
other funds were distributed. Almost without dissent, our board and
shareholders approved. To the end, we were all in it together.

Laurie and I also did not want to forget the staff. We proposed to
give them one thousand dollars for each year they had worked. The
board and shareholders again concurred, knowing that this money
would come out of their own proceeds from the sale. Our most loyal
employee got a check for nine thousand dollars. Others got enough
for major dental work, a better automobile, or paying off their bills. I
wished we could reach back through the years, and reward all those
who had cast their lot with the Reporter *and nourished it with their*
life force and their love. But that was impossible.

These unusual disbursements cost Laurie and me each eighteen
thousand dollars from our share. But we had no complaints. We knew
all along that the Santa Fe Reporter *was much, much more than the*
two of us at its center. We did not come out rich, or with enough to
live on indefinitely. But we did have enough to relax for a time, while
pondering what to do with the rest of our lives. And we did come away
with the satisfaction of a job that was done, if nothing else, at least as
well as we could do it.

But now all of it was fading into the past. The Motel 6 in Little Rock
looked like all the others, and the hour was much later than I had planned. I
would not be well rested for tomorrow morning's meeting with the publisher
of the *Arkansas Democrat*. But adrenaline would get me through. In the
thousand miles between Santa Fe and Little Rock I had caught some clues,
but I still was not sure what I was doing. Maybe it would all seem clearer
in the morning light.

16

The Battle of Little Rock

WALTER E. HUSSMAN JR. WAS probably the most intense man I had ever met. He was as trim and taut as a long-distance runner, and despite a receding hairline seemed younger than his forty-three years. His bearing was patrician. His big smile made me feel welcome. But as soon as the subject turned to Gannett, he was all business.

I knew something of Hussman's situation. The war in Little Rock between his *Arkansas Democrat* and Gannett's *Arkansas Gazette* had been covered extensively in the trade press. In 1974 Hussman and his father had bought the *Democrat* and added it to the five papers in rural Arkansas and several cable television properties already owned by their Little Rock–based Wehco Media Inc. But though it was by far their biggest operation, the *Democrat* was a loser from the start.

Totally dominated by the then family-owned *Gazette,* the Pulitzer Prize–winning, statewide "Voice of Arkansas," the *Democrat* had only half the circulation and barely a fourth advertising of its rival. It was also considered lowbrow, with little appeal to upscale readers or advertisers. Worst of all, it was an afternoon paper, in an era when morning papers were prevailing in almost every competitive situation in the country. In 1978, after four years of heavy losses, the Hussmans gave up. Hat in hand, they asked the *Gazette* for a joint operating agreement, to keep their paper alive. They sought only crumbs, 10 percent of the profits. To their horror, they were turned down.

The *Democrat*'s demise seemed both imminent and inevitable. But just before folding it, the younger Hussman made a last-ditch effort to save it. He converted to morning delivery, gave free classified ads to individuals, sold advertising to major stores at the unheard-of rate of one dollar per column-inch. He offered sharp discounts on subscriptions. He hired a tough new editor.

The immediate effect was to compound the multimillion-dollar losses already suffered by the *Democrat.* Hussman admitted later it was truly a last stand. Unless it produced results within ninety days, he was ready to quit. But the response was instantaneous. Readers flocked to the free want ads, advertisers jumped at the low rates, subscribers liked the gruff, down-home style of the new editor. Heartened, the Hussmans decided to stand behind their revitalized flagship newspaper, though they knew the task would take years and cost tens of millions of dollars.

At first the *Gazette* seemed unconcerned. But as the *Democrat*'s challenge grew more serious, the *Gazette,* according to one account, "reacted like a Southern gentleman whose honor had been affronted." Refusing to roll up its sleeves and wade into the brawl by matching Hussman's flamboyant ploys, the *Gazette* kept doing business in the same old way. Meanwhile, its dominant position was slipping. By 1984, after losses of $40 million, the *Democrat* had built its market share to almost 40 percent—and posted its first profit, a tiny one of fourteen thousand dollars, which Hussman divided among his employees. The *Gazette* responded by suing the *Democrat* on antitrust charges.

The lawsuit was one of the oddest in antitrust history, because it was filed by a larger, profitable newspaper against a smaller, money-losing competitor. The laws are weighted heavily in favor of the underdog. While huge companies are restricted in using their resources to crush small competitors, little guys are fairly free to try anything that might enable them to survive. Thus when the *Gazette,* "The Oldest Newspaper West of the Mississippi," one that had never had an unprofitable year since its founding in 1819, claimed it was the victim of antitrust abuse from the upstart *Democrat,* the concept was a novel one. And when the case went to trial in 1986, the jury did not buy it. The Hussmans and their paper were found innocent of all charges.

The owners of the *Gazette* then decided to sell. Losing in court seemed to take all the fight out of the once-haughty paper. Late in 1986, the *Gazette* announced it had been bought by Gannett. Everyone watching was sure the sale was dire news for Hussman. "Gannett declares war in Little Rock" stated *Editor & Publisher,* quoting Allen Neuharth telling *Gazette* staffers that he would commit the resources necessary "to help you win the war." *E&P* added: "*Democrat* publisher Walter E. Hussman Jr. called Neuharth's remarks 'sobering' and said he interpreted them to mean that Gannett intends to drive the *Democrat* out of business."

The *Gazette* moved quickly. Soon it too was offering free classifieds, discounted subscriptions, almost every incentive initiated by the *Democrat.* Gannett also launched cash-giveaway promotions, filled its pages with color, and poured $16 million into capital improvements, while the Gannett Foundation poured hundreds of thousands of dollars into charitable causes all over Arkansas. Soon advertisers and other observers of the "war" were reporting that the *Gazette* was wheeling and dealing, with an array of under-the-table departures from the prices on its rate card. Such allegations were routinely denied by Gannett, but the denials were laughed at. Analysts estimated that the "war" was causing the *Gazette* to lose $10 million a year.

Then in September 1988, Gannett crossed all established boundaries. It slashed the price of a *Gazette* subscription to just eighty-five cents for a full week, including a two-inch-thick Sunday edition. The price was less than half the *Gazette*'s previous rate of $1.97, and was the lowest subscription cost of any American newspaper with a circulation of more than twenty thousand. It did not even pay for the paper on which the *Gazette* was printed. By one estimate, the cut was costing the *Gazette* $7 million a year in lost revenues. If the *Democrat* matched the rate, its loss would be $5 million. Yet while the chain could afford ever-mounting deficits, Hussman was already at his limits.

"This is just wholesale price-cutting, which is really unheard-of," *Editor & Publisher* quoted Bob Picard, a newspaper economics professor at Emerson College in Boston. "It doesn't appear to be warranted by the competitive situation in Arkansas." Hussman agreed. "From an antitrust standpoint, I don't think anybody ever made as bold a move as Gannett made in Little Rock by cutting subscription prices across the board by 50 percent," he said. "We are definitely discussing it with our attorneys." Even so, most observers were convinced that Gannett had launched the final offensive in a war that Hussman had always been destined to lose.

But somehow he never acted like a loser. Instead he fought back with gusto and relish. Like a dashing Confederate cavalry commander, he led his outmanned troops on raid after raid, often inflicting minimal damage but leaving his enemy nervous, confused, and defensive. Drawing on his roots, Hussman lost no opportunity to portray Gannett as a giant invader, down from the North. When the *Gazette* was sold, he welcomed the chain to Arkansas on a full page of the *Democrat*—which featured a map of the state, to help Gannett find its way around. In another dig, the *Democrat* adopted the title "Arkansas' Newspaper." The *Gazette*'s somewhat lame response was to declare itself "Arkansas' Best Newspaper."

Hussman emphasized the mismatched nature of the war, with charts contrasting Wehco Media's annual revenues of $67 million to Gannett's more than $3 billion, and his half-dozen papers' total circulation of two hundred thousand versus the chain's six million. Nor did he fail to point out that his company was family-owned and based in Little Rock, while Gannett was owned by the "New York Stock Exchange" and directed from "Washington, D.C." Literally, the headquarters were across the Potomac River in Arlington, Virginia, where the chain had relocated its base from Rochester, New York.

To debunk Gannett's denials that it was making secret deals to advertisers, Hussman announced that the *Democrat* would match any rate, no matter how low, as long as it was supported by a *Gazette* invoice confirming the price. Soon he had dozens of cut-rate invoices, which he gladly showed to journalists writing about the war. He also filed them, as evidence for an antitrust case.

When Gannett announced its startling cut in subscription rates, Hussman responded with typical humor and audacity. In large house ads he pointed out that a full week of the *Gazette* now cost about the same as one copy of the *National Enquirer.* More important, however, he decided not to match the slashed rates. He announced that he could not afford to, and appealed to the people of Arkansas to understand why. If Gannett succeeded in driving out the *Democrat,* he said, everybody would pay in the long run. He asked advertisers and readers to stand behind him.

And they did. Three years into the war, the *Democrat* had made significant gains in advertising against the *Gazette,* and had closed the circulation gap so rapidly that it was calling itself "America's fastest-growing newspaper." Although it was still second to the *Gazette* in sales and circulation, the *Democrat* now was near the lead in both areas.

To halt the *Democrat,* the *Gazette* had tried one thing after another, including a change in editorial identity. Traditionally a "good gray lady" in style, like a Southern version of the *New York Times,* the *Gazette* stressed stolid layouts and in-depth reporting of weighty matters. Gannett changed all that. At the time of the sale, Gannett pledged to uphold the *Gazette*'s traditions and retain its longtime editor, who had never worked for another paper and was the publisher's son. But scarcely a year later, one week before Christmas, he was demoted to a meaningless job. He resigned a short time later.

The *Gazette*'s new editor transformed the paper overnight. Color photos, charts, and frothy features popped up everywhere. Story length was cut sharply, to reflect Gannett's idea of the attention span of "today's reader." Articles on tanning salons and dogs displaced national and international affairs on page one. The *Gazette* said it was just shedding its "elitist" image. But loyal readers were aghast. They responded with a barrage of outraged letters to the editor. Wags suggested that the paper's name be changed from the *Arkansas Gazette* to the *Arkansas Gannett.* The *Democrat,* meanwhile, was beefing up its news coverage in all areas, particularly the weighty ones it had conceded in the past. It filled a huge amount of editorial space, month after month. The *Gazette*'s editor termed the *Democrat*'s news hole "astonishing," and griped that it was hard to compete with.

Not even the circulation rate slash worked for the *Gazette.* After an initial surge in subscriptions, each of which was a money-loser, the Gannett paper kept losing ground. Soon the campaign was recognized as a flop. Then reports that the *Gazette* was fraudulently inflating its circulation figures began getting out. A former circulation worker who sued Gannett for wrongful dismissal testified he was fired for refusing to falsify records. And a tiny article in *Editor & Publisher* reported that two other circulation workers had also filed suit, claiming that in addition to being fired they had had their lives threatened when they refused to go along with a scheme to inflate the figures.

Such was the war in Little Rock. Both newspapers were still losing vast sums of money, and conventional wisdom still was saying that Gannett would win in the end. But so far at least, Walter Hussman was hanging on. He was someone I needed to learn from.

When we met, I explained my mission. Hussman knew my name, from "The Newspaper That Was Murdered." When he asked what I was planning to do in Green Bay, however, I had to admit I did not know.

"Then how can I help you?"

"I was hoping you had gathered information that helped you form your own strategy. If so, I would like to look through it. Then I'd like to pick your brain for ideas that we might use."

"Yes, I do have a file on Gannett," he said, pointing to a ledge behind his desk. It was piled high with magazines, newspapers, manila folders, sheets of paper, in three stacks, each about two feet tall. "You're welcome to go through it." He led me to a conference room with a long table and comfortable chairs. "You can work here," he said. "There's the copying machine, and if you need help, just ask my secretary."

I dug into the file. Though disorganized, it was an amazing resource. In it were blow-by-blow accounts of the Little Rock war, in dozens of stories from the *Democrat,* the *Gazette,* and many other publications. In addition, there were articles on Gannett from magazines and newspapers all over the country. Most of the articles were critical, ranging in tone from open contempt to a mixture of grudging admiration for the chain's financial prowess and disdain for its journalism. The few fully complimentary stories tended to come from business journals. I was surprised. I had not realized that apprehension about Gannett was so widespread, or so outspoken. I thought it was found mainly in places like Santa Fe, Salem, and Green Bay, where competitors had felt firsthand the chain's terrible might. This proof of national-level concern was encouraging.

Also in Hussman's file were financial analyses of both the *Gazette* and the full Gannett company, from brokerage houses and media consultants. Notes in the margins showed he had combed them line by line, looking for anything that might help him. Equal attention had been given to circulation audits, and to the statements of circulation required by the Postal Service of papers sending copies through the mail. Whenever Hussman caught the *Gazette* in an obvious or possible exaggeration, he noted it. There were dozens of letters from Hussman—to advertisers, subscribers, civic leaders, lawyers, newspaper people in other cities, the shareholders of Wehco Media. Every letter had the same purpose: bolstering the *Democrat* in its battle with Gannett.

One thick section concerned legal matters: briefs filed for and against the proposed JOA in Detroit. The lawsuit of a fishing-tournament organizer claiming that the *Gazette* broke its promise to promote the event, after luring his advertising out of the *Democrat.* The testimony of the fired *Gazette* circulation worker, who won his job back plus a large cash award after stating he was ordered to file fraudulent reports. Juiciest of all were accounts of the suit by the female circulation workers who claimed that their lives were threatened. I noted the name of their lawyer.

The most telling document was a long, detailed chronology of the Little Rock war, compiled by Hussman. Starting with the *Gazette*'s unsuccessful antitrust suit against the *Democrat,* it listed almost 150 events affecting the competition between Wehco and Gannett. Many events, such as the *Gazette*'s circulation slash, were public, and had been extensively reported. But many others were private. Every employee hired away from the *Democrat* by the *Gazette* was named. Conversations with advertisers describing secret deals with the Gannett paper were duly noted.

Noted also were conversations with a former *Gazette* employee who apparently had been bothered by his conscience. After leaving his job he had gotten in touch with Hussman, to say he was told by his bosses that Gannett "was going to throw everything they had" at the *Democrat,* and that it would be out of business or sold within twelve months. The same former employee also alleged that the *Gazette* had falsified records for its circulation audit. I understood immediately what the chronology was for. Hussman was amassing evidence for an antitrust suit against Gannett.

For two days I worked through the file. In sharp contrast to the discomfort and anxiety that attended my foray into the secret file in Oregon, I took lunch and coffee breaks, spread the material out, and made photocopies of everything I wanted. On Friday morning I had a long meeting with Hussman. He teemed with ideas that had worked for him and might work for Frank: the free classifieds, special advertising sections, zoned editions, appeals to local pride, ways to keep Gannett off-balance. We had lunch with the paper's lawyer, at a club in downtown Little Rock. Hussman saw the publisher of the *Gazette* across the room. They waved at each other. I was not introduced.

When I said good-bye to Walter E. Hussman Jr., I knew the secret of his remarkable record against journalism's most fearsome foe. He was not merely committed to the battle with Gannett, he was obsessed by it. Leaving the daily operation of the *Arkansas Democrat* to an able general manager and editor, and letting the other units of Wehco Media more or less take care of themselves, he concentrated day and night on tactics that might someday win this war. Making time for me was one.

There's a lesson in there for you, old buddy Frank Wood, I thought as I walked to my car. If you hope to have a chance in Green Bay, you must do the same thing.

My work in Little Rock was not yet finished. At the office of their lawyer, I had an afternoon appointment with Gale Reamey and Julie Wilson, the former employees now suing the *Gazette* and three of its circulation officials for $8.5 million in damages, for "emotional distress, including, but not limited to, severe depression, anxiety, fear, anger, agoraphobia, loss of self-esteem, feeling of being isolated, and loss of concentration." They struck me as somewhat zany plaintiffs. In their twenties by my guess, they wore blue jeans and T-shirts. They talked in a scattered manner, wandering off on tangents and interrupting each other. I wondered how a jury would respond to them.

But though they were not easy to interview, the story they told was bizarre. According to Reamey and Wilson, early in 1988 in the course of their work, they discovered that the *Gazette* was routinely reporting nonsubscribers as subscribers and was manipulating records to hide the discrepancies. When they reported it to their superiors, they were told that the scheme was much bigger than they suspected, that "dangerous persons" were involved, and that their own safety was in question.

The lawsuit said the *Gazette* officials named as defendants met several times with Reamey and Wilson and told them, among other things: that their phone was tapped; that they were "in danger"; that they were "targets"; that they must stay together at all times; that they should take a different route home every day and make sure no one was following them; that they should move immediately to another county and check into a motel under assumed names; and that the *Gazette* would pay their expenses while they were in hiding.

Because of these warnings, the lawsuit said, Reamey and Wilson moved to an adjacent county, where they lived first in a motel and then in a trailer. While in hiding they were told that the *Gazette* had begun an "internal investigation," but that it would probably last several months. Then, the suit charged, one of the defendants told them that the *Gazette* was going to "drag this thing out" until after the circulation audit was completed.

Eventually Reamey and Wilson returned to Little Rock, where no harm came to them. In June 1989, more than a year after their experiences, they filed their suit. The *Gazette* and its officials denied all charges. Several meetings with Reamey and Wilson did take place, the *Gazette* confirmed, and they were paid for some meals while living in the adjacent county. Nothing else was admitted.

In Reamey's and Wilson's absence, the circulation audit was completed. It found that for both the daily and Sunday editions, Gannett's *Arkansas Gazette* had overstated its true circulation by the highest discrepancies of any newspaper in the United States in 1988.

Before leaving Little Rock I bought two copies of a new book I had seen advertised: *Confessions of an S.O.B.* It was written by, and its title chosen by, Allen Neuharth, who had just retired as Gannett's chairman. One copy I left at Hussman's office, in thanks for the help he had provided. The other I took with me.

I spent the next day at Hot Springs National Park, an hour southwest of Little Rock. Once a posh resort for wealthy patrons seeking curative powers in its geothermal waters, Hot Springs was now a relic. Only a handful of its fabled "baths" remained open, and curiosity seekers such as I were served by bored attendants. But the hot, aromatic waters still could induce a temporary trance. As I slipped into it, I wondered: Who are these people from Gannett? Where do they come from? What makes them what they are? And can anything stop them from doing the things they do?

17

A Hard Landing

JUST TWO BIG STATES, MISSOURI and Iowa, separated Arkansas from Wisconsin, and now I was eager to cross them. But again I chose back roads. The journey is as important as the destination, I reminded myself, and I resisted the speed of the interstates.

Walter Hussman's example had inspired me. For the first time I was letting myself think that this thing just might work. I pulled out a battery-operated tape deck, and dictated into it any idea that might prove useful for the Green Bay Project. Curving through the Missouri Ozarks, I suggested that the *News-Chronicle* should solicit more legal notices from lawyers. Skirting the state capital at Jefferson City, I listed ways for readers to get involved. Passing Mark Twain's birthplace near Hannibal, I pictured a better obituary section. Leaving Missouri, I felt that Frank should sell off some of his operations to finance the struggle. Inhaling Iowa's pungent signature aroma of hog manure, I revised the paper's graphics. Zipping by the clock museum at Conover, I mobilized the staff. Pausing at "the world's smallest cathedral" near Festina, I called for "tradeout" ads on television and radio.

The ideas tumbled out. Each one fed my zeal. But a final roadside attraction pulled the mission back into perspective. "Effigy Mounds National Monument," said a sign near the bridge that crossed the Mississippi River into Wisconsin. I turned. The monument was the shrine of an ancient Indian culture that vanished seven hundred years ago, leaving behind great earthen mounds shaped like birds and bears. Eighty to one hundred feet long, the mounds were already grown over with foliage when white men came. For decades no one realized they were not just part of the landscape. But eventually they were recognized, and now they are a federal preserve.

A small museum displayed tools, fetishes, personal items, pottery shards, and swatches of clothing—all that remained from the daily life of the mound builders. *So fleeting, so fleeting,* said the voice of my familiar spirit. *We live our lives, do our work, serve our gods, fight our battles, and so quickly it passes, until nothing is left and no one remembers. It is all illusion.*

Yes, but in the meantime we must pretend, to make something out of it, I answered as I pressed on in darkness to the city of Madison, 137 miles south of Green Bay. *Even if it is nothing but a dream, my race is not yet run, and I have promises to keep.*

In the Madison Motel 6 the next morning, Monday, October 9, 1989, I felt odd—clammy and nervous, a little scared. I knew why: The journey from Santa Fe was about to end. This day the insulation of the road would yield to the next phase of the Green Bay Project. The comfortable would give way to the unknown.

Squeezing the remaining miles for all they were worth, I found little farm roads to bring me to Green Bay. Despite every stalling tactic, I arrived by noon. Over lunch I read that day's issue of the *News-Chronicle,* the newspaper I had come to save. The front page celebrated the Packers' defeat of the hated Dallas Cowboys. Shaking off its loss to Tampa, Green Bay had won three straight. Its offense led the league, and a win next Sunday would leave it tied for first in its division.

After lunch I called Frank Wood. He was at the third number I tried, St. Norbert College. "Welcome to Green Bay, Dick," he said. "Come on over." In his book-lined office Frank seemed as tired as I remembered. But now he also seemed eager. "I've called a meeting for some people in the company for 6:30 tonight," Frank said as soon as I sat down. "All they know is that it's about the *News-Chronicle.* I want to introduce you, and tell them that the time has come to fight. What do you say?"

I gulped. Things were moving too fast. Two hours after landing in Green Bay, I wished I were still on the road. I had nothing to present at a special meeting of the Brown County Publishing Company the first night I arrived.

This was typical of Frank. He loved dramatic gestures, even half-baked ones. When one came to mind he lunged for it, while I preferred to move quietly until all was ready, then to strike boldly. My idea of an appropriate first step was to meet with the libel lawyer—assuming that Frank had found one. Groundwork: That was what was needed now, not pep rallies. My impulse was to beg off, to say I needed time. But canceling the meeting would be an even worse first step. "Good," I said. "Let's hit it. And when can I meet with the lawyer?"

"I'm still working on that," Frank said.

Before leaving for a class, Frank called his secretary at the printing plant in the village of Denmark, where the apartment I was to take was located. "Mary has the keys ready," he said. The secretary was a sturdy sort, more efficient than friendly. I did not try to overcome her reserve at this first meeting. As we proceeded, a loosening-up would come in its own time.

The apartment was half a mile down Denmark's main street, on the second floor of a stone building that might once have been the general store. Now it was a unit of the Brown County company, housing production facilities and the Denmark Press. A long, dark stairway led from the street to the apartment. I counted the steps: twenty-three, with a small landing partway up. At the top were two old Green Bay Packers pennants. And my new home.

Just inside was the bathroom, an ordinary one except for black-and-white wallpaper picturing toilets through the ages. Hooked on the door was a rack for hanging clothes. The rest of the apartment, a fifteen-foot-square room, waited down a short hall. The room held six pieces of furniture: a beige, brown-striped sofa that pulled out into a bed, two wooden chairs, a small desk, a white porcelain lamp, and a bookcase. Two large windows, facing east and south, let in the daylight. There was no hint of a kitchen, not even a refrigerator.

"Pretty basic," I thought. But the room was clean and cozy. In contrast to the autumn chill outside, it was toasty warm, and its carpeted floor was soft. Fake wood paneling gave the walls a nice hue, offset by yellow curtains. Above all, it was a true retreat, my one essential requirement. "This will do fine," I concluded. "This is just fine." Unloading the car took several trips up the stairway. My new home was a mess. The floor was strewn with suitcases, files, boxes, and other items. Organizing it would be tricky.

The time was near for the meeting at the printing plant, which was company headquarters. With no presentation and no plan, I decided on a low profile. I did not know what Frank had told this group, but I did not want to seem like a blowhard the first time out, by coming on strong with nothing to back me up. The best use of this occasion was to take a read on Brown County Publishing's key people. I would need their help on the Green Bay Project, and until I had a feel for their strengths and weaknesses, I could not speculate what they might be capable of.

When they had gathered, Frank presented me to a somber and somewhat puzzled group, a task force he had assembled for the purpose at hand. On previous visits I had met two of them: the company's dour, toupeed vice president for publications, and the vice president for personnel, an affable chap whose wife had roomed with Frank's wife in college. The other five men were strangers.

A strikingly heavyset man was the editor of the *News-Chronicle*. The thin man next to him was the company's vice president for printing. The business manager was a gray-haired Dutchman, exuding self-control. Considerably looser was the part-time controller, who taught with Frank at the college. The remaining man I liked instinctively. Younger than the others and quicker to smile, he was not an officer but a company troubleshooter. Thinking he might play a part in my project, Frank had asked him to the meeting. His name was Al Rasmussen.

After introductions, Frank plunged into the sole topic on his agenda. But instead of confronting it head-on, he lurched and stumbled around the point. With a long and gloomy recital of the *News-Chronicle*'s finances, he made a better case for shutting it down than going on. And instead of saying that I had come to try to save the paper, he did not explain my role at all. The others looked at me furtively, wondering why I was there. Then abruptly Frank sprang me on the group. "Dick here knows a lot about Gannett," he said. "What can you tell us?"

On the spot, I discarded my intention to be an observer this night. Some enthusiasm had to be pumped into the Green Bay Project, and it seemed to be up to me to do it. So I told them why I had come. I admitted I did not yet know what was going to happen. I talked about Little Rock. I told how Walter Hussman was gaining ground not by outspending but by out-thinking Gannett. And the people of Arkansas were rallying behind him. "At first, nobody gave him a chance," I said. "Now they aren't so sure."

The assemblage stared impassively. They did not seem to be buying. I closed forcefully, stressing that the *News-Chronicle*'s only hope at this point was imagination. "By all the odds, even that won't work," I conceded. "The paper is so deep in the hole that technically it's already dead. There's no way it can economize its way back into profitability. Nor does it have enough time to wait for things to get better. Maybe nothing will work in the end. If so, we'll find that out. But in the meantime, you never know the power of a new idea until you try it—or what will happen if you put up a fight. Sure it's a long shot, but that's why Frank asked me to come. He and I are ready to give it a go—and I hope you are, too."

The Brown County Publishing Company task force did not say a word. *My god,* I wondered. *Are they dead, or merely comatose?*

Finally Frank spoke. "Let's hear from each of you. Doug?" The vice president for publications shook his head slowly. "I don't know," he said. "It'll only cost money, and we can't stand any more losses. Morale is already shot—and what if we get sued? I'll level with you: I've got money invested in this company, as well as my job. I'm worried about my security. I don't like it."

The controller came next. "From what I hear, we still have those circulation problems on the south side," he said. "How can we do something like this when we can't even deliver the paper?" Were my ears playing tricks? These were the men Frank was counting on to rally behind the *News-Chronicle* and the Green Bay Project? There seemed to be no fight in them.

But maybe there was. "Gannett has slapped us from pillar to post," said the printing vice president through clenched teeth, "and up to now we've just taken it. I don't know if fighting back will do any good. But I say it's time we stood up to those goddamn sons-of-bitches! I'm for it. You can count me in." The repressed fury in his voice riveted me, and everyone else. It defied resistance, and it carried the day. The four remaining men agreed in turn that the time had come to make a stand. The issue was settled. No vote was taken, but there was a consensus. As he acquiesced, however, the vice president for publications wanted the record to show that he still had his doubts. The session had been short on fervor, but Frank had achieved his purpose. He had gained his company's declaration of war.

Munching a sandwich in my apartment, I reflected upon the evening. Though slow to crank up, these men would probably come through. They were capable newspaper people, tired of being pushed around and willing to fight for their company if they thought it would do any good. They lacked not brains or guts, just imagination. Well, we'd see what we could do about that. As sleep came, I could hardly remember that just that morning I was on the road. The day had moved swiftly. If not sure before, I now knew I was immersed in the Green Bay Project. Up to here.

The next morning I gazed down upon the village of Denmark. It was hard to say which was more drab, the weather or the town. No precipitation fell, but the sky was the color of lead. From my windows everything seemed withered and inert. Downtown Denmark had seen better times. A brown-and-gray row of storefronts stretched downhill from the Brown County Publishing building. Some were boarded up, others were still operating. All were old. Vacant lots and abandoned foundations peppered the streets.

On a brief cruise the night before, I had counted about two dozen businesses. Six were bars, including two across the street from my room. There were two banks, one grocery store, and a wood-products factory in the central area. Ringing it were tree-lined blocks of houses. The leaves were already brown. The atlas listed Denmark's population as 1,475. It seemed to be a farm community that was fading, as its sons and daughters chose life in the cities. Tall grain silos, eight or nine, rose alongside the weedy railroad tracks that cut the town in half.

Thrusting into the leaden skies were Denmark's two dominant structures. Through a snarl of overhead utility wires, both were visible from my room. One, a block away, was a huge gray water tank atop a spindly steel skeleton, with the name of the village spelled in bold black letters. The other, half a mile off, was a towering smokestack of once-red bricks. I wondered what noxious emissions the industrial plant below it was pumping into the air.

More than anything else, Denmark, Wisconsin, was dreary. Unrelievedly, emphatically *dreary*. It was a world of gray and brown, the colors worn by everything in town: the sky, the earth, the roads, the structures. Gray and brown: the colors of decay.

I met Frank at the printing plant. He introduced me to the dozen or so people in the business office, where my desk would be. There was an awkwardness in it, however. Because of the need for in-house secrecy, which I had insisted upon at the previous night's meeting, all Frank said was, "Dick will be doing some special projects." I saw curiosity in more than one pair of eyes, but there was nothing to be done about it. My presence would just have to be mysterious for a while. In my office I wrote down each person's name. Even in these strained circumstances I wanted a friendly working environment, and remembering names was the first step.

At lunchtime I found only a couple of restaurants in town, both quick-fry, one in a bowling alley. With a smile I recalled Green Bay's other claim to fame, a distant second to the Packers: the highest number per capita of bowling alleys of any city in America. But bowling-alley food would not get me through. I was in a town without restaurants, in an apartment without a kitchen. Something had to give. In a discount store I bought a hot plate, an electric coffeepot, and a camping mess kit. With my picnic cooler they made a kitchen equal to the one in the tent in Santa Fe, when I first arrived there. If I had done it then, I could do it now.

A steaming cup of coffee in my room the next morning was a treat. A greater one followed a hearty knock on the door. My visitor was Chris Wood, Frank's thirty-five-year-old son. We had met years ago, and had stayed in touch through his world travels, employment in the national parks, and bout with cancer, which he had overcome. Now Chris worked for Brown County Publishing, as the printing division's top salesman. In two weeks, he was planning to marry.

"Dick!" Chris belted out my name in his exuberant voice. "How in the hell are you? I am so glad to see you! Would've come by earlier, but I just got in last night from Minneapolis. Boy, I'm glad you're here. So—how does it look after two days?"

As Frank's son, Chris knew exactly why I had come to Green Bay. Letting down my guard with him was a great relief. "Hard to say, Chris. We've definitely got our work cut out for us. I guess you heard about the meeting the other night."

"Sure did. Dad said it went great. He hasn't been so revved up in years. And I feel the same. We've just been waiting for a chance to stand up to the *Press-Gazette*. They've been kicking us around for so long. It's time we stood up to them. I'm ready!"

When he left a short while later, I too was ready. Here was some real in-house enthusiasm for the Green Bay Project, and it helped. If a few more like Chris emerged from the ranks of Brown County Publishing to bolster Frank's fading energy, we might make something out of this yet. After all, we were just getting started. I had been in town only two days. Like anything else, the work here must be put together one piece at a time. And with a little help . . .

But a little help proved hard to find.

18

The Resistance Within

As I suspected, Frank did not have a libel lawyer. He still was counting on his wife's brother-in-law, recently retired from a labor-law career. I did not see the connection between labor and libel, but Frank seemed to feel that skill in one area was readily transferred into another. Also, Jack FitzGerald would donate his services, and that was not a minor consideration. "When you talk to Jack, you'll see," Frank assured me. "He is nobody's fool. I think you'll be surprised." So the lawyer and I had lunch. And Frank was right: I was surprised.

Jack FitzGerald was a graying, craggily handsome man, and a pipe smoker. Spare of words, he let me do the icebreaking. Over coffee, I raised the subject that had brought us together. "I don't know exactly what form this project will take, but it's got to hit hard. To avoid lawsuits, or at least win them, we must be careful about every word. It'll be a lot of work for you."

He stared back at me. "I want to say something to you, Dick," he finally responded. "Frank and Agnes have worked all their lives for what they have. I don't want them to lose it all now, in some half-cocked fight he has no chance of winning."

My face flushed red. Emotions churned inside me, but what were they? There was anger, quick and hot, and betrayal, for I stood accused by this man who was supposed to help me. Even stronger, however, was the sinking sensation of dismay. Jack FitzGerald was right, of course. This was indeed a foolish venture, as I had known all along. The fragile spark of encouragement, which I had been sheltering, was snuffed by his words. It was a mistake to be here. All I wanted was out.

"Then talk him out of it, Jack," I said. "This isn't my idea, you know. I never wanted to come to Green Bay in the first place. Or did Frank forget to tell you that? So you just go talk him out of it tonight, and I'll get in my car tomorrow and drive right back to New Mexico. What do you say, Jack?"

"I'm not going to talk him out of it. Frank has made up his mind, and it's not my place to tell him what to do."

"Then I guess I don't understand just what the hell your place is," I spat back. Nothing further was resolved at lunch. Jack FitzGerald remained the Green Bay Project's lawyer.

Similar progress was made at the *News-Chronicle*'s quaint offices, in a former Catholic convent, when I met with the newspaper's editor to discuss the logistics of getting the project typeset, produced, and printed, all without tipping our hand. The editor had been present for the first-night meeting, and there he had voted to fight. Yet now at his desk, he had the pained air of being interrupted. As we talked he went through his mail, placing news releases in one stack, letters in another, and tossing everything else into the trash.

In-house confidentiality would be a problem, he said. The paper's electronic word-processing system gave any reporter or editor access to everything in the file. If articles concerning the *News-Chronicle*'s very survival began accumulating, they were sure to be noticed. Then word would fly through the company, and probably would leak across town to the Gannett paper. "That's no good," I said. "How can we get around this?"

"Beats me," the editor replied, displaying more impatience than concern. "I could swear the staff to secrecy, but you know how that goes. It would probably have just the opposite effect."

"Let's keep thinking. There must be a way to keep it quiet."

"The best thing I can suggest is some bland label for the report, something that would not arouse curiosity when it appears on the story menu. Instead of slugging it 'war' or 'Gannett' or something hot like that, we might call it 'zoning' or 'obit.' But if it keeps appearing day after day, somebody might pull it up to see if it should be erased. Then the cat would be out of the bag."

That sounded like a certainty to me. "How about if we waited till the last minute, then produced the whole thing overnight?"

"Doubtful," he shrugged, chucking another handout into the round file. "The reporters keyboard their own stories, and the few full-time typesetters we have wouldn't want to work all night. I say we just enter it under a blind slug and see how long we get away with it. Who knows? It might just work. Well, if that's all you need today, I ought to be getting on with other things."

"It is all I need today," I said, masking my exasperation. "But we don't have the answer yet. We have to keep thinking, to come up with something else." Unlike me, he made no attempt to hide his own annoyance.

I left carrying our best solution: a field-unit keyboard, for reporters away from the newsroom. I would typeset the report myself, onto disks to plug into the system at the last minute. Theoretically the plan was not a bad one. Preparing a disk as I typed my stories would reduce the workload for someone else. And total secrecy could be maintained. The hitch was that I was not familiar with the *News-Chronicle*'s system. The instruction manual, which I took along, seemed written in a foreign tongue. But others had learned it, and I guessed I could too.

Still, I felt tricked. Instead of spreading the work around, the editor had left me with more of it to do myself. Maybe this really was the best solution, but I wondered. Did anyone but me care whether the Green Bay Project swam or sank? As more days passed, even Frank was strangely detached. Now that he had uprooted me, he was seldom available. Duties at the college, at home, elsewhere in the company, all seemed to take precedence over my work. Several times I sought to go over my memos on strategy. Several times he was too busy to meet, at least until "next week."

Going to the office at the printing plant made my spirits sag. Every pair of eyes pointed downward as I walked through the central area. If I stopped at a desk and bade its occupant "Good morning," the eyes would lift just long enough to extend a quick "Oh—good morning" in return. Efforts at conversation with the workers whose names I had carefully memorized went nowhere. I wondered what I had done to offend them. Nor was there welcome in the streets or stores of Denmark. Buying groceries or gasoline, I would smile and say, "Hello. How are you today?" Usually I got back a blank stare, sometimes a brief word, never a pleasant exchange. These people were weird.

The first time I spotted the village police car in my rearview mirror, I cautioned myself to mind the speed limits and the stop signs. The second time, I mused that these guys must not have much to do. The third time, I wondered if they were out to get me. The fourth time, as the cruiser tailgated me five blocks while I resolutely held the posted speed of thirty-five miles an hour, I was certain. "Of course," Frank explained in one of our infrequent telephone talks. "You're driving a foreign car, where it's an article of faith to buy American. You have out-of-state plates. Everybody in town has seen you by now, but nobody knows what you're up to. Sure, the cops want to nail you. It's a point of pride."

So, I thought, a cat-and-mouse game. OK, I'll play. At least it's more fun than going down to the office each morning.

Each evening I returned to the apartment, whose single room was beginning to close in on me. The worst part was the mess on the floor: files, magazines, newspapers, cardboard boxes. I needed a worktable. I had a key to the offices below. Surely somewhere in this rambling structure was an unused table—or something resembling a table—that I could appropriate.

The downstairs housed the production facilities for most of Brown County Publishing Company's newspapers, including the *News-Chronicle.* There were typesetting machines, a darkroom, paste-up tables, and other devices with which I was familiar. Twenty miles away in Green Bay, the *News-Chronicle*'s editorial office was wired electronically to the production center, and several courier runs each day made deliveries between the two bases. It was a strange way to put out a paper, but I was coming to realize that not much in Frank's little empire was normal.

I had avoided meeting the people who worked below. Chilled by my reception at the printing plant, I did not want to repeat that scenario here. I did not enjoy giving evasive explanations of what I was doing. I preferred to remain a stranger. But now that I wanted a table, I had no one to ask for assistance. I waited for Saturday, the only day the building ceased its around-the-clock operations. Slipping down creaky stairways, rummaging around gloomy basements, poking into closets and storage areas, coughing through the smoke-break room, I pursued my quest. I felt like the Phantom of the Opera, secretly violating a space to which I had no legitimate claim.

In one room I found a three-foot-tall metal frame, separated from whatever had been fastened to it. Under a staircase was the perfect top: a forty-inch-square section of particle board. Against a wall were two wide planks, each eight feet long. I pictured them running side by side between cardboard boxes in my room—a fine surface for getting things off the floor. Several trips up many steep stairs later, the apartment worked at last.

Chris Wood's wedding relieved the dreariness of my routine. It was a joyous occasion, but it had a downside. He left at once for a three-week honeymoon. My most ardent supporter would be absent in the formative stages of the Green Bay Project. Feeling more and more alone, I struggled to the printing plant each day and walked the wordless gantlet. Not until I was at my desk did a sense of purpose infuse the work. Then my blood quickened, for the work was going well.

At last there was time to catch up with the court records, published articles, academic studies, books, advertising rate cards, Walter Hussman's thick file, and the other information I had been gathering for weeks. By telephone, by sifting through Brown County Publishing Company records, and by investing long hours at the city library and the even finer library of the University of Wisconsin at Green Bay, I gained more material each day. As I absorbed it, I was learning remarkable things about Gannett.

19

"A License to Print Money"

THE ORGANIZATION THAT WAS TO become the nation's largest newspaper chain was from its beginnings a distinctly American institution. Like the country that drove out native inhabitants from coast to coast behind the motto "the only good Indian is a dead Indian," Gannett lived by the principle that the only good market is a dead market—that is, one without competition.

"The company was founded in 1906, when Frank Gannett bought the *Gazette* in Elmira, N.Y., for $20,000," reported *Dun's Review,* a business journal. "Although the *Gazette* was profitable and its competitor, the *Evening Star,* was not, Gannett reasoned that he could make even more money if there were only one paper in town. So he bought the *Star* and merged it into his own. Working exactly as monopolies are supposed to, the paper generated so much cash that Gannett decided to use the same strategy in other cities." Thus was born a philosophy that now rules journalism in America, where 98 percent of the cities have no daily competition.

For decades, this eminently pragmatic view of newspapering remained a regional one. Under Frank Gannett, the company showed little interest outside the Northeast. When he died in 1957, he owned twenty-one papers in small cities, most of them in upstate New York. His successor as chairman, Paul Miller, stepped up the acquisition pace, moving into markets larger and more distant, as far away as Honolulu and Guam. But like the founder, he avoided competition.

In 1967 the company went public, offering its shares on the New York Stock Exchange and thus accepting an incessant demand for profits from shareholders and security analysts, whose concern was not journalism but the bottom line. It was a challenge easily met. In the next decade, under Miller, Gannett grew from twenty-eight papers in five states to seventy-three in twenty-eight states. Annual revenues surged from $185 million to $558 million. Earnings rose from $15 million to $69 million. The price of stock went from $9.67 to $38 a share.

The figures were stunning testimony to the power of monopoly economics, a power summed up succinctly by the newspaper industry's foremost analyst, John Morton. "In monopoly situations," he noted, "newspapers can be a license to print money." Other observers concurred. "Even at the industry's present level of profitable performance," stated one, "Gannett is in another league. While most papers average pre-tax operating profit margins of about 15 percent, Gannett comes in at nearly 30 percent. And Gannett does it in what has become the contemporary formula: by searching out monopoly markets and buying into them. Most Gannett papers operate in markets all to themselves."

"With no significant competition to worry about," added the *Los Angeles Times,* "a company like Gannett can—and does—jack up its circulation and advertising prices almost at will, a practice Gannett boasts of openly when speaking to security analysts about what a good, safe investment Gannett stock represents."

In company terminology the ability to raise prices at will was called "flexibility," and indeed it was invoked without apology. As Gannett's chief of operations bragged to investment brokers in 1986: "We've had 40 price increases thus far and anticipate nine more later in the year." Such statements were music to the investment community's ears. Giving Gannett a "do buy" recommendation, one analyst called it "virtually an unregulated monopoly." Another admiring trader wrote: "Gannett's management lives, breathes and sleeps profits, and would trade profits over Pulitzer Prizes any day."

But Gannett's priorities did not impress media critics as easily as they did Wall Street brokers. The *Los Angeles Times* was blunt: "The publishers of most of these papers are, in fact, largely scorned for looking on their papers as 'cash registers'—for sacrificing quality to profit, for producing newspapers that are too often timid, parochial and mediocre."

The *Times* continued: "Every business—every company—has its own unique lexicon, and the words that make up that lexicon often reveal a great deal about the company's priorities. At Gannett, for example, newspapers are often referred to as 'products' or 'units,' and budgets are called 'profit plans.' Each paper—each department—has a 'profit plan,' and each is expected to meet that plan, to produce the annual profit that Gannett desires."

Time magazine similarly found little to praise: "The stereotypical Gannett paper has a circulation of 40,000, profit margins that dazzle Wall Street and a reputation for lassitude. . . . Most exemplify the new blenderized newspaper, which leaves no mark because it has so little sting." And a

Columbia University journalism professor summed up the disdain of many professionals by noting that Gannett talked "as if the business of journalism is business and not journalism."

The *New Republic* saw little hope for improvement. "As the Gannettoids swallow more communities and profit centers, spewing out more of their banal newspapers, reporters and editors who want to bring some passion to their work will be crowded out. The Gannett world has little room for criticisms, differences, conflicts," said the writer, who also offered an explanation: "The problem with Gannett isn't simply its formula or its chairman, but the company's corporate culture. The product *is* the company—cheerful, superficial, self-promoting, suspicious of ideas, conformist, and implicitly authoritarian."

Such descriptions did not sit well with Allen H. Neuharth, who succeeded Miller as chairman in 1978. So he decided to dress up Gannett's image—but not by diligently raising standards at the newspapers in the chain. Neuharth had bigger things in mind. While buying ever more newspapers, Neuharth was laying plans for his dream: a color-filled new nationwide daily, to be called *USA Today.* In September 1982 that dream became reality. With its splashy graphics, lavish use of color, abbreviated articles, and emphasis on sports, entertainment, and weather, *USA Today* was praised, ridiculed, debated, and imitated from the start. For the next several years, no other paper had more impact on the industry.

Like everyone else in the business, I had been curious about *USA Today*'s much-ballyhooed debut. I disliked it instantaneously. With happy chatter about TV shows and sports stars passing as front-page news, with often meaningless graphics sprinkled throughout, with an enormous amount of space devoted to cheesecake and the weather, Gannett's national newspaper, I felt, made a material contribution to the "idiot culture" overrunning our television-benumbed country. In place of intellectual nourishment, *USA Today* provided only "chewing gum for the mind." But I knew, of course, that I was prejudiced.

I was not, however, alone. Many media critics ridiculed the Gannett flagship. One of them, noting the high-quality paper on which *USA Today* was printed, commented: "It doesn't rub off on your hands, or on your mind." At an investigative journalism conference, where the *Santa Fe Reporter* had won a major award, I laughed when a speaker facetiously announced two new competition categories: "Best Investigative Paragraph" and "Best Investigative Weather."

The critic for the *Washington Post* wrote: "Like parents who take their children to a different fast-food restaurant every night and keep the refrigerator stocked with ice cream, [*USA Today*] gives its readers only what they want." His observation gave Gannett's pride and joy a permanent nickname: "McPaper."

Nevertheless, Neuharth's brash creation was indeed giving large segments of the public exactly what they wanted. Seven months after the paper was launched, it was distributing more than a million copies a day. Within two years, the only American newspaper with higher circulation was the *Wall Street Journal.* Yet behind the big numbers, *USA Today* was a financial disaster. Though heavy start-up deficits were projected, the actual losses stunned even the country's richest chain. In its seven years before my arrival in Green Bay, "The Nation's Newspaper" had never shown a profit. In many months it had lost more than $10 million, and its total cumulative deficit exceeded half a billion dollars.

At most companies, such a hemorrhage of red ink would be fatal. Gannett, however, had an easy answer to its $500 million problem: Just jack up the return from its other papers to cover the shortfall. Throughout *USA Today*'s early years, the chain managed not only to avoid a decline but also to keep raising profits, by squeezing its captive markets ever harder. While I was researching my project, the chain reported its eighty-eighth consecutive increase in quarterly earnings.

Newspapers were not the only source of Gannett's riches, though they were by far the largest. In addition to eighty-four dailies in thirty-six states and two U.S. territories, with a total circulation of 6.4 million, Gannett owned some forty weeklies, ten television stations, sixteen radio stations, the largest billboard advertising company in North America, and the Louis Harris polling firm. It had posted total revenues of $3.3 billion the previous year and profits of $364 million—despite the bottomless hole of *USA Today.*

Presiding flamboyantly over it all was Neuharth, a short, energetic man known for his ego, intelligence, combative nature, temper tantrums, genius for making money, and determination to emerge the winner in every situation. In his trademark gray sharkskin suit, Neuharth had become the most striking figure in contemporary American journalism. "With Al," a fellow publishing executive summed him up in an oft-quoted remark, "you never know where the suit stops and the shark begins." Yet the most frequently repeated quotation had come from Neuharth's own lips. Asked how to pronounce his company's name, he replied: "It's pronounced Gan-NETT—with the accent on the NET."

Though he had inherited rather than initiated the policy of rapid expansion, he pursued it with more vigor than either of his predecessors as chairman, and with more boldness. Along with *USA Today,* the Neuharth era was marked by the biggest acquisitions in Gannett history. Irked by the criticism that his huge chain did not produce good journalism, Neuharth decided to go out and buy it. Accordingly, in the mid-1980s Gannett paid top dollar for some of the most respected mastheads in America: the 100,000-circulation *Clarion-Ledger* and *Daily News* in Jackson, Mississippi, for $110 million; the 200,000-circulation *Arkansas Gazette,* for $51 million; the 375,000-circulation *Des Moines Register* and *Tribune,* for $165 million; the 320,000-circulation *Louisville Courier-Journal* and *Times,* for $305 million; and the 830,000-circulation *Detroit News,* for $717 million. The outlay totaled more than $1.3 billion.

It was a price Neuharth was willing to pay for respect, without spending years earning it. Before being sold, these papers all had proud heritages. Among them, they had won twenty-six Pulitzer Prizes. Thus Neuharth's checkbook enabled him to say in his memoirs: "Lest you wonder, Gannett newspapers have won their share of Pulitzers. Thirty-seven in all. Some before they joined Gannett, some since." Yet by actual count, only eight of the Pulitzers claimed by Neuharth were won under Gannett direction. All the rest were bought.

While shopping for respectability, Neuharth kept an eye on the bottom line. The papers in Des Moines, Louisville, and Jackson all were monopolies. In Detroit and Little Rock, however, things were different. Both of those cities had daily competition. Noting that Gannett had little experience competing, observers waited to see what Neuharth would do. Events soon revealed that his plans for Detroit and Little Rock were not the same.

After first denying it, he later admitted in court that before buying the *News* he had struck a secret deal with the owner of the competing *Detroit Free Press* to seek a joint operating agreement. In Little Rock the plan was not secret deals but open warfare, an all-out campaign to put the *Arkansas Democrat* out of business. Yet somehow, both his southern and northern campaigns did not unfold as planned. After the Detroit JOA bid became known, adamant opposition from several quarters tied up the application for years. And in Little Rock, Walter Hussman proved a far more tenacious adversary than Gannett had bargained for.

In Louisville, Des Moines, and Jackson, however, Gannett's monopolies surpassed all expectations, with the lethal combination of "flexibility" in pricing and sharp cost reductions amassing unheard-of profits. Nowhere was the Gannett difference more clear than in Des Moines, where in 1985 Neuharth had by a wide margin topped other bidders for the family-owned *Register* and *Tribune*. "Our investment paid off quickly," he reported in his memoirs. "Earnings quadrupled in our first four years of ownership. Says Charles Edwards, a member of the Cowles family who remained and is now our publisher: 'If my grandfather had known these newspapers could make this much money, he never would have died.' "

Gannett's sealed bid in Des Moines was $35 million higher than the runner-up offer. Later a losing bidder, from another chain, was asked whether Gannett had overpaid. Not at all, he replied. But how could he think that, considering the huge difference? "Simple," he said. "Gannett is prepared to do things we won't do to make money."

20

An Enthusiasm for Fraud

BEFORE ALLEN NEUHARTH TOOK COMMAND, the Gannett chain was lightly regarded as "a bunch of little shit-kicker newspapers." But at least it was considered a clean outfit. With his ascendancy, however, things changed. He emerged as chairman in 1978—the same year that Gannett went on trial for fraud in Connecticut.

The alleged fraud had taken place a few years earlier, when Neuharth was still president. As detailed in U.S. District Court, it stemmed from Gannett's attempts first to salvage, then unload a failing newspaper it owned in Hartford. Most uncharacteristically, the chain had gotten into a competitive situation in Connecticut's capital city. And it was not competing very well. The *Hartford Times,* one of Gannett's biggest newspapers at the time, was in a head-to-head struggle with the *Hartford Courant.* Yet the harder it struggled, the more ground the *Times* was losing, in both advertising revenues and circulation. Gannett saw only a dismal future in Hartford. So in 1973 it decided to sell. But there was a problem: If a prospective buyer knew the true circulation figures, and how badly the battle was being lost, the *Times* would be difficult to unload. At best it would bring a bargain-basement price, and it might not sell at all.

For years falling circulation had plagued the *Times.* Admitting to advertisers that fewer and fewer readers were getting the paper would only hasten its decline, so the management devised a number of schemes to falsify the figures. Although the fraud was devised and implemented by local managers in Hartford, knowledge of it eventually reached corporate headquarters. But when seeking to sell the *Times,* Gannett made no attempt to correct the circulation figures or admit they were inflated. Instead, some of the company's highest executives made sure that a prospective buyer, Register Publishing Company, remained deceived until the sale was completed late in 1973, at a price of $7 million.

Shortly after taking over the *Times,* Register discovered the discrepancies. Realizing that the newspaper's market position was far weaker than it had seemed, Register asked to renegotiate the purchase price. Gannett refused. When Register withheld payment because of the discovered fraud, Gannett sued to collect. For three years Register tried to save the *Times.* But its deficits continued to mount, and the situation became hopeless.

In 1976, the paper shut down. Gannett's lawsuit to collect full payment, however, remained in the courts. Then Register filed a countersuit, seeking to recover damages caused by Gannett's deception. Eventually the suits were merged into one case. In 1978 an eighteen-day trial was held in Hartford before Judge Jon O. Newman, who issued a thirty-eight-page decision against Gannett almost two years later. During the trial, Gannett's schemes to inflate the *Times* circulation were revealed. They were spelled out in the judge's decision, which I got from my *Santa Fe Reporter* friend at the *Courant.*

The fraud at Gannett's Hartford paper was not an impulsive incident or a one-time desperation tactic. Rather, it was practiced routinely over a three-year period, up until the sale. First, in 1971, the *Times* began claiming as paid circulation hundreds of thousands of free copies given away as samples. In time the practice was questioned by a circulation examiner, and early in 1973 it was discontinued. Yet the very next month, as noted by Judge Newman in his verdict, "the management of the *Times,* its enthusiasm for fraud apparently undiminished, initiated another scheme to inflate circulation figures."

This plan was much more sophisticated. Under it, the Gannett paper created a totally fictitious company, called "Metropolitan Survey Services," and claimed that the firm had been hired to do market surveys. Then the *Times* made some $142,000 in payments to the phony company, for services that were never performed. Later the money was returned to the *Times,* and went onto the books as payments for subscriptions. Though bogus, the false subscriptions made the *Times*' competitive standing seem stronger than it was. It was a complex money-laundering operation—and it succeeded, duping first Hartford's advertisers and then Register.

Because of the subterfuge, the *Times*'s circulation was presented by Gannett as 113,000 instead of the real figure of 105,000. The difference was 8,000, a crucial number. As the closing date for the sale drew near, Register officials began to suspect that something was askew. For reassurance, they asked for a guarantee of the stated 113,000 circulation. But since that number was known to be false by Gannett controller Robert Eisenbraun and other executives, the request was cause for alarm. According to the judge, "Eisenbraun discussed the matter with Douglas McCorkindale, Gannett's general counsel, but neither chose to tell Register what they had discovered, despite the fact that Eisenbraun was again asked about the market survey by officers of Register when he had dinner with them on October 9."

Feeling pressure from the suspicious buyer, McCorkindale finally presented the situation to Gannett's president, Neuharth. According to the court's decision, the two of them decided to seemingly go along with Register's demand, by giving a guarantee that the 113,000 figure was correct—"provided that a cushion of approximately 8,000 copies per day were included in the guarantee to allow for changes based on later information." By creating this "cushion" of 8,000 copies—the amount of reported *Times* circulation that they knew to be false—Gannett's president and top legal officer were providing a non-guarantee guarantee for their company's claims. Unaware of what was behind it, Register accepted the adjustment, and closed the deal.

In finding Gannett guilty of fraud, the judge used tough language. Referring to the company's awareness of the 8,000-issue exaggeration, he wrote: "It was a knowing falsehood not to reveal this fact when asked directly about it." And to Gannett's defense that the scams were operated by lower-level employees instead of top officials, Newman ruled: "It is the corporation's duty to exercise control over the employees who are authorized to represent it. Any other rule would grant the modern corporation, with its complex internal structure, a virtual license to defraud." Therefore, he concluded: "All these misleading actions, having been taken by policy-level employees, can be attributed to Gannett itself."

Yet despite these pronouncements, Newman ruled that Gannett's fraud was only one of several factors in the demise of the *Times*. He particularly looked askance at the buyer's decision to try to save the paper for three years instead of immediately demanding a revocation of the sale as soon as the fraud was discovered. Thus he turned down Register's request that the sale be canceled and the purchase price repaid. Instead he came up with a complicated formula ordering Gannett to pay Register $966,450. The restitution, however, provided little comfort to the duped buyer. According to Register's lawsuit, the total losses it suffered for trusting Gannett— including the *Times* purchase price, broker commissions, operating costs for the doomed newspaper, and interest—exceeded $17 million.

Responding to the decision, Neuharth said in a statement: "From the beginning we acknowledged that some circulation figures had been unintentionally misstated by the *Hartford Times,* but that any damages as a result were minor. We are pleased that the judge has concurred and has awarded nominal and reasonable amounts to settle the claims of both parties."

In a bitter retort, Register senior vice president Lionel S. Jackson Jr. declared: "It is striking news and worth considering by all in the newspaper industry that a media conglomerate such as Gannett has been found guilty of fraud. Mr. Neuharth apparently takes some satisfaction from the fact that the judge set damages at $1 million rather than $15 million. His callous attitude about Judge Newman's finding of fraud says as much about Gannett's integrity as the court's opinion, which we invite all the public to read."

21

"The Highest Level
of Dishonor"

ANOTHER CITY WHERE GANNETT WAS stung in federal court was my own, Santa Fe. There the chain was sued for fraud and breach of contract by the former owner of the *New Mexican,* Robert McKinney.

Charging deliberate betrayal of the contractual promises made by Gannett in order to acquire Santa Fe's daily paper, McKinney sought to cancel the sale altogether. Though I had never much cared for this haughty man, he became a sympathetic figure when the longest jury trial in New Mexico history disclosed the manner in which the chain had honored its solemn obligations to him. "Gannett's conduct, as revealed in the trial of this case," wrote the judge in a scathing fifty-two-page opinion, "may be acceptable in its executive suites or in the marketplace in which it moves and trades. It is not acceptable in this, or any other, court of equity."

McKinney bought the *New Mexican* in 1949, and for the next quarter century ran it in a high-handed manner that left him influential if not universally admired in the city and the state. His nicely profitable, seventeen-thousand-circulation, daily-monopoly journal was the very archetype of the properties Gannett had strung into the nation's biggest chain. Moreover, as a state-capital paper it carried a status coveted by the rich but lightly regarded group. As early as 1970 Gannett expressed interest in buying the *New Mexican.* But not until 1975, when McKinney learned he had a heart condition that would make it impossible for him to live even part-time in Santa Fe's seven-thousand-foot altitude, did the talks get serious.

Ill and sixty-five years old, McKinney was willing to hand over the newspaper's ownership and profits to Gannett. But he still wanted the *New Mexican* to be his personal instrument, and he insisted on retaining full control for several years. When Gannett tried to reduce the power to be left in McKinney's hands, he angrily broke off negotiations. Rich, proud, authoritarian, a former ambassador to Switzerland and former board member of TWA and Martin-Marietta Corp., the *New Mexican*'s owner was not a man to be pushed around even by a giant like Gannett. Only after the chain agreed to his demands was the sale completed, in February 1976.

Those demands were spelled out in an "Employment Agreement," termed by the judge an "airtight contract." McKinney got "complete charge" of all operations for five years after the sale, and "complete authority" over editorial policy for another five years.

From his lower-altitude home in Virginia, McKinney intended to run the *New Mexican* through a trusted general manager, Stephen E. Watkins—the accountant with whom I had fought during my time at the paper. But two years after the sale, Watkins was fired without McKinney's approval and replaced with a Gannett appointee. At the trial, Watkins testified that he was fired because he did not meet Gannett's "impossible" profit goals of from 36 to 38 percent, to match other papers in the chain. Such a return could not be realized without destroying the *New Mexican*'s quality, he said.

Failure to meet profit demands was not the only clash that McKinney's man had with Gannett's way of running the *New Mexican.* Not long after taking over, Watkins testified, the chain pressured him to hire a circulation manager named Steve Pope, who proceeded to implement what the judge called "the Pope circulation fraud scandal."

According to Watkins, Pope proposed to increase circulation revenues by fraudulently reducing the number of papers delivered to prepaid subscribers. A memo in Pope's handwriting, presented as evidence at the trial, suggested that customers with fifty dollars in their accounts should receive twenty-eight fewer papers than they had paid for. Subscribers with lower balances would also get fewer papers. Apparently Pope felt that most subscribers were not precisely aware of when delivery of their newspaper expired. But to be safe, Pope suggested that customers who had previously complained about service should not be included in the plan. And anyone who noted the shortfall and asked about it would be told it was caused by a computer error, and immediately given the full prepaid subscription. Watkins's objections to the plan hastened his exit, he testified.

Other irregularities in circulation also became part of the trial record. Included were manipulations of accounts receivable and the disappearance and presumed destruction of "crucial records." Because of the discrepancies, the Audit Bureau of Circulations refused to accept the *New Mexican*'s reported numbers.

Shortly after his general manager's dismissal, McKinney suffered a further indignity from Gannett. For the 1978 New Mexico gubernatorial campaign, he instructed the paper to endorse the Democratic nominee. When the endorsement was written, however, it contained passages highly critical of the candidate. Reviewing it in Virginia, McKinney demanded by telephone that the passages be deleted. The Gannett-appointed management refused. Furious, McKinney then tried to fire the officials who had disobeyed him. The Gannett hierarchy, however, did not recognize his authority, and left them in place. Then McKinney was officially stripped of all management power. Despite this emasculation, however, Gannett left his name on the masthead as "publisher and editor-in-chief" and maintained an office with his name on the door.

Late in 1978 McKinney sued Gannett for fraud and breach of contract, and asked that the sale of the *New Mexican* be canceled. Gannett denied all wrongdoing. When it came to U.S. District Court in Santa Fe in 1980 before a jury and Judge Santiago Campos, the case became a fourteen-week trial. At its conclusion, the jury found Gannett guilty of six breaches of McKinney's contract. Because the trial failed to prove that Gannett had intended to violate the contract at the time it was signed, the fraud count was not upheld.

After the verdict was returned, Campos ruled that Gannett must return the paper to McKinney. Further details of his ruling would be forthcoming in a full memorandum of opinion, he added.

At Gannett headquarters, chairman Allen Neuharth issued a statement dismissing the jury's findings as "minor technical violations." As for the judge's ruling, Neuharth called it "a preposterous miscarriage of justice," as well as "an outrageous decision based on politics and provincialism." Responding later, Campos frostily declared: "Out here in the provinces, we have a three-letter word that describes that kind of distortion and a four-letter word to describe people who traffic in that kind of distortion." He stopped short of spelling out the word "liar" to characterize the head of the nation's largest newspaper chain.

When Campos's full opinion was issued in March 1981, it left no doubt as to his assessment of the corporate behavior that had been brought to light in his courtroom. "Gannett's breaches were wrongful," the judge wrote. "Rather than a few isolated incidents amounting to merely technical breaches of the Employment Agreement, Gannett's course of conduct, evidenced by the actions of the highest-level Gannett executives, created an ignoble showdown. McKinney's authority was superseded without legal justification. McKinney was stripped of rights which had been bargained in good faith. There is no market where McKinney can replace what Gannett has wrongfully taken from him."

Repeatedly the judge expressed a low regard for Gannett's way of upholding its end of a bargain. "One of the greatest sources of wonder to me at the trial was the attitude of some of the Gannett men when they addressed McKinney's right of 'complete charge' and 'complete authority' under the Employment Agreement. It appeared incomprehensible to them," the judge wrote in one passage. " . . . Neuharth, for example, cavalierly characterized McKinney's solid and substantial contract rights of 'complete charge' and 'complete authority' as 'window dressing.' "

Elsewhere Campos stated: "My observation of the Gannett men who appeared and testified in court, consideration of their testimony and the exhibits admitted into evidence, and reflection on testimony of others regarding the conduct which molded the breaches of the Employment Agreement tell me that these are hard-charging, willful men who, almost without exception, were fully cognizant of the dimensions of Gannett's obligations and McKinney's rights under the Employment Agreement."

Quoting internal memos written by executives in the chain's West region, Campos noted that Gannett's idea of a general manager for the *New Mexican* would be one who, in dealing with McKinney, "would be nice to 'the old coot,' would tell him what had been done after it had been done, and would keep his office dusted in case he dropped in."

Finally, Campos summed up what he had seen unfold in his court: "I believe that Gannett went into this deal with its eyes wide open. It knew the Employment Agreement would interfere with the way it wanted to run the *New Mexican.* It also knew that McKinney was old and physically infirm. It knew he would be residing in Virginia. It wanted the *New Mexican* very badly. Gannett took a gamble." With acid pen he added: "Gannett could have responded by fully honoring McKinney's contract. Instead, it escalated its pattern of breaches to the highest level of dishonor."

As things turned out, McKinney did not quickly resume ownership of the *New Mexican,* for an ironic reason: The Gannett stock that he had acquired in payment for his newspaper had appreciated so much in value that he stood to lose about $5 million if he returned it in exchange for taking the paper back. Compounding the problem was the diminished condition of the *New Mexican* after five years under Gannett's control. Noting its plunging circulation and sharply reduced editorial content, McKinney argued that Gannett should be held accountable for undermining the paper's value. In increasingly acrimonious clashes, McKinney even accused Gannett of deliberately trying to destroy the *New Mexican*'s worth through a vengeful "scorched-earth policy" when it realized he was likely to win the paper back.

"Unscrambling the egg," as Judge Campos termed the task of sorting through the financial complexities of the case, proved so difficult that for six more years after the 1981 opinion, Gannett and McKinney continued their legal struggle. Eventually McKinney dropped his insistence that the paper be returned to him. Instead he demanded that the full terms of the original Employment Agreement be honored, though years had passed in the meantime. Gannett again resisted, however, seeking in a series of appeals to buy off the contract rather than comply.

In mid-1987 Gannett lost its last appeal. Only then did it agree to honor the contract it had signed with McKinney more than a decade earlier. Under the terms of the reinstated contract, McKinney would resume "complete charge" of the *New Mexican* for three more years, then would have "complete authority" over editorial policy for the next five years. In essence, the clock began ticking on the contract again, resuming at the point that Gannett had violated the agreement.

On September 1, 1987, the embattled McKinney, now seventy-six years old but surprisingly sturdy after living at lower altitude, marched triumphantly into the *New Mexican*. As he reclaimed the newspaper for which he had fought so long, he declared: "I have returned." Two years later, he bought the paper back in its entirety, thus laying claim to a title virtually without precedent in American journalism: The Man Who Beat Gannett.

22

The Conspirators

IN JUNE 1989, JUST FOUR months before I came to Green Bay, still another federal court, this one in Los Angeles, revealed a secret of Gannett's success in the outdoor advertising field: a criminal price-fixing conspiracy.

Gannett Outdoor, a wholly owned subsidiary, is the nation's largest roadside advertising company, with forty-five thousand billboards in almost three hundred markets covering 85 percent of the population. One of the most lucrative markets is Southern California, presided over by the Los Angeles–based Gannett Outdoor Company of Southern California. After a three-week jury trial, Gannett and a codefendant, Metromedia Inc., entered a plea of "nolo contendere," or "no contest," to U.S. Justice Department antitrust charges that they had conspired for years to reduce the rents paid to billboard-site property owners by secretly agreeing not to compete in the leasing of those sites.

Each company was fined $850,000 for criminal violation of the antitrust laws. In addition, the former chief executive officer of Gannett Outdoor, Hal W. Brown Jr., and a former vice president of Metromedia, Michael F. Tobey, were convicted of price-fixing. Each was fined $100,000, given a suspended three-year prison sentence, placed on probation for five years, and ordered to perform one thousand hours of charitable service.

"Defendant has been convicted as charged," stated the judgment against Gannett, issued by the U.S. Court of the Central District of California. Stories from the *Los Angeles Times,* sent by my former *Santa Fe Reporter* colleague, indicated that the charges resulted from a federal grand jury investigation. In the hands-off, deregulated, let-business-be-business political climate under Presidents Reagan and Bush, such a case—and particularly such an outcome—was indeed unusual. Under the Republicans, antitrust enforcement had been honored largely in the breach. And deferential regard for Gannett was apparent in the highest echelons of government.

When *USA Today* was launched, the ceremony was attended by Reagan and the First Lady, Nancy, under a tent on the grounds of the national Capitol in Washington. When the paper concluded its first five years of enormous circulation gains and incessant financial losses, Reagan sent a message of congratulations: "Your success is truly a turning point in the news business." Dignitaries at the five-year anniversary party included United States Supreme Court Chief Justice Warren Burger and House Republican Whip Dick Cheney, later named secretary of defense.

Within the Justice Department, Gannett's influence reached all the way to the top. Less than a year before the Southern California trial, controversial U.S. Attorney General Edwin Meese III had overruled both his antitrust division and a federal administrative law judge to approve the joint operating agreement sought in Detroit by Gannett and Knight-Ridder. Both the antitrust unit and the judge had concluded that the losses cited by the chains as justification for the Detroit JOA were not caused by irreversible market forces but were a deliberate strategy, whose sole purpose was to win approval for the proposed dual monopoly—and the millions of dollars in extra profits it promised to make for the already rich chains. The judge's negative recommendation was a historical precedent. No previous jurist in his capacity had ever ruled against a JOA. But the final word rested with the attorney general.

In the months leading up to his decision on Detroit, Meese had been under constant media fire on numerous accusations of influence peddling, improper business dealings, and other activities not suitable for the nation's chief law enforcement officer. Buckling under the attack, he had announced his intention to resign. Yet while cartoonists and editorialists throughout the country were pillorying Meese as one of the worst examples of the excesses of the greed-driven 1980s, Gannett and Knight-Ridder were laying low. If their newspapers found any fault with the attorney general, evidence of it was hard to find on their pages.

Several political heavyweights were recruited to support the Detroit JOA, including former Republican President Jerry Ford, who was from Michigan. The public-relations firm of a Meese adviser was hired by Knight-Ridder to promote the cause. And Clark Clifford, a former secretary of defense, later to be indicted, then acquitted, in the multibillion-dollar BCCI banking scandal, sat on Knight-Ridder's board of directors. Meese, however, insisted he was not influenced by anyone in reaching his decision to ignore the findings of the judge and his own antitrust staff, and approve the largest JOA in history. A day later, he vacated his office.

In the world of realpolitik, I was amazed that a regional subdivision of the same Justice Department could come down hard on Gannett in the

Southern California case. The only possible explanation, I felt sure, was that the chain's violation of the antitrust statutes out there had been so flagrant, so egregious, so illegal on the face of it that no court, and no administration, could openly condone it. When I called the Justice Department prosecutor of the case, I discovered I was not wrong.

"As far as the criminal process is concerned, a nolo contendere plea is the same as a guilty plea," said John Greaney, a Washington-based assistant chief of litigation in the antitrust division. He pointed out, however, that in technical terms, a plea of no contest does not carry an admission of guilt. "Theoretically, they can say later that they were not guilty," he explained.

Greaney said the Justice Department had objected strenuously to the no-contest plea, because a conviction or an outright plea of guilty would have made it easier for parties injured by the price-fixing conspiracy to file their own suits to collect damages from Gannett and the other defendants. Without such evidence on the record, he said, plaintiffs in civil suits must bear the burden of proving guilt, a process often prohibitively expensive to victims without much money. Greaney said the case against Gannett and the other defendants was so strong that the prosecutors were sure they could get a conviction. But the judge accepted the nolo contendere plea instead.

Late in 1988 the grand jury in Los Angeles had spelled out the charges against Gannett and its coconspirators, who were indicted for engaging in a number of illegal activities over at least a twenty-year period, from 1964 to 1984. According to the indictment, the defendants had agreed not to enter competitive bids on billboard sites, even when previous leases had expired and the sites were back on the market. The conspiracy had the effect of holding rentals on the sites artificially low, decreasing revenues for the land owners and increasing profits for Gannett and Metromedia. The defendants were further charged with lying to property owners about why bids were not submitted, training employees not to submit competitive bids on the affected sites, and destroying evidence of the conspiracy after it was discovered.

When the charges were filed in December 1988, both Gannett and Metromedia denied any wrongdoing. "We believe the charges are without merit," said Metromedia's general counsel. "The case will be vigorously defended and we expect to be fully vindicated." A statement from Gannett took a similar position. The charges were based "on a misunderstanding of the facts and the law," and "will be contested vigorously," Gannett declared. Furthermore, stated company spokeswoman Mimi Feller, the alleged illegal activity took place before Gannett bought the Southern California billboard operation, which it acquired in 1979. Therefore, she insisted, her company could not have been a party to the alleged conspiracy.

Yet John Greaney of the Justice Department had a direct answer when I asked him if the $850,000 fine levied on Gannett indicated that the company had played a knowing and active role in continuing the conspiracy after taking over the outdoor operation. "Yes, it does," he said.

23

Eviscerated Shells

NOT EVERY GANNETT CITY HAD spawned a lawsuit, or a widely reported drama like the ones in Detroit and Little Rock. I knew of other markets where Salem-style tactics were alleged. "The Newspaper That Was Murdered" brought many such tales. But the victims were too poor, too cautious, and even too smart to sue. Going one-on-one with Gannett required exceedingly deep pockets.

Emotionally draining, ruinously expensive legal battles were a fool's game for anyone without either a sure case, like the *Community Press,* or adequate resources to fight to the end, like Robert McKinney. Otherwise, with its in-house lawyers and its riches, Gannett could delay and wait, wait and delay, while victims slowly bled to death trying to move the wheels of justice. So most struggled and suffered in silence, and many gave up.

For the purposes of the Green Bay Project, I needed to push beyond the court record and the publicized battles. In even the places where it was not making waves, I needed to know what effect this largest of all chains was having. In a more perfect world, the effect might have been a good one. A monopoly newspaper with almost no limits on its ability to make money in the town it dominated might be expected to use part of that money to improve the product it gave its readers. In the real world, however, what usually happened once a paper got a stranglehold was that its editorial quality was gutted.

No chain better illustrated that curious maxim than Gannett. Despite its wealth, it was known more for stripping newspapers of proud journalistic heritages that took generations to build than for elevating so-so papers into great or even very good ones. The reason was the usual one: the bottom line. Raising or even maintaining a newspaper's quality was a costly proposition, with expenditures for salaries, supplies, even the cost of the space needed to print the stories that a large staff produces. Long ago Gannett had learned it could make more money by not investing too much in such things.

There were variations from place to place. In some towns Gannett bought dreadful newspapers and converted them into the chain's typical product, which was an improvement. In others Gannett imposed its flashy style on staid but respected papers, and suffered local wrath as a result. In most places, however, Gannett simply put out its paper in the way that made the most money, without regard for journalistic quality or tradition.

The Gannettization phenomenon had been studied by Pulitzer Prize winner and journalist-turned-scholar Ben Bagdikian, dean of the graduate school of journalism at the University of California–Berkeley. His 1983 book *The Media Monopoly* gave sharp rebuttal to chairman Al Neuharth's full-page ad in the *New York Times* that posed the question "What happens to a family newspaper when it joins Gannett?"—and gave this answer: "It gets better."

In Bagdikian's dissenting opinion:

> How can one know if it gets better? Neuharth believed he knew. In a *Los Angeles Times* interview in 1978 he said a locally owned newspaper that gives too much sophisticated news is "out of touch with its community." Chain papers, he said, are realistic, give the readers what they want, and consequently gain circulation.
>
> The Gannett papers fail their own test. From 1973 to 1978 Gannett papers lost 6 percent in circulation while other dailies of the same circulation size gained circulation. . . .
>
> Neuharth himself may have disclosed one cause of the Gannett chain's failure to gain circulation for its monopolies. In a 1978 speech to the American Society of Newspaper Editors, in Washington, D.C., he ridiculed smaller papers that try to be too serious. When it comes to national and international news, he said, "Coffeyville, Kansas, Muskogee, Oklahoma, they don't give a damn. The less they hear about Washington and New York the better they feel about it."
>
> The editor of the *Emporia Gazette,* still owned by heirs of [legendary American journalist] William Allen White, was in the audience. Coffeyville, a site of a recent Gannett acquisition, is near Emporia. The Emporia editor wrote:
>
> "It was my first meeting, so I was too shy to go to the microphone and tell Mr. Neuharth that Coffeyville is not a backwoods hillbilly town . . . and that his remarks were an insult to the then-newest Gannett property, the *Coffeyville Journal.*"
>
> The *Coffeyville Journal,* it turned out, had been greatly respected and its circulation had grown steadily before Gannett bought it. Its former owner, Richard Seaton, and editor, Daniel Hamrick, had won prizes for their fight against attempts by the John Birch Society to take

over the city council. After Gannett bought the paper, the amount of news was reduced. When an accurate news story offended an advertiser, the Gannett headquarters told the local editor to make peace. When reactionaries complained about stories the paper had always run, a Gannett regional director supported the complaints and a Gannett senior vice president said he was grateful for being informed that the local editor was "failing to do a proper news reporting job for its community."

The editor of many years, Daniel Hamrick, quit. A nearby paper, the *Parsons* (Kansas) *Sun,* editorialized: "Its neighbors have watched with dismay the decline of the *Journal* in recent months. Its news content, under chain ownership, had become increasingly small. . . ."

What happened to news in Coffeyville and in other Gannett cities was not unusual for Gannett local papers or for almost all chain-owned local papers. Profit squeezes and indifference to comprehensive local news is the norm. Systematic studies by researchers over the years make clear that despite grandiloquent rhetoric, chain papers give their communities less serious news than do independent papers.

A study reported in the standard scholarly journalistic publication *Journalism Quarterly* found that papers that were once competitive but were made monopolies by chains produced "higher prices and lower quality." Another study at Brookings Institution showed that chain-owned papers charge 7 percent more for ads than independent papers, but where the chains have competition their rates are 15 percent lower than for counterpart monopoly papers. . . .

The most pervasive changes made in independent papers acquired by chains are typically to increase advertising and subscription rates, to introduce cosmetic alterations of page design and makeup to give the impression of modernity, and to quietly reduce the amount of serious news. It is conventional wisdom among publishers that readers are uninterested in "serious" news. As we will see later, this is not true. The real reason publishers shun "serious" news is that it is more expensive than features. . . .

In 1966, before Gannett began its drive to create its international empire, its 26 daily and six Sunday papers averaged approximately 45 news employees per paper. By 1980, when it had 81 daily, 53 Sunday, and 23 less-than-daily papers (and had added Saturday editions to acquired papers that previously had none), it averaged 26 news employees per paper.

More pointed and plaintive than Bagdikian's broad overview were local assessments of the damage Gannett was doing to once-respected mast-heads. I found several such critiques, usually in magazines or alternative newspapers—often the only voices left to mourn the passing of a city's journalistic integrity.

"The Decline of the *Idaho Statesman*" was the title of one such article, in a 1985 issue of *Northern Lights,* a spirited young journal covering economic, environmental, and energy issues in Montana, Idaho, and Wyoming. The story, by Boise writer Pat Ford, disclosed that the publisher of Gannett's *Statesman* had ordered a key paragraph deleted from a news article, for fear of offending a commercial developer. His tampering cost the paper a scoop, and caused twenty-five newsroom employees to confront him with a letter of protest.

Northern Lights continued:

> The incident is only the latest in the long trail of decline by the only daily newspaper in the largest city in the Northern Rockies. The *Statesman,* which ought to be the best paper in the region by virtue of its location in Boise, is facing mounting criticism from its readers, its competitors and the reporters who work there.
>
> News space is much reduced, there has been a shift in news empha- sis, and the paper's editorial policy is weak-kneed. The responsibility for the paper's decline belongs with the *Statesman*'s management, the Gannett chain, which owns the paper, and, surprisingly, on Gannett's national flagship paper, *USA Today.* . . .
>
> In 1922, then-publisher Calvin Cobb said, "I think we should run the *Statesman* as a subscribers' paper, rather than as an advertisers' paper, as for instance, if we have to leave out an advertisement or a good news item, leave out the advertisement." Cobb's sentiment seems to have been abandoned by modern proprietors.
>
> Jim Fisher, political reporter and columnist for the *Lewiston Tribune* [a respected independent newspaper in the state], says, "The amount invested in news at the *Idaho Statesman* today is pitiful. The local news hole (the amount of space devoted each day to local news) is very small. The local section is lucky to have two pages of news before the classifieds start." Marc Johnson, who edits and reports *Idaho Reports,* a 30-minute evening public affairs program on Idaho public television, agrees: "On most days, it's probably smaller than most dailies in Idaho."
>
> To test these assertions, I measured the column inches of local and state news from March 1 through March 15 in the years 1975, 1980 and 1985. For those 15 days in 1975, the news averaged 228 column inches per day. In 1980, the average was 241 inches per day. But by 1985, those same days averaged 173 inches per day. The reduction for the period was about 28 percent.

For comparison, I measured state and local news content of two other Idaho dailies. The *Lewiston Tribune* averaged 251 inches per day, and the *Twin Falls Times-News* averaged 243 inches per day. . . .

This decline in coverage seems also to have affected the quality of what remains. Says Jim Fisher, "I get the feeling not many demands are made on the news staff. A small news hole doesn't make for a dynamic, inquiring paper." Frustration about the news space and resources, a *Statesman* reporter says, "is general within the news staff. But most of us are resigned to it. There's absolutely nothing you can do."

The reasons for this powerlessness seem to lie squarely with the *Statesman's* parent company. The Gannett Company recently purchased its 87th daily newspaper [it subsequently sold a few], the *Des Moines Register.* Company-wide [revenues] in 1983 were over $1.9 billion. The company boasts over 60 consecutive quarters of higher earnings and profits.

"It's the opinion of the Gannett management that the foremost thing is to keep its stock healthy," says former *Statesman* editorial page editor Rick Ripley. Another former *Statesman* reporter is more blunt: "Gannett belongs to the Blackbeard school of capitalism. Gannett people are the ultimate bottom-line people. Their formula is, "If it makes money, do it; if it doesn't, don't." . . .

Reporters believe that one reason the *Statesman's* news staff and space haven't returned to former levels, despite the [mid-1980s national] economic improvement, is Gannett's national newspaper venture, *USA Today.* . . . "We all suspect a certain amount of *Statesman*-profit goes into that," says one reporter. "You would have to be naive not to think there's some connection between less news space and *USA Today.*"

A more bitter lament was sounded in the *Jackson Journal of Business* in Mississippi's capital city. There Gannett had been presiding over the town's daily journalism since 1982, when it bought the *Daily News* and the *Clarion-Ledger,* newspapers with a tradition of digging and a Pulitzer Prize for public service. Noting that Gannett had at first made a show of upholding the papers' heritage, writer Rebecca Pittman saw nothing but a downhill slide in more recent years. Her October 1988 article was headlined "The Gannettization of the Daily Press in Jackson (Or How a Parent Company Milks a Local 'Cash Cow')."

Like its title, the text pulled no punches:

> You have to wonder whether or not John Johnson, executive editor
> of the *Clarion-Ledger* and the *Jackson Daily News,* knew what he
> was getting into when he agreed to be on a local talk radio station's

afternoon call-in show not long ago. Certainly he's a brave man if he anticipated the response his appearance generated from WJNT's listening audience.

For nearly the entire show Johnson was subjected to continual caller criticism of the two daily newspapers he oversees. Recalls Randy Grammar, host of WJNT's "Randy in the Afternoon": "I would say that between 85 and 90 percent of all the comments were negative. He got hammered for two hours."

Arguably, talk radio aficionados are a tough-minded bunch with overly evolved opinions on the proper delivery of their daily news mix. But there's a good case to be made that these callers indeed reflect a widespread sense that Jackson's daily newspapers are falling down in their efforts to provide quality coverage of local, state, national and world events.

There is, for starters, obviously less actual news copy in the *Clarion-Ledger/Jackson Daily News,* compared to years past, and what gets in is too often superficially reported or just plain superficial. Page counts are much lower than in previous years. Investigative reporting is virtually non-existent. . . .

It would appear that Jackson's daily newspapers have fallen victim to what is recognized among journalists as a classic Gannett syndrome: in the beginning, the unique editorial strengths of a newly acquired newspaper are well cared for, but over time this gives way to an editorial direction more in line with Gannett Inc.'s over-arching passion for profit.

Increasingly, the *Clarion-Ledger* has come to resemble Gannett's flagship newspaper, *USA Today.* On the plus side, the *Clarion-Ledger* now routinely prints color graphics, color weather maps and page one color photographs, as pioneered in *USA Today.* But—in typical Gannett fashion—*Clarion-Ledger* stories are now significantly shorter, while frothy features often find their way to the front page at the expense of hard news. . . .

Even executive editor John Johnson allows he's troubled by his shrinking news hole. "It bothers any editor," he says. "No editor ever has enough space."

But there always seems room for animal stories, dear to the heart of gung-ho Gannett editors (who other journalists have labeled "Gannet-toids"). In the past year Jackson readers have been served up page-one pieces on such matters as a deer residing at the city pound, an Ocean Springs couple who annoyed neighbors by keeping ducks, and a four-legged chicken in Pearl.

"They're trying to pander to a so-called 'reader,' and that philosophy is different from my philosophy," says former *Jackson Daily News* reporter Willie Rabb, now with the *Charlotte* (N.C.) *Observer.* "They feel like the reader doesn't want to expend any energy at all to learn about the problems of society. . . ."

Thus many accomplished writers move on to other papers, as reflected in the high turnover rate for *Clarion-Ledger/Jackson Daily News* reporters. Such turnover holds down payroll costs—at the expense of high-quality reporting. "They just don't invest in anyone with any institutional knowledge of what they cover—anyone with any depth or perspective," says *Tampa Tribune* reporter Gaynell Terrell, a former *Clarion-Ledger* business reporter.

Nevertheless, the *Clarion-Ledger/Jackson Daily News* has long been regarded by industry observers as a "cash cow." Since the days of the Hedermans [the former owners], Jackson's daily newspapers have raked in profits one former *Clarion-Ledger/Jackson Daily News* editor describes as "bordering on the obscene."

Eight months after this article appeared, Gannett merged the morning *Clarion-Ledger* and the evening *Daily News* into one paper.

But what about Gannett's *Green Bay Press-Gazette*? How had it fared? To reach the people I must reach, I needed to know. Like the industrious writer in Boise, I decided to take a ruler to the pages of Gannett's paper. More precisely, because it would take a lot of time, I sought someone to do the measuring for me. As usual, I invoked the *Santa Fe Reporter* Connection. One hundred miles to the north, out in Lake Michigan on a place called Washington Island, was a meticulous former reporter from our staff. She had left journalism, and now was raising goats on her brother's farm. Yes, she would do it.

I packed off a week of the *Press-Gazette*. In a few days she called with some figures. The tale they told was decidedly unusual for Gannett. In every way that could be measured with a ruler, the *Press-Gazette* was giving its readers a more generous editorial package than almost any other paper in the chain. Astonishingly, the industry's standard equation of 60 percent ads and 40 percent editorial was turned inside-out.

In the measured week, the *Press-Gazette* had devoted 57.4 percent of its total space to news, features, columns, and other reading matter, while filling only 42.6 percent with advertising. The paper had published a total of 398 pages, and 228 had been nonadvertising. If the normal news-to-ad ratio had been observed, only 159 pages would have been editorial. The difference was 69 additional full-size pages of reading matter for Green Bay.

I ran some figures and pushed the comparison. During the week, the *Press-Gazette* had sold 170 pages of advertising. If those pages had been the standard 60 percent of the total, the 40 percent given to editorial content would have numbered just 115 pages, instead of the 228 that actually had been published. By abandoning the industry norm, the *Press-Gazette* was giving its readers almost double the ratio of news, sports, and features that most Americans find in their daily newspaper. And to fill all the extra space, Gannett was maintaining a larger and costlier editorial staff in Green Bay than those in the chain's typical cities.

There had to be a reason, and it was obvious: competition. The only other Gannett paper facing daily competition was in Little Rock. And the news hole there was even more enormous than the *Press-Gazette*'s. Meanwhile, Gannett's other readers throughout the land were getting, on a take-it-or-leave-it basis, eviscerated shells of newspapers that once had been their cities' pride.

None of this, of course, was understood by the man or woman on the street in Green Bay. They did not know or care that half the features they took for granted in the big, fat *Press-Gazette* were provided courtesy of the puny, dying *News-Chronicle*. But once the competition vanished from the scene, they would learn soon enough what Gannett's idea of a good newspaper was.

24

Numbers Do Not Lie

As TELLING AS THE CONTRAST was between Gannett's editorial product in Green Bay and elsewhere, it was not nearly as crucial as another comparison I needed: a financial one.

Although readers might have been a paper's reason for existence in pre-chain days, those days were gone. In the hard world of business, readership figures were just a tool to convince advertisers that their messages would reach the desired number of potential customers. Except for a few specialty publications that got by on subscriptions, almost every paper in the land was utterly dependent on advertising to pay the way. The *Santa Fe Reporter* had been, and the *Green Bay News-Chronicle* certainly was.

The only chance for survival that Frank's paper had was to persuade Green Bay's advertisers that using the *News-Chronicle* would serve their own self-interest. Yet the claim of highest circulation belonged fivefold to the *Press-Gazette.* An entirely different case must be found to lure retailers into the *News-Chronicle.* That case had to be simple enough for even the most boneheaded advertisers to grasp. And as I knew from experience, the only arguments they responded to were monetary. To gain their support we had to show them that preserving the *News-Chronicle* was of direct importance to their pocketbooks.

Knowing Gannett, I was sure that the newspaper rivalry in Green Bay, unbalanced as it was, was benefiting every merchant in town. Where the chain had no competition, it shook down the community for every last dollar. It was the normal way for a monopoly to function, and was cause for open boasting at Gannett. "A colonial power exacting tribute" was a term used by a former employee to describe the chain in a 1987 article in the *New Republic* titled "Invasion of the Gannettoids."

Perhaps no single action better illustrated Gannett's imperial attitude than a 1979 directive that came straight down from the top. From now on, the order stated, all bank deposits except daily operational funds would be transferred by local papers to national headquarters *every night.* The drain on local economies around the country was considerable—about $1.5 billion a year when the order was issued, and more as the chain kept growing. The day Gannett got it, all this homegrown wealth ceased to nourish its own communities. Coupled with the monopolistic prices that Gannett was free to charge, this daily flight of capital was a direct siphoning off of economic vitality in dozens of cities. In terms of balance of trade, Gannett was running up a huge surplus, while its captive trading partners fell ever deeper into deficit.

Only where the chain faced competition was there any reason to deviate from the policies that had made it rich. I knew this—but unsubstantiated convictions would not help the Green Bay Project. I needed proof. Finding it did not prove difficult. Scholarly analysts of the newspaper industry had watched with concern as the chains were locking up American journalism. Some of them considered it a phenomenon worth academic scrutiny. The conclusion they reached was that the advent of the chains—Gannett in particular—amounted to a bright promise betrayed.

When chains were first emerging, naive analysts foresaw benefits for both subscribers and advertisers. The reasoning was that by consolidating administrative, accounting, personnel, and other expenses, plus the ability to buy supplies in vast discounted quantities, chains could operate far more economically than independent papers, and would pass along the savings. But just the opposite happened. Though the chains did indeed economize greatly, they *raised* prices instead of lowering them. As franchises answerable only to corporate headquarters, America's newspapers were now devoted first and foremost not to serving their communities, but to making money. And of all the chains, none was more obsessed with profits than Gannett.

As early as 1971 a report in *Journalism Quarterly* confirmed the obvious. A Southern Illinois University professor named Gerald Grotta analyzed financial data from 154 newspapers across the country, both independent and chain-owned, seeking a statistically supported answer to the question: "Have the consumers of the industry's products received any of the potential benefits from economies of scale made possible through concentration of ownership, as is often claimed by the industry, or have the potential benefits been absorbed by the industry?" His answer: "Not only did the purchaser of advertising receive no benefits from consolidation, he actually paid significantly higher prices after consolidation."

"The evidence indicates that consumers pay higher prices under consolidated ownership," he found, "with no compensating increase in quality or quantity of product received, and perhaps a decrease in quality." He summed up his study with a truism: "No economist will be surprised to find that monopolists charge monopoly prices."

A later survey was more specific, and of all the nation's chains, it targeted the largest. Seeking to compare Gannett's advertising rates with those of other chains in monopoly markets, William Blankenburg of the University of Wisconsin–Madison gathered local rate cards from fifty-four Gannett papers nationwide and fifty-four papers in other groups, then made a detailed comparison.

The summer 1983 *Journalism Quarterly* gave the results. In his article "A Newspaper Chain's Pricing Behavior," Blankenburg reported: "Not only does Gannett not offer lower prices, it sets higher prices." He found that Gannett's "significantly higher" rates traced to company policy rather than external factors, and were as much as 18 percent more than rates of other chains. In dry, academic prose, he summed up: "The hypothesis that Gannett ownership is associated with higher retail advertising prices is supported."

Bringing the findings of professors Blankenburg and Grotta home to Green Bay would require statistics of my own. To test my own hypothesis that the *News-Chronicle* was holding down prices at the Gannett paper, I needed to compare the *Press-Gazette*'s advertising rates with rates of the chain's similar-sized papers elsewhere. Because Green Bay was the only midsize market where the chain faced daily competition, I needed facts and figures to thrust at doubting advertisers. In essence, I needed a two-by-four to hit the mules on the heads with, to catch their attention.

Like the professors, I devised a methodology. According to *Editor & Publisher Yearbook,* there were eleven other cities where Gannett owned a paper with circulation in the 45,000–80,000 range. Because the cost of advertising is linked to the number of readers a newspaper delivers, my comparison must be made with circulations roughly similar to the *Press-Gazette*'s 56,190 daily, 79,215 Sunday. Bigger or smaller markets would not be relevant. I had been trying to get the advertising rate cards of these eleven newspapers ever since starting the Green Bay Project. I had succeeded in getting only eight, but this sample was large enough to provide a meaningful collective comparison with the *Press-Gazette*'s rates.

A typical rate card lists several prices for advertising, depending on how much is bought. The higher the volume, the lower the cost per column-inch.

Volume discounts, a standard procedure throughout the industry, were in effect at the *Press-Gazette* and every other Gannett paper whose rates I studied. Thus a client who buys a single ad, one time only, pays the highest, or "open," rate. A supermarket, on the other hand, with several pages of advertising every week, might use twenty thousand or more column-inches a year, and pays a sharply lower rate per inch. Papers also have a "national" rate, for institutional or brand-name advertisers such as General Motors or Coca-Cola.

To get an across-the-board comparison of all the papers in my study, I chose eight different volume levels, from open rate to twenty-thousand-inch, on each card. I added up the prices charged by each newspaper at each level, then averaged them to produce a representative composite rate at each paper. Then for precision, I adjusted this rate to reflect each paper's actual circulation. Despite my best efforts to simplify the study, I did not expect most readers to understand it very well. It had so many numbers from the dense realm of newspaper economics, presented all at once, that many people would find them incomprehensible. But that was all right: The key target for this piece of the Green Bay Project was advertisers, and they knew about such things.

The calculations were tedious and time-consuming. So after working out the formula, I sought assistance, again from the *Santa Fe Reporter* Connection. I telephoned a journalist now living in Boulder, Colorado. Always for the underdog, she was quick to lend a hand. When her calculations and mine were run together, they told an amazing tale. For local advertising, the *Green Bay Press-Gazette* was charging rates a full 46 percent lower than the average at similar-size papers in the chain. For national advertising, the difference was even more dramatic. Gannett's rate in Green Bay was 59 percent lower than the norm.

With my pocket calculator, I punched out an example of the savings for a typical merchant. With a five-thousand-inch contract at the *Press-Gazette,* he was currently paying $1,597 for a full-page ad. If the paper were charging Gannett's average, however, that same ad would cost $2,332—$735 more. Similar differentials applied to the cost of advertising at every rate level.

By my estimate of the *Press-Gazette*'s annual advertising revenue, the dramatically lower rates meant that the Green Bay business community was paying at least $7 million a year less than it would if Gannett were free to operate at its monopolistic norm. By extension, that same multimillion-dollar reduction was being passed on to consumers, thus benefiting everybody in town. At least $7 million a year. That was how much Frank Wood was saving an ungrateful city that refused to support his failing newspaper—which could be prospering if even a fifth of that total were diverted into its pages. That was the hell of it.

The presence of the *News-Chronicle* was the only possible explanation of the *Press-Gazette*'s incredibly low rates. The eight other Gannett papers in my survey came from all parts of the country, from diverse communities, and from a spectrum of economic conditions. Some were located in expensive urban areas. Some were in isolated rural areas. Some were in the Far West, some in New England, some in the Midwest. Some were in depressed regions, others in the midst of booming economies. The only factor unifying them was that none faced daily competition. While captive advertisers in Sioux Falls, South Dakota; Stockton, California; Bridgewater, New Jersey; Springfield, Missouri; Burlington, Vermont; Boise, Idaho; Poughkeepsie, New York; and Salem, Oregon, were coughing up almost 50 percent more per ad, the complacent merchants of Green Bay were riding cheap.

But their sense of security was false, for I knew something they did not. I knew what was going to happen as soon as Gannett succeeded in driving the *News-Chronicle* into the grave. It had been spelled out in a business-journal article called "Blues for the News": "Once the second paper fails, the business of running a paper becomes easy: Just open the mail and pull out the checks. In fact, it's typical for a monopoly newspaper to jack up advertising rates within six months of its competitor's death. After all, who's left to complain?"

If further evidence were needed, it came from Oregon. In 1982, one year after Gannett settled the *Community Press* case, a Salem shopkeeper filed a class-action lawsuit, charging that eliminating the only competing paper had hurt all advertisers in the city. Gannett was accused of "numerous illegal, unfair and deceptive trade practices." The effect was "to raise, fix and maintain all rates for display and classified print advertising in the Salem market at artificial and non-competitive levels." The lawsuit asked for a trial, but none took place. Like the *Community Press* case, this too ended in secret settlement. With another check, Gannett bought its way out once again.

In 1980, when Gannett was worried about making a courtroom explanation of its pricing policies in response to the *Community Press* suit, the base advertising rate in its Salem paper was a flat $8.60 per column-inch, daily or Sunday. In 1989, after almost a full decade of standstill inflation everywhere in the nation, the daily base rate in Salem was $22.68 per inch. The Sunday rate was $24.31.

Would the advertisers of Green Bay be serving their self-interest by tossing enough business at the *News-Chronicle* to keep it alive? Overwhelmingly, the evidence indicated that they would. But did they have brains enough to understand? Only time, and the publication of my report, would tell. But now I had the statistics to prove the point—and presenting them to the world would be the Green Bay Project's best shot.

25

Gray Days, Dark Nights

IT WAS A GOOD THING the research was going well, for nothing else was. As October marched toward November, huge gray clouds rolled in off Lake Michigan and took up residence in the skies above Wisconsin. The sun disappeared for days, then weeks, on end. The only sign of its passage was a muted brightness that crept across the dark heavens. I shriveled in the endless shadow. Not even the Packers brought a ray of light. Instead of taking the division lead, they dropped two quick games to teams they should have beaten. The city seemed to resign itself to yet another year of mediocrity from the once-vaunted Pack.

Frank continued to be elusive. My three- and four-page memos on strategy, innovation, and timing for the Green Bay Project drew no response. He was teaching a full load at the college, and those duties seemed to take precedence. He found time for me only once or twice a week, usually on the run. If we met at night, after his long day of work, he was too tired to focus. His unavailability rankled me, but it was not yet a major problem. Research on Gannett in other places was keeping me busy, and until it was done I did not have to find out what was happening in Green Bay. Each thing in its time, I told myself.

Meanwhile, I sought to coordinate the project with the Brown County Publishing departments that must play a role in it. For the report to be effective, it must become the talk of the town. And before it cooled down, we must convert it into dollars and cents for the *News-Chronicle*. While readers and advertisers were still stirred up we must hit them with special promotions, to boost circulation and revenues. For all of Green Bay to know what was happening, we must publicize the report beforehand, then distribute thousands of extra copies in every corner of the city. Before the project was done, the company's circulation, advertising, printing, production, and editorial departments all would be involved, and preparations could not wait until the last minute. Yet as I enlisted the troops, I had to be cautious. Each person who knew was one more risk of a leak.

Choosing words that revealed only as much as necessary, I met with those who were to help. But help came grudgingly. I felt their resentment of me, this outsider who for some reason had Frank Wood's backing, but would not confide in the longtime employees whose assistance he was seeking. Under the circumstances, the extra work I represented was perceived as a burden. The *News-Chronicle* editor did not see how he could free a photographer. The printing foreman seemed oppressed. The circulation director, however, was enthusiastic, and that helped.

But a disheartening lack of encouragement came from Frank's pride and joy, the political cartoonist Lyle Lahey. A gangling, lopsided man, Lahey had the penetrating insight and devastating wit that mark the best practitioners of his somewhat loony craft. For years his irreverent, trenchant cartoons had been the *News-Chronicle*'s strongest element. They were its editorial voice. Lahey was good enough for a big-city daily, yet he seemed content in Green Bay.

Frank insisted that Lahey be part of the Green Bay Project. I shared Frank's regard for Lahey's work, and was eager to pool our efforts. But when we huddled, he proved testy. Openly supportive but slyly resistant, he was quick to undercut me with a doubting word, a barely perceptible sneer, or alternative ideas presented with an air of superiority. I wanted his help and appreciated his suggestions. Some were better than mine, with more understanding of Green Bay than I had gleaned in my short time there. At first I thought I was imagining the uncooperative undercurrent. But it kept recurring. It was just more baggage, when I already had too much.

The most helpful support came from Al Rasmussen, the company troubleshooter at that first night's meeting. His role was still undefined, but he sat in on several sessions, and did not withhold his backing. His style was low-key but competent, the kind that gains respect without demanding it. In his innate understanding of my work, Al was like the company's other true believer: Frank's son Chris. But Chris was still away on his honeymoon. I missed him sorely.

Going to my office each day was taking on the aspect of a minor ordeal. Passing wordlessly to and from my desk, I could almost see suspicion and hostility swirling in my wake. So I closed the door, and began writing articles for the report.

The first was about Gannett Outdoors' price-fixing trial in Southern California—and there was a reason why it was first. Of all the examples of Gannett wrongdoing I had found, this was the simplest and most straightforward. The outcome of the trial was a matter of public record. Other papers had reported it. Gannett's "nolo contendere" plea was tantamount to a guilty verdict. I had spoken with the Justice Department prosecutor, who was unequivocal in his condemnation of the chain's conduct. This story was uncomplicated, fully substantiated, open-and-shut.

And I wanted to see how Jack FitzGerald, the Green Bay Project's lawyer, would respond to it.

We met in his comfortable retirement condominium on a Saturday morning. I had mailed him the article, and he had gone over it. He began chipping away, with questions that were intelligent but naive, and irrelevant to libel law. "Did you record your conversation with the prosecutor?" "Did you verify the information you took from other articles about the case?" "Did you speak to the judge?" "If Gannett denies these charges after the story is published, can you prove them independently of the court record?"

In a theoretical sense, his questions were good ones. Theoretically, all the information used by every journalist in every article would indeed be more libel-proof if cross-referenced, tape-recorded, and sworn to in affidavits. His lawyerly compulsion to avoid trouble at all costs was admirable in its way. But in terms of real life and the need at hand, Jack FitzGerald's cautionary nit-picking did not bode well.

He displayed no familiarity with this country's hard-won press freedom, grounded in the First Amendment and hammered out over two centuries in countless court cases addressing the very points he was raising. He clearly did not know what journalists were allowed to do under the law, what information was legally protected by "privilege," or at what point printed material was sufficiently supported to be defended in court.

I did not pretend to be an attorney or to know every jot and tittle of the libel and slander laws. That was why I had insisted from the start that we must get such expertise. But I had been a working journalist for more than twenty years, and I did know two things for sure: that there was not a line in the story that was not totally defensible in legal terms, and that if everything I wrote had to pass such unrealistic scrutiny, the Green Bay Project would never see the light of day.

The strained cordiality that we both were trying to maintain was fraying fast. "Your questions are careful and thoughtful, Jack," I said, looking for complimentary words to make my point less bruising. "But speaking as a journalist, I don't think they show an understanding of the law."

"For your information, Dick, I've tried over a thousand cases in court," he bristled. "And I've won most of them."

"I don't doubt that," I replied, my own hackles rising. "But tell me, Jack—how many of those cases involved libel?"

He glared back icily, not wanting to concede the point. "None of them," he finally acknowledged.

That night by telephone, as delicately as I could, I stressed to Frank that if we valued our necks, the Green Bay Project had to get a trained libel lawyer. "I have no doubt that Jack FitzGerald is one of the best men ever to practice in his field," I said. *"But this is not his field."*

"I'll discuss it with him," Frank said calmly.

Equally draining was the everyday business of living.

Meals were a problem. After a week of cans and a hot plate, I had to find a better solution. In time I discovered two truck stops that served a robust lunch—or "dinner," as lunch is called in Wisconsin, to distinguish it from "supper." Each was about fifteen miles away, however. Driving back and forth three times a day would take too much time. So I drank coffee all morning, broke for lunch around two o'clock, then ate enough to get through the evening. It was a workable, if not healthy, plan.

Returning one day, I spotted a liquor store. I came home with a bottle of scotch and a bottle of vodka. Most evenings I worked late in my room, boosted by a stiff belt or two. Pushing me was my desire to get the Green Bay Project over with, and get myself back to New Mexico, the land of sunshine and friends.

I came to know the dull ache of loneliness. From time to time Frank and Agnes invited me out with them and their friends. These occasions were enjoyable, but also stressful. As Frank kept stalling on his end of the Green Bay Project, I felt a growing resentment toward him, for pulling me up here to fight a fight he now seemed uneager to fight himself. Tones of frustration and rebuke were slipping into my talks with him. Though my anger was seething instead of boiling, I feared it might erupt in sharp words. I did not want Agnes, an innocent bystander, to be present if it did.

Most particularly I missed the company of women. Unadept at con-viviality with strangers, I did not seek acquaintances in the bars across from my apartment. As for the women at the office, they were even less accessible. That was too bad, especially concerning a blonde in advertising. But there was no way. Spending time with them would be impossible without discussing what I was doing. I had cloaked myself in secrecy, and now that it chafed and rubbed, I could not take it off.

I spoke by telephone with Bonnie in Santa Fe. But my calls, too infrequent for her, were hollow and unfulfilling for me. Using her as an outlet for feelings I could not vent in Wisconsin, I dumped negativity upon her poor blond head. When we hung up I felt sour and unnourished, as did she. But my burden was worse, for I was to blame. We were drifting apart. Laurie too was out of reach. Involved with someone else, she was traveling, weighing career possibilities, shaping a new life after the *Santa Fe Reporter*. Our long professional and personal collaboration was fading into the past.

I did not have a television. But I did go to the movies, once or twice a week, twenty miles away in Green Bay. My small radio and tape deck became my best friend. With the splendid programming of Wisconsin Public Radio—in-depth news, soothing or provocative music, arts reports, comedy, interviews, panel discussions—it helped me through each day. But sometimes even the radio got me down. One morning the poll of a Boston College professor who had asked economics majors their attitudes toward life and business was reported. Two-thirds agreed that "There is nothing more important to me than my own economic well-being." Three-fourths believed "It's everyone for himself or herself in the American economy." Fully 88 percent agreed that "In our society, everyone has to look out for number one." And two-thirds of them concurred: "People do not let moral scruples get in the way of their own advancement."

I tested these findings a few nights later, over dinner with a St. Norbert College literature professor, whom I had met at Frank's house. "What do the kids at your school—a small, Catholic, liberal-arts college—want from life?" I asked.

"Money," he said. "Big salaries, big houses, Porsches, BMWs."

"They think those things will make them happy?"

"Yes."

"They won't find it there."

"They think they will."

The tape deck played a different role when I was working in my room—writing, reading, taking notes, plotting strategy. Then it was the tape deck that relieved the barrenness of my one-room home and after-hours office. The strains of Dvorak, Ravel, Wagner, Strauss, Puccini, Rachmaninoff, and company gave a pleasing backdrop to my labors, and kept them moving onward.

Around midnight, when I knocked off and went to bed, often bristling with resentment toward Frank or outrage at the latest Gannett atrocity, or maybe just slipping into loneliness, the tape deck helped in a different way. It coaxed me into sleep, with music that loosened the stone grip of my mission. Emmylou Harris would sing me lullabies, or Frederica von Stade. But to my surprise, the most soothing sounds were the Southern gospel songs I had brought along at the last minute. "Peace in the Valley," they promised. "Take My Hand, Precious Lord," they cried. "Lead Me, Guide Me," they pleaded, and "Stand By Me." "Who Am I?" they asked, and accepted that "There Are Secrets Known Only to Him."

There was nothing directly religious in my response to these old, familiar songs. My Southern Presbyterian upbringing was years and years behind me, and its message too suspect to guide me now. But the soft haze of nostalgia was in this music, as well as a mystery that dwarfed such petty endeavors as the Green Bay Project—or the Gannett newspaper chain. Before the tape ran its course, I usually was lost in welcome slumber.

Denmark's two-man police force continued to assert its presence, in my rearview mirror and on side streets. I was scrupulous at all times about speed limits, stop signs, even parking close to the curb. I wanted to win this little game. It was the sole amusing aspect of life in Denmark, and I was determined to thwart my stalkers. But they got me anyway. A ticket on my windshield one morning mystified me. The car was on the street below my room, where I had parked since coming to town. The wheels were right on the curb. Yet there was the ticket, with my license number, demanding that I pay the village of Denmark three dollars—for a violation I did not comprehend.

I asked about it at the printing plant. Because of the possibility of sudden snowfalls, someone explained, the streets were closed to overnight parking from November through April, to enable snowplows to keep them open. Yesterday was the first of November—therefore I had broken the law last night. "There are signs posted around town," said my explainer, in a tone more smug than sympathetic. "Haven't you seen them?"

Chickenshit, chickenshit, I thought, reflecting upon the just-turned calendar and the bone-dry roads. The cops in some towns might have left a note instead of a ticket, at least once, on a New Mexico car they had seen for weeks. But not these guys. I paid the fine that night, slipping the ticket envelope and three bucks under the village hall door. Any delay, I figured, and they'll probably tow my car. From then on, I parked in the Brown County Publishing lot.

One night, only minutes after falling asleep to the gospel tape's calming reassurances, I was jerked back awake by ruder sounds. "Shithead!" came a vicious male voice through the window slit that let in fresh air. "Stand up and fight, you pussy!" For a moment I thought I was under attack. Then I realized the insults were coming from the street, and were not directed at me. I slipped to the window, and looked down upon half a dozen rough-cut young men, spilling out of the bar across the way.

"Shithead, I'm talking to you!" taunted the largest of them, poking a much smaller man in the shoulder. "I say you're a cunt and an asshole, and I want to know what you're going to do about it."

The victim showed no stomach for a fight. But his tongue was a match for his tormentor's. "You're the shithead around here!" he screeched, on the edge of desperation. "You're nothing *but* shit!" Yet his arms hung limply at his sides.

"Looks to me like you're scared, Sammy," mocked one of the onlookers. "Guess Hubert's right—you are a pussy."

Big Hubert struck again, with another shove and more words. "You're not only a pussy, you're also a cocksucker and a son of a bitch. I'm calling your mother a fucking bitch, shithead, and that's what she is, unless you can prove different."

Still Sammy refused to fight. He tried to walk away, but the circle of men, which seemed to hold no allies, closed around him. "No real man would take that kind of talk," said one of them. "You're pure-shit yellow, ain't you?" said another.

Sammy still did not raise his fists. Pathetically he endured several more pokes and insults, from Hubert and the other thugs. Except for an occasional "You're the shithead around here!" flung back hysterically, he offered no defense.

Long before the young men of Denmark grew tired of their sport, I grew tired of watching. Even with the window shut tight, however, the sounds from below still filled my room. *This is just so ugly,* I thought, *so incredibly ugly.*

After maybe fifteen more minutes, with Sammy's humiliation complete in the eyes of his peers, the street scene broke up, without physical violence. I rewound the gospel tape and played it again from the top. But sleep was a long time coming.

26

Why Am I Doing This?

THE GREEN BAY PROJECT LURCHED painfully onward. For each two steps it gained, it slid back one. There was progress, but not enough. The work within my control—research and writing—was advancing rapidly. Work that needed assistance, however, was not.

A month into the project, Frank called another meeting of the Green Bay Project task force, the company officials I had met with on that first night. Unfortunately, the financial books for October had just been closed, and they told a disastrous tale. The losses that month were heavier than ever. The *News-Chronicle* was inexorably pulling down the entire company, and the people who depended on Brown County Publishing for a livelihood were running scared.

It was a morose group of men who listened as I ticked off the Gannett misdeeds that soon were to become public knowledge. They stared back impassively as I described the plans to mobilize Brown County Publishing for the charge. When my presentation coasted to a halt, silence followed. After many seconds, Frank broke it. "Sounds to me like things are right on track," he said. "What do the rest of you think?"

Nobody said a word. *It's a game,* I thought. *They're playing a game with him. They know he's going to do this thing no matter what they say. They remember all the times they've already urged him to fold the* News-Chronicle, *to no avail. They do not understand the Green Bay Project, and never have. But they know that telling Frank to pack it in will not do any good. So they're using the silent treatment to make their point.* Gone was the fighting spirit that flared briefly the last time they assembled. They had seen no miracles yet from this strange miracle worker Frank had hired, and now they had been kicked in the teeth again by another month of horrific losses.

A word from the rural South came to mind. This bunch was "whupped." Not one among them believed the Green Bay Project would accomplish anything at all. They had been willing to humor Frank, but their faith in him had just about run out. Yet short of open defiance, a step they were not quite ready to take, they knew they could not deter him. So they just stared in wordless protest.

Frank got the message. It made his back stiffen. "I want an answer from each one of you," he said, his eyes defying the resistance in the room. "We'll start with you, Doug."

"You know how I feel," came the forced reply from the dour chief of publications. "I've said all along we can't save the *Chronicle*. I still say so, and the sooner we face it, the better."

"Fair enough," Frank said heavily. "How about you, Jerry?"

"I just don't know. I was for this thing last month, because I was tired of being kicked around. But after listening to Dick's report, I don't get it. I don't know what good it will do, or how much more time it will take. In the meantime, we're going down the tubes."

"A good point," Frank responded. "When do you think you'll be ready, Dick?" he asked me without warning.

I did not know, but admitting it would be worse than making a guess. "Hard to say," I hedged. "Maybe the week before Thanksgiving. Not before then."

"That's not so long," Frank said. "Just a couple of weeks. If we've come this far I think we can hang on until then."

Laboriously he worked his way around the room, wringing a response from each man present. There were no surprises. There were misgivings aplenty, but the group bowed to the foregone conclusion that Frank was going to go through with his folly, whatever it cost him or the company.

"Maybe it won't work," he admitted in conclusion. "I know that. But it's something we've got to try. And Dick, if there's anything we can do to speed things up, just let us know." *What would help the most, Frank, would be for you to get your own ass in gear,* I said to myself. But I did not say that aloud. I just kept thinking it as I tried to fall asleep that night.

I blamed myself, however, for another obstacle. I could not get the hang of the word-processing unit the editor had given me. In Santa Fe the computer age had passed me by. Its language was cryptic, and while I might break the code someday, the midst of the Green Bay Project was neither the time nor the place. The editor had no ideas when I told him another plan was needed. Somewhere within the mechanical capabilities of Brown County Publishing Company the solution would be found. But I set the search aside. The important thing now was to generate copy. And so I did, several pages a day, on a machine that even I could master: my Smith-Corona

PWP-40 word processor with its built-in printer, all no bigger than a portable typewriter.

No more helpful were other Brown County Publishing workers. With Frank forever unavailable until "next week," I could no longer wait to start gathering stories of Gannett's practices in Green Bay. Case histories presumably were known by people in the company. Yet my talks with them were not productive. If I asked for a specific document, they dug it up for me. But questions regarding the circumstances drew a blank. "I don't know." "I don't remember." "That was a long time ago." "I'm not the one to ask about that." Such were the answers I got.

Passive aggression was at work here. My reportorial skills were unequal to the challenge. Things might be different if I could take these people into my confidence. If I could say, "I plan to write a report on how Gannett is trying to put the *News-Chronicle* out of business, and this will be part of it," maybe they would help gladly. But I was not willing to take the risk.

Was I being entirely too cautious? Paranoid? Obsessively secret instead of intelligently so? Was I losing the ability to tell the difference? Yet down deep I felt sure that if Gannett heard of it, the Green Bay Project could be deflated like a flat tire. If Gannett issued a preemptive denial of any improper actions against the *News-Chronicle,* then whatever disclosures the report made would lose their punch. They would not take the town by surprise. They would be burdened with skepticism and doubt.

Surprise was of the essence. When we struck we must put Gannett on the defensive, scrambling to refute our accusations. If the *Press-Gazette* were ready and waiting, our chance of even a fleeting victory would be gone. Psychology must be on our side. The audacity of the attack made it all the more imperative that every accusation be supported by solid evidence. Anything less would damage our credibility—Frank's and mine and the *News-Chronicle*'s—and could land us all in court. Thus rounding up facts for every case going into the report was vital. But until all was ready, the Green Bay Project had to remain Top Secret.

The dilemma confounded me. Tracking down each lead with the workers who knew about it was impossible without blowing the cover of secrecy. What I needed was an inside operator, someone familiar with each case, and with the workings of the company. Someone who knew where records were kept and who was in charge of what. Someone who could ask questions without sparking rumors. I had assumed Frank would be this person. But he could not be pinned down. And without such help, I was spinning my wheels.

On even the simplest matters, cooperation was hard to find. The report was going to need many illustrations. Trying to round up some, I asked a vice president where to find the Brown County Publishing logo and other company graphics. "Gee," he responded, "I don't think we have anything like that. Sorry."

I did not believe it. In fifteen minutes of rummaging around I came up with stationery, employee handbooks, and other items with the images I sought. "I found what I was looking for," I said, arraying them before the unhelpful vice president.

"Oh, good," he replied. "I didn't think about those things."

The resistance from Lyle Lahey, the cartoonist, was harder to circumvent. He was responsible for illustrating the national stories on Salem, Hartford, Southern California, and other places. Yet each time I asked about the work, he said he had not started. There was no immediate rush, for the report would not be ready for several days. But until I saw some sketches, I could not relax.

The illustrations must be neither too hard nor too soft. If too soft, they would not add impact. If too hard, we could be sued. Like the words, the pictures must be strong enough to pack a wallop, yet responsible enough to defend in court. Convinced that Lahey was stalling to show that no outsider could order him around, I prayed that his work would be good when it did come in. If not, I had nothing to use in its place.

One afternoon when I had no phone calls to make and no story to write, I was reading in my office. Through the door, which for once was not closed, I overheard two workers talking in low voices. "What's the latest on the hired gun?" one asked. Suddenly I saw it clear: I was indeed a hired gun. From the noble journalist working selflessly to save the town I was reduced to a gunslinger, paid by a scared owner to save his spineless ranch from a band of outlaws. I had become a clichéd actor in a bad western movie. Worst of all was the hackneyed plot's lone twist: I was not sure this ranch was worth saving.

Why am I doing this? The question would not leave me alone. *Frank Wood refuses to get involved in his own fight. Nobody in his company gives a shit. They're all just waiting to say "We told you so." The newspaper I'm trying to save is really not distinguished—solid enough, but not exceptional. And in the end, this is not a fight we can win. Even if it finally does get off the ground, the Green Bay Project was always doomed to fail. In the meantime, it sure as hell isn't any fun. So what is the point? Why am I doing this?*

Unless I could find a reason to stay—a reason I could put into words and understand—I was ready to quit and go home.

27

One More Warning

I felt hoodwinked and betrayed by Frank. He should not have brought me here just to drop his fight in my lap. I thought we were in this thing together. I was doing my part, but he was not doing his. If I called off the deal now, I would be justified. That was what I told myself. I composed words for breaking the news, and rehearsed them in my mind. I thought of the things I wanted to do back home, the people I missed. It would be best for Frank too, and for his company. The sooner I left, the sooner they could do what they had to do. That was what I told myself.

But it was a false exercise. I was stuck. I had made a commitment. Now it existed in the world, with a life of its own. Others could drop their end of an agreement, but whether I would uphold mine was up to me. I could not picture squirming and writhing all the way to New Mexico, knowing I had cut and run. No, I resolved bitterly, I will do the Green Bay Project—because I said I would. I will do it with or without Frank Wood's help, and obviously without the help of anyone else in his company. I must scale back the plan, scale it back to what I can do myself.

There will be no four-pronged effort from the editorial, advertising, circulation, and printing divisions. I will just put together the best journalistic report I can, publish it in Frank's paper, and call it the Green Bay Project. Then I will get the hell out—and let the chips fall where they may. But maybe, just maybe, they would fall in useful places. Beyond my sense of self, I felt a second, stronger reason to stay until something got printed. The story of Gannett must be told.

Day after day in my research, I had been angered, depressed, disgusted, and sickened by just how far Gannett would go to ensure its monetary gain. If fraud seemed necessary in Connecticut, Gannett would commit fraud. If price-fixing seemed helpful in California, Gannett would fix prices year after year. Price-gouging was just standard practice. Antitrust violations, breach of contract, extermination campaigns, deceit, bribes, lies, threats, under-the-table deals, circulation scams, broken promises—anything that would make a buck, journalism's most strident champion could be counted on to do it all.

And this was the calling I had loved.

Every now and then, when it got caught, Gannett whipped out its awesome checkbook, forked over a quick million dollars or two or three, and resumed doing what it was doing before. The occasional slap on the wrist was just a cost of doing business. All that is needed for evil to flourish, I remembered, is for good men to do nothing. Or remain silent. Well, at least I would not remain silent. I would get this profile of Gannett on the record. Then anybody who was interested could look it up.

I did not expect to alter the way Gannett did business. Making money was the primary value in American life, and Gannett had mastered the art. It was succeeding at success, while the nation was embracing the idea that the end justifies the means. No, the Green Bay Project would be only a sniper shot at an advancing army. Nevertheless, I felt there was value in firing it. Two decades as a newsman made me respect the power of unleashed information. Once sent into the world, it cannot be called back. And though it might wait, it can someday make a difference. I was determined to add one more warning to those that had already been sounded. But in Gannett's case, I saw no change in store. Not only was the national mood unperturbed by this company's ways, so was the newspaper business itself.

There were several reasons why journalism would not police itself against Gannett. Foremost among them was the chain's own scope and reach. In more than eighty American cities, including some of the largest, never would the only daily paper be concerned with its own ethics. By the simple device of purchase, Gannett had neutered many of the most aggressive mastheads in the country.

Nor was the silence caused only by all those papers' editors' sure sense of what would happen to their careers if criticism of their employer's business practices appeared on the pages they presided over. Also shielding Gannett from scrutiny was the invisible line separating newsrooms from business departments. High-minded journalists, in love with words and ideals, generally felt there was something distasteful about the financial side of their organizations. They knew, of course, that money was necessary to provide their paychecks. They understood vaguely that money was generated by advertising. But they chose not to soil their minds by dwelling on such things.

In my early years, I too had looked disparagingly upon the advertising and business departments. But the *Santa Fe Reporter* had taught me that they are as vital as courageous editors—if not more vital. Without a courageous editor, a paper will go flat. But without a sound business department, it will go away. This understanding came slowly, but in time I became comfortable with it. There was nothing wrong, I now knew, with a paper making money, even lots of money—if it did not violate laws and ethics in the process. Yet that was what Gannett was doing, confident that most of journalism would look the other way.

The likelihood of non-Gannett newspapers lodging a protest was not much better than the chance of one coming from within the chain itself. The vast majority of newspapers were owned by other chains, many of which had learned from the biggest and were emulating it. The nation's second-largest chain, Knight-Ridder, was in bed with Gannett in Detroit, and had shown its willingness to abandon its integrity to achieve its business purposes there. Business, in fact, was the driving force of almost all the chains.

Then there was the "old boy network." As Gannett grew in prominence and clout, its officials had assumed high positions in the industry's professional organizations. From Al Neuharth down, Gannett operatives had been president, board members, and other officers in the American Newspaper Publishers Association, the Associated Press Managing Editors Association, and other similar organizations, which represented almost every daily in the country. The more Gannett mixed and mingled at conventions, and took leadership roles, and cultivated friendships within journalism's ruling circles, the less likely was it to be held accountable for the practices that had taken it to the top.

A few of the country's strongest and most independent papers, including the *New York Times, Wall Street Journal,* and *Los Angeles Times,* had indeed looked critically upon Gannett. And because of a long-standing personal feud with Neuharth, the executive editor of the *Washington Post,* Ben Bradlee, relished taking swipes. Reports in these papers had proved quite useful in my research. But except for the situation in Little Rock, which had been covered in some detail, these accounts tended to be generalized, weighing the pros and cons of the Gannett concept rather than the chain's specific, abundant, and well-documented transgressions. As far as I knew, I was the only reporter ever to gather evidence to support a multiple-count indictment.

The nation's magazines, uncompromised by the clubbiness of the newspaper world, had been more bold. Long, tough-minded articles in various periodicals had helped my work immensely. Yet not even the magazines that concentrated on journalism had ever mounted a comprehensive investigation.

Nowhere was the lack of scrutiny more evident than in *Editor & Publisher*. Unbothered by the Salem revelations, *E&P* barely acknowledged that the case existed. *E&P* was similarly uninclined to look into the fraud case in Hartford, the price-fixing trial in California, or the charges of circulation irregularities in Arkansas, although each of these matters was noted briefly. Considerable space, however, was given to Detroit and Little Rock; and Robert McKinney's lawsuit in Santa Fe was written about several times. When a situation got too loud to ignore, *E&P* reported it. But seldom did journalism's foremost magazine find fault with anything Gannett did. As long as the biggest chain kept buying full-page ads, it seemed, the industry's watchdog would have little bark or bite.

A lone voice crying out against Gannett and other huge chains was Ben Bagdikian of the University of California–Berkeley. His *The Media Monopoly* issued an urgent warning, one highly regarded by professionals. But among the general population its call to arms went largely unheard.

One twenty-two-page chapter in the book was devoted to Gannett. Titled "From Mythology to Theology," it ticked off a list of abuses around the country, and noted that Gannett's strategy for deflecting criticism was to falsely glorify what it was doing. In speeches, advertising campaigns, and articles in publications such as *Editor & Publisher,* Gannett touted traditional virtues in public while dismantling them in private, Bagdikian pointed out.

As he put it: "Gannett Company Inc. is an outstanding contemporary performer of the ancient rite of creating self-serving myths, of committing acts of greed and exploitation but describing them through its own machinery as heroic epics." His scorn was reciprocated. "Ben Bagdikian," said Neuharth, dismissing the author's Pulitzer Prize, "is an academician who lives in an unreal world and who very briefly learned a little bit about the newspaper business on the East Coast. Since then, he has been living in a never-never land in California."

The only two full books about Gannett I found were examples of the self-generated myths that Bagdikian had flagged.

The first, *The Making of McPaper,* told of the birth and early years of *USA Today.* With Neuharth's help, it was written by Peter Pritchard, a Gannett man who later became *USA Today*'s editor. Insisting he had a "free hand" to tell the story warts and all, Pritchard was understandably mindful of the company that signed his paychecks. His tale of monumental vision and epic struggle was hailed by *E&P* in a four-page prepublication spread.

The other book was one of the most curious I had ever seen. *Confessions of an S.O.B.* was Allen Neuharth's autobiography. In it he took glee in recounting times he had flouted societal norms to make a "success" of himself and the company he headed.

He congratulated himself for many things: for his boyhood "tantrum" that prevented his widowed and destitute mother from remarrying; for his skill at forcing the man who hired him at Gannett, Paul Miller, into an unwanted retirement; for his sly outmaneuvering of a business associate by eavesdropping on a telephone conversation; for defeating adversaries in numerous business deals, then rubbing salt in their wounds. He celebrated all the money he made, complete with figures, and all the money made by Gannett. "Money is thicker than blood," declared a chapter heading. "Expect others to do unto you what you would do unto them," he listed as a secret for success, along with: "Somebody has something you want. Go for it."

He extolled the pleasures of his "first-class" life, among them: "a $17 million Gulfstream IV jet," "a $360,000-a-year nine-room hotel suite in the Waldorf Towers in New York City," and "limousines and drivers at every destination." He did not mention, however, the time he was so abusive to a company chauffeur on the way to a Florida airport that the driver stopped the car, ordered Neuharth out, and left the head of the nation's largest newspaper chain hitchhiking to catch his plane.

Nor did the book make any reference, even in the index, to Salem, where Neuharth's henchman fed him reports about the annihilation of the *Community Press*. There was not a word about Santa Fe, where Neuharth testified in court that his company's contractual agreements with the ill and old Robert McKinney were "window dressing." Also absent was mention of the time when Neuharth conspired with Gannett's top lawyer to consummate the fraud that their company had perpetrated in Hartford.

All autobiographies are self-serving, but Neuharth's twisted the norm. He relished depicting himself as a rogue, a scoundrel, a bad boy, an imp, a rule-breaker. Or, in his oft used phrase, a "lovable S.O.B." But when his actions were venal or criminal, or revealed him as an asshole, he omitted them.

Few critics thought much of his book. "My beef with this sort of nonsense is really not with Mr. Neuharth but with the here's-how-I-became-such-a-huge-success books in general," said the *New York Times* reviewer in dismissing *S.O.B.* as lightweight. *Fortune* magazine commented: "Judging by what he relates, the man who built Gannett into America's largest newspaper chain and created *USA Today* is a conniver, backstabber and liar, an executive so utterly without principle and so totally self-absorbed and so self-indulgent he could startle even the most cynical muckraker."

Even syndicated humorist Dave Barry took swipes at *S.O.B.,* as well as its author's quick-punch writing style. "Neuharth says that to win," Barry wrote, "you have to:

* Work hard.
* Attend to details.
* Strive for excellence.
* Be a scumbag.

"But in the end, people will love you anyway. Also, you'll be rich. Exactly how rich Neuharth got is discussed frequently in his book, 'Confessions of an S.O.B.' It's at your local bookstore. And if it's not, Neuharth will have somebody's knees broken."

The reading public, however, seemed to disagree with the critics. For weeks Neuharth's book was on the *New York Times* best-seller list, rising as high as number two. (Not until months later was the reason for this sales record known. Determined to have his book recognized as a best-seller, Neuharth ordered the Gannett Foundation to buy large quantities of *S.O.B.* at key bookstores on whose reports the *Times* based its list. When his manipulation was discovered, the *Washington Post* reported it on page one—a fact considered strange by those unaware of the bad blood between Neuharth and *Post* editor Bradlee, who was gratuitously insulted in the book.)

Nor had the country's journalism schools confronted Gannett. Charged with shaping future newspaper people, and with infusing them with ethical concepts as well as marketable skills, the J-schools had their reasons for keeping quiet. A J-school's success was measured by the professional advancement of its graduates. With Gannett the largest employer of journalists, the risk of alienating it and jeopardizing job possibilities was a risk few schools would take.

Gannett was also buying the schools' silence with grants, scholarships, and donations, as reported almost weekly in *Editor & Publisher.* With a sense of irony I clipped one announcement. "Gannett Grant Aids Ethics Workshop" said the headline, and the item below reported: "The National Workshop on the Teaching of Ethics in Journalism returns to the University of Missouri–Columbia School of Journalism for its second consecutive year in 1989 as a result of a $26,000 grant from the Gannett Foundation."

The foundation was also an effective tool for stilling protest in the cities paying the price of Gannett's monopolies. Even as these cities were being squeezed, the Gannett Foundation was striking the pose of a civic benefactor. By returning a tiny fraction of its profits in the form of charitable contributions, Gannett bought the gratitude of organizations getting the crumbs it threw—and the silence of groups hoping for some in the future. Not one citizen in a thousand, including elected officials, had a grasp of economics sufficient to understand that the chain was draining more financial strength out of the community each week than it was giving back all year. To sustain the illusion, Gannett's donations were always well publicized in its papers.

As long as mayors issued commendations, as long as volunteer chairmen wrote letters of thanks, as long as the man or woman on the street felt gratitude instead of outrage, Gannett was free to operate behind a smoke screen. As Ben Bagdikian pointed out, all that is needed for black to become white is a little myth-making.

And all that is needed for evil to flourish is for good men to do nothing . . .

All across the land the Gannett way was alive and well, and nowhere did I see anything in place to change it. Certainly there would be no political solution. As demonstrated in Detroit, the Justice Department was not inclined to stand in the way. Even less likely to do so were elected officials. In several state capitals Gannett ran the only newspaper, whose favor was coveted by legislators. And it was a brave national politician indeed willing to provoke the master of eighty-plus daily newspapers in thirty-six states, ten television stations, and the Harris polling firm.

Oddly and sadly, the little Green Bay Project seemed the best hope for sounding the alarm one more time, in one more place, in hopes that sooner or later it would be heeded. Too much work had been done, too much had been learned, for it all to come to nothing. So with or without the help of Frank Wood or anybody else, I vowed to see it through.

28

Painful Progress

"I'M TELLING YOU AGAIN, FRANK: It's not going to work out with Jack FitzGerald. We need a libel lawyer." It was the same old discussion. But this time Frank surprised me.

"Jack agrees with you."

Over the telephone, Frank did not see my mouth drop open.

"We've talked it over, and he thinks you're right. A friend of mine is a partner in the best media law firm in the state, LaFollette and Sinykin in Madison. Their top libel man is Brady Williamson. He wants to have lunch on Friday. Can you make it?"

"Can I ever! This is the best news I've heard in weeks. Just be sure to get a private dining room. We've got to come straight to the point—and all we don't need is for someone at the next table to be working for the *Press-Gazette.*"

"I'll take care of it."

Just before noon on Friday, Brady Williamson arrived at the *News-Chronicle* with two associates. All were experts on libel law. With their tailored suits and shiny briefcases, the lawyers looked like business. The Green Bay contingent presented quite a contrast. Frank and I wore rumpled sports coats. Jack FitzGerald, who was there to size up these guys, had on an old sweater. The most jangling note was sounded by Al Rasmussen, whom Frank had asked along at the last minute. Expecting to spend the day pushing papers at his desk, Al had come to work in an old high-school athletic jacket instead of his usual coat and tie. Its purple-and-gold brightness clashed merrily with Williamson's neat gray herringbone. I thought it was funny, and hoped Al did too.

The comedy continued at the restaurant. Frank's request for a private room had gone awry. The only one available was not set up. The hostess suggested a corner of the main area. Frank was amenable but I was not, so a disgruntled waitress led us to the room and began spreading silverware.

To help, Frank began bringing chairs, from a stack along the wall. From the first one he lifted, the seat fell out and crashed to the floor.

Finally lunch was served. The time had come for Frank to explain what was going on. And he did so, forcefully. With emotion and resolve, he described the battle between the *News-Chronicle* and the *Press-Gazette*. He cited the losses of recent years and stated his belief that Gannett was trying to drive him under. He gave my background and the reason I had come. It was a taut, powerful presentation.

I recognized it as impressive—but I was no longer buying. *It's an act,* I kept thinking. *A damn good act. It was good enough to get me here, Frank, and now it's good enough to get the lawyers cranked up. But where will you be when they need you?* My reflections were sour, but were also beside the point. I now had my own agenda: telling the Gannett story. Saving the *News-Chronicle* had become secondary. More than ever, I saw that task as hopeless. But getting the word out—that could still be done, and these lawyers could help me do it.

When Frank was finished, Brady Williamson responded. His questions were crisp, his points clear, his cautions wise, his spirit eager. My own spirit rose in turn. It mounted higher as Williamson described his law firm. Founded by Frank's friend Gordon Sinykin and a son of Wisconsin's legendary political reformer "Fighting Bob" LaFollette, the company was rooted in the traditions of the old Progressive Party, and often went to bat for the little guy. It all sounded good to me.

"Let me emphasize just one thing," I said when my turn came. "Most lawyers are primarily concerned with keeping their clients out of trouble. But we already know how to stay out of trouble. There's nothing to it: Just don't take on the biggest and meanest newspaper company in the country. We need you to do something different. We need you to say how far we can go in exposing Gannett and what's happening here. Nobody wants to be sued, but we'll run that risk, as long as we can defend our work. So we don't really want you to keep us out of trouble—we want you to help us make trouble."

"We understand the distinction," Williamson replied. "You might be glad to know, Dick, that the libel laws of Wisconsin are among the most liberal of any state. There's a strong tradition of press freedom here. Our job will not be to stop you from doing what you need to do, but to make sure it's done right."

My sigh of relief was probably audible. The Green Bay Project had proper legal counsel at last.

Other areas, however, were standing still. I was resigned to scaling back my plans for an all-departments effort to boost the *News-Chronicle*. Now I was content to just make the report. But even that was not in hand. There was still no production plan, and I could not pin Frank down to get the local cases. His constant avoidance made me suspect, now that push had come to shove, that he did not have the goods. What he showed was wishful thinking, the naive belief that because I had blown the whistle on Gannett in Salem I could do it again in Green Bay, whether or not he provided names, dates, facts, and figures.

The more I pressed him to sit still and produce hard data, the more otherwise engaged he became. My apprehension mounted. Without a link between what Gannett had done elsewhere and what it was doing in Green Bay, the report would be an irrelevant enterprise to its readers. It would lack immediacy. If it failed to evoke hometown pride, indignation, and self-interest, it would be strictly for the archives, for it would not answer that most crucial of all journalistic questions: So what?

If, after everything else, even the report fell flat, the Green Bay Project would be a waste. This thought gnawed at me constantly. It got me down and kept me down. Like the skies above, my mood had only hues of gray. Not even the snows of winter came, to add whiteness to the landscape. The climate was not unlike the gray people who lived in it. Did living for generation after generation under sunless skies seep into these people's genes, drying up laughter? Whatever it was, something had drawn down their life force. I understood only too well. Mine too was ebbing, and would not revive until I went home. But first whatever was left of the Green Bay Project must be completed.

The writing was going well. First drafts were becoming finished products, now that the lawyers were on the job. Their proposed changes were few— they too wanted the report to be strong—but their services were indispensable. Occasionally my indignation spilled over in my text. They red-flagged such indiscretions, then together we toned down the language.

After a while, I got a telephone in my room. Immediately I abandoned the office at the plant and worked at home. It deepened my isolation, but was still a change for the better. At home my energy was not sapped by the silent resistance of the people I had come to help. I was at my desk early and late. Some nights I went to a late movie. On nights when I stayed home, my stiff drink or two became three or four.

Early in November the national segment of the report was ready. But the Green Bay part was not. Then I got a break. Frank came down with the flu. Too sick to tend his duties in the company, he was under doctor's orders to stay home. It was my chance and I took it. It was time for him to answer questions, I insisted, even from his sickbed.

One endless Saturday in his unpretentious condominium home, with him bundled up in an easy chair and me seated on the sofa, I grilled Frank. His skin was sallow and his eyes red, but I gave him no quarter. He was not going to get away this time. While Agnes fretted in another room, I pressed Frank for anything that might be useful: The story of how his company got started and how it grew. Crises it had survived. Its successes and failures. And, most vital, case studies of what Gannett was doing to eliminate Green Bay's competing paper.

For eight grueling hours the session went on, punctuated by a lunch break and the quarter-hourly bonging of the two ancient grandfather clocks that ruled the house. At one point we paused to mark the southbound flight of a line of long-necked geese, visible through a picture window. How I envied them.

I was merciless—and worse—in my questioning. I rebuked Frank for every vague answer, every contradiction, every slip of memory, every time he could not provide the missing piece of information that my reporter's training told me was needed. All too frequently I heard myself being exasperated, critical, superior, sarcastic, condescending, even insulting. Though I was gathering needed information, these lapses of civility only hindered the process. Worse, some of them were sharp enough to test the boundaries of friendship.

I understood the psychology driving me, but seemed incapable of controlling it. All the frustration that had been building through the dreary weeks in Wisconsin was coming out, now that sickness had made Frank my captive. I wanted him to squirm for tricking me, for cutting out on me, for not holding up his end of the deal even though my promise still bound me. It was a down-and-dirty psychology, but I could not rise above it. Through it all, Frank maintained his equanimity, replying to my digs as though they were normal give-and-take. Now and then he bristled, but suppressed his anger at once. I did not know if his composure came from maturity, a calm disposition, or the enfeebling effects of the flu.

Whatever the source, it kept things from breaking out in acrimony. And so we lurched onward.

I was getting local material I could work with at last. But some parts of Frank's memory were more useful than others. His memories of Brown County Publishing Company, even of its earliest days, were sharp and clear. But his evidence implicating Gannett in a systematic campaign to snuff his newspaper lacked precision. He had plenty of tales to tell, but when I demanded facts to back them up, he grew vague. Time and again he undercut his charges with a maddening string of qualifiers: "To the best of my recollection," "Unless I'm mistaken," "As nearly as I can recall," "If memory serves," "It seems to me," "I'm not certain, but . . ."

When I wanted more, he passed the buck. "You could get the details from Clyde," he would say, or "Doug probably kept records on that," or "Talk to the advertising staff." Yet the people he referred me to were the ones resisting me every day. The more he tantalized me with half-stories, the more I longed for that inside operator. Frank himself should be playing the role, just as Walter Hussman had personally rounded up every piece of information that might help him beat Gannett in Little Rock. But Frank did not think like Walter Hussman.

Now that we had finally come to cases, I saw that Frank's mind did not work like an investigative reporter's. It did not snap like a steel trap onto the logic of a situation. My own instincts, sharpened through years of experience, said that Frank was not wrong in his allegations. Properly supported, the incidents he cited would make a powerful case against Gannett in Green Bay. Yet his evidence was incomplete and inconclusive. I did not need the lawyers to tell me it had too many gaps. But I did not know where, when, or if I could find the missing pieces.

I limped home to determine what to make of the bruising encounter. I was somewhat closer to the all-important local case against Gannett, but it kept receding before me. It could not yet be pulled together. In the meantime, if I ever intended to follow those fortunate geese south, I had to keep moving. At least I could now sit down and write the story of Brown County Publishing Company.

29

Lives That Matter,
Flesh That Bleeds

WITH THEIR LIFE SAVINGS OF $700 and a borrowed $17,460, Frank and Agnes Wood bought the weekly *Denmark Press* in 1953 and became country publishers. Both were twenty-four and two years married, and Agnes was pregnant with their second child. Both of them had grown up in the newspaper business. In his Michigan hometown, Frank had wandered into the local weekly as a boy of ten, and soon was regularly being shooed out of the shop. Then he won his high school's journalism award. Agnes's father ran a Wisconsin weekly. He advised Frank to choose another line of work. When they bought the *Denmark Press* he did not hesitate to tell the young couple that in his opinion they would never make it.

The *Press* had four employees and annual revenues of twenty-two thousand dollars. Taking seventy-five dollars a week for themselves and their growing family, the Woods paid their dues. While Agnes tended the books and obits and weddings and subscriptions and the children, Frank sold ads, wrote stories, took pictures, set type, ran the press, and got the paper out every week. They rented for five years, then made a down payment on an old house, and installments on a washing machine.

Slowly the enterprise grew. By 1956 it employed six people. Then Frank made a modest bit of journalism history, with the first employee pension plan at any weekly in America. His paper withheld 3 percent from each paycheck, matched it, and put the funds in a trust account. The idea was so novel that some employees were suspicious. "The only way we got the last guy in," Frank remembered, "was when we convinced him it was the same thing as a 3 percent raise."

The next breakthrough for the company came in 1960. A shopper was going broke in the area's largest city, the county seat, Green Bay. Taking a gamble, Frank bought it cheap, changed its name from the *Green Bay*

Advertiser to the *Brown County Chronicle,* and kept it going. He just about lost his bet. Heavy deficits continued for several months, wiping out everything he had made in seven years in Denmark. But in 1961 the *Chronicle* stabilized, then became profitable.

Late that year the company bought a used press big enough to print the *Chronicle,* instead of sending it out as a job. In 1965 Frank upgraded his equipment and progressed into the then-young field of offset printing, becoming a commercial printer of advertising inserts and other publications. Later he added a state-of-the-art heat-set press, capable of the most sophisticated work. By the early 1970s Brown County Publishing, as Frank now called his company, was a major printer in northeastern Wisconsin. It also was expanding in number and variety of publications. In some communities Frank started shoppers. In others he launched specialty periodicals, aimed at tourists, senior citizens, farmers, and other groups. And in several small towns, he purchased long-established weekly or twice-weekly papers and maintained their traditions.

Through the years Frank built a reputation for fair dealing and a fair price. As his company grew, he made a point of visiting the area's remaining independent publishers, to assure them he had no plans to move into their territory—and to ask them to call him first if for age or any other reason the time ever came when they wanted to sell. In time, many did. In at least one case Frank struck such a friendly deal that it was completed without lawyers.

By far his most ambitious acquisition came in 1976, with the *Green Bay Daily News.* Started four years earlier by union strikers from the *Press-Gazette,* the *News* was on its last legs, with annual losses of four hundred thousand dollars. But Frank felt that Green Bay needed to keep its second daily newspaper. So he bailed out the *Daily News,* first as a substantial investor, eventually as outright owner. As the new publisher, he renamed it the *News-Chronicle* and merged its operations to some degree with the weekly *Brown County Chronicle.* Together they were known as the Chronicle Group. For eight years, profits from other divisions subsidized the daily's losses. Then in 1984, the *News-Chronicle* showed a tiny profit. A larger one came the next year. But in 1986, its fortunes turned the other way. The losses returned, and now were approaching five hundred thousand dollars a year.

Brown County Publishing's growth peaked in the mid-1980s, when it owned some thirty mastheads in Wisconsin and nearby in Illinois. But partly because the company had become too far-flung and partly to cover the losses in Green Bay, Frank began consolidating and selling publications, always taking care to preserve the jobs of employees. By 1989 he was down to a dozen publications, with circulations ranging from seven hundred to sixty-seven thousand. All were Wisconsin-based, in or near Green Bay. Together they grossed about $7 million a year. Printing sales added another $7 million, for a company total of $14 million.

As his personal wealth grew along with his enterprise, Frank felt a need to thank the community that had generated it. So he and Agnes set up the Wood Family Foundation, which over the years quietly channeled many thousands of dollars into charitable causes in the Green Bay area. Then when times got tough for Brown County Publishing, Frank had dipped into his pocket for another reason—to keep the company solvent, and to preserve its workers' jobs.

More than three hundred full- and part-time employees were on the payroll, which totaled more than $5 million a year. And though the firm never had been flush enough to pay high wages, it had taken care of its workers in other, extraordinary ways. The precedent-setting pension plan at the *Denmark Press* was a forerunner of other benefits in store. Every full-time worker now had a life insurance policy paid for by the company. Both long- and short-term disability benefits were covered by the medical plan. So was dental care. In the 1960s Frank began an employee stock program. Now the majority of his company's shareholders traced to it.

In job security as well, Brown County Publishing had taken care of its workforce. Preserving jobs was an article of Frank's creed, more important than the bottom line in good times and bad. Yet living up to that creed had not always been easy. As the circular-distribution business burgeoned in the early 1980s, Frank realized he could save money by buying machines to replace the large crew of manual inserters who gathered weekly in Denmark to stuff the preprints into various publications. But he also realized that the seventy or so part-time workers depended on these paychecks to make ends meet. Humble as it was, the operation was a crucial element in the economy of this small, decaying town of only 1,475 residents.

To reconcile the company's needs and the needs of the workers, Frank called a meeting and made a promise: If the inserters could increase their productivity to cut expenses, he would maintain the operation as long as there were enough people to keep it going. "Afterwards," Frank remembered, "I totally melted when a woman who appeared to be retarded came up

and said, 'Does this mean if I can't insert fast enough I can't have a job?' "
Frank told her not to worry, then quietly made sure she was kept on the
payroll. For almost another decade Brown County Publishing maintained
the inserting crew. Machines did not replace it until other jobs had drawn
off most of the workers. Even then a few people were kept.

Another challenge came in the "Reagan Recession" of 1982. More than
most places, industrialized Green Bay was suffering. Hundreds of workers
were laid off, business was bad in almost every store, and advertisers were
cutting back sharply. Brown County Publishing watched revenues shrink
in both printing and publications, and tightened its belt. Then came a loss
that seemed insurmountable. Two huge printing contracts were canceled.
Overnight, the company lost more than a million dollars in revenue, with
no quick way to make it up. There seemed no alternative to laying off
thirty workers. It hurt, for in thirty-six years, Frank had never let anyone go
because of harsh times. But there turned out to be another choice, after all.

Wrestling with his difficult decision, Frank presented it as a hypothetical
case to a business class at St. Norbert College. The students quickly identified it as his own company. He said there was no way to avoid layoffs.
The students disagreed. "The kids told me, 'You're not doing it right. You
should go back and ask the people what they want, and what they're willing
to do,' " Frank recalled. Then the class stayed two extra hours to devise
ways to avoid layoffs. "They came up with some great ideas."

Frank did go back and ask his employees what they wanted. Their
message was plain. "Many of the people said, 'Look, my spouse has already
been laid off, and we don't need two people on unemployment at the same
time. I want to keep my job.' " Instead of layoffs, Brown County Publishing
came up with an array of other cost-cutting measures. Some were suggested
by the students, others were proposed by the workers. Profit-sharing and
pensions were reduced. Paid holidays were eliminated. Sick-leave benefits
were cut. Vacations were halved. No one was let go. When things got better,
all the benefits were restored. "We're very paternal," Frank summed up
his company's attitude toward its workers. "When times get hard, we get
protective."

Frank's paternalism extended to the town of Denmark. As malls and
discount stores lured its shoppers into Green Bay in the 1970s, he noted with
dismay the withering of what had once been a thriving commercial district.
It was taking on the look of a ghost town. Brown County Publishing was
tempted to take similar flight, especially after acquiring the *News-Chronicle*.

The labor pool was greater in Green Bay, and savings could be realized by centralizing operations there. But instead of adding his company to those already boarded up in Denmark, Frank expanded it into vacant buildings.

Over several years he purchased the sites of a brewery, three auto dealerships, a tractor repair shop, and Denmark's general store—which now housed my apartment, among other things. He converted these sites for his company's use, so that Denmark would remain a place where people worked, parked, walked the streets, and shopped. Though the decline continued for years, Frank's efforts slowed it considerably—long enough for Denmark to finally start growing once again, as a bedroom community for Green Bay.

Many townspeople credited Brown County Publishing with anchoring things until the resurgence came. Nor had this blend of economics and humanity gone unnoticed in official quarters. Just weeks before my arrival, Brown County Publishing was named Denmark's "Business of the Year," for both its "excellence in business accomplishment and community involvement."

My story was written, purposely kept brief. There was more that could be told. I thought back on other incidents Frank had mentioned over the years: workers he had steered into college, and helped pay their way; employees' relatives he had hired in family crises; ill and elderly people he had kept on the payroll long after their productivity declined; alcoholics, addicts, even overweight staff members he had sent off for treatment, at company expense; former prison inmates he had put on the payroll, sometimes with success; the employees he had helped through divorce, illness, financial catastrophe, deaths of loved ones; all the people who, before me, had been given shelter in this little apartment.

No, Frank's way could probably not be called good business. But maybe it could be called something better. I recalled a conversation with another guest on a raucous weekend at the hideaway cabin in the north woods of Wisconsin. "Frank Wood is considered a legend around here," said the other, who taught with him at St. Norbert. "A legend in his own time." And I remembered one time in his car, when Frank told me the story of his romance.

During college, he and a good friend took jobs on Mackinac Island, a resort in Lake Huron, for a carefree summer before moving on to other things. Quickly they paired up with two young women. All summer they played, around campfires, on long walks, at dances and picnics and beach parties. It was the best time of their lives. But Frank had a secret. While escorting one lady, he had fallen in love with the other, the pretty, vivacious, and devout Agnes McHale. Yet he could not show it, for she was his best friend's girl.

He hid his feelings, even after summer ended and the island friends were staying in touch largely by correspondence. But then they got together again, and afterward Frank drew his buddy aside. "If you and Agnes are serious," he said, "I wish you all the happiness in the world. But if you're not, then I'm going to go for her—for I know she's the girl I want to marry." The friend was surprised. But he gave Frank his blessing. For him, Agnes had been a summer love, a pal. Thus freed, Frank began his courtship. Within a year, he and Agnes were married.

"Since then, there has never been a day when I have not known that marrying Agnes was the best thing I ever did," said my friend, with something like awe in his voice.

"And what's the worst thing you ever did?" I asked flippantly, perhaps because the emotion of the moment could not be held.

"Oh, I don't know," he chuckled. "Maybe buying the *Daily News.*"

GODDAMMIT! I raged, late that night in my room. *When the Gannettoids decide to kill something, don't they even care that their victims are real people, with lives that matter, flesh that bleeds and hearts that break? Is money the only thing they know? Is there no human face on anything Gannett does?*

I tried to sleep. After a long while, I reached for the gospel tape, and put it on. But it did not help. Then, for maybe the first time, I actually heard the words of the old hymn "Stand By Me."

> When the storms of life are raging, stand by me.
> When the storms of life are raging, stand by me.
> When the world is tossing me, like a ship out on the sea,
> Thou who rulest wind and water, stand by me.

It was too much. I got out of bed and paced the floor.

> When I'm growing old and feeble, stand by me.
> When I'm growing old and feeble, stand by me.
> When I do the best I can, and my friends misunderstand,
> Thou who never lost a battle, stand by me.

Long after the song ended I sat awake, in the hard chair in the dark room. I felt humbled and ashamed. In my peevishness and self-absorption I had forgotten why I had come to Green Bay, and who I came to help. Was it any wonder that Frank was out of strength, swimming and sinking in deep, deep waters? More than anyone, I ought to understand. Fifteen years of running the *Santa Fe Reporter* had been enough for me, yet he had been at his post for thirty-six. And his way had been harder. Where I employed twenty-five people, three hundred looked to him. Where I paid workers with challenges and pride, he was setting up pension plans. While I had opted for the unencumbered life, he was still helping others. When I was hitting the road, he was making a stand. While I fantasized about saving the town, he was actually doing it.

And when I needed his help, he was there.

If he now was meeting his obligations at the college and at home before pouring the last of his energy down the black hole of the *News-Chronicle,* could I not forgive him? If he now needed someone to fight not with him but for him, could I not give him that much?

Well, partly yes and partly no. To tell you the truth, Frank, I'm still pissed. But you're doing the best you can, and I will too. So don't worry, my friend. I'm going to see it through. And yet, make no mistake: I am not that guy who never lost a battle. Already I've lost my share, and you and I are about to lose another. But I will stand by you, and we will lose it together.

30

The Ticking Clock

WITH RENEWED DETERMINATION I KEPT at the Green Bay Project. The obstacles remained, but now my task was to work past them. The greatest hindrance, my own attitude, was finally under control. External problems, however, were getting serious. The calendar had become an enemy. My quick prediction of springing the report before Thanksgiving was clearly an impossibility. Yet going with it after that date was a dismaying prospect.

Each year Thanksgiving kicks off this country's Christmas buying binge. Everyone is distracted in that season; and every newspaper—even a scrawny one like the *News-Chronicle*—gets an advertising surge that strains its capacities. In short, the Christmas rush was the worst possible time for the report. For the readers we hoped to arouse, it could get lost in their holiday shuffle. For the employees of Brown County Publishing, it would be an extra burden when they least could handle it.

"I think we should wait till January, when things slow down," I said to Frank after his bout with the flu. We were getting along much more smoothly. Now that I had come out of my snit, Frank was in turn becoming more involved and less defensive.

"Yes, that's what we ought to do," Frank seemed to agree. *"But I can't wait that long."* There was desperation in his voice. "I need something before the end of December. If we close the books on the losses we've taken this year, without some sign that things could get better, I'll have to shut down the *News-Chronicle*. The board of directors is ready to revolt, and I've got to show them something. The report is the only hope. It has to come out in December."

So he does know about the resistance in his company, I noted silently. *He just chooses not to let on sometimes.*

In my retooled frame of mind, I once again wanted the Green Bay Project to be effective—as effective as possible. That was why I suggested waiting. But I heard the truth in Frank's words. And to be honest with myself, they brought more relief than regret. Though I would do it if I had to, returning to Wisconsin after a Christmas at home was almost too grim to contemplate. Better by far to stay and get the job done, once and for all. We would do it in December.

"All right, then," I replied. "I thought you might say that. So let's set our plans right now. Most of the writing is done, and I have a feel for how long the report should run. I would say the better part of two weeks, maybe ten days, at two or three pages a day. The deeper we get into the Christmas season, the less impact it will have. So let's start it on the Monday after Thanksgiving—November 27. How does that sound?"

"It sounds good. But can we be ready by then? We haven't even started production. Can we get it all done in sixteen days?"

"We can if we have to. You know that, Frank—it's just another deadline. Let's put a deadline on this sucker, or else it will never be ready. There's only one way to make things happen in the newspaper business, and that's with a deadline."

"You're right. Then November 27 it is. D-Day."

"No, Frank. That was June 6."

The instant we set the date, the pressure tightened. Frank's misgivings were accurate. There was indeed too much work for the time available to do it in. Mathematically the equation was impossible. Yet I remembered all the times at the *Santa Fe Reporter* when the same was true. Never did the paper fail to appear. And the Green Bay Project would appear, too. On November 27, 1989.

The key, as usual, was doing most of the work myself. I was skilled at layout and headlines. I also was pretty good at paste-up, the hands-on construction of the pages. This was how to prevent the Green Bay Project from becoming onerous to the production crew in their busiest season. I could work odd hours, or all night if necessary, and do all sorts of things unreasonable to ask of hourly wage earners. And the fewer who got involved, the easier it would be to maintain secrecy.

The job I could not do was the typesetting. This problem had confounded me from the start. Yet when it could be delayed no longer, it got solved. A staff compositor named Floyd Ferdon was assigned to my project, and was sworn to silence. A calm, middle-aged man, Floyd was one of the original strikers who had started the *Daily News*. "Sounds good to me," he said, when I dealt him in. When he knocked off at the end of the day, several stories were in type.

With production accounted for, I worried next about the other loose ends: the in-house promotions, the advertising and circulation pushes, the radio and television trade-outs to announce the report. There was no way I could personally tend to those things by November 27. What the Green Bay Project needed was a special assistant, and when I put the question to Frank, he said the words I wanted to hear: "How about Al Rasmussen? He just might be the answer to a maiden's prayer."

And indeed Al was the answer to my prayers. He jumped upon the job. Quickly he arranged swaps with three of Green Bay's four television channels, plus several radio stations. Without disclosing the subject, Al booked a blitz of fifteen- and thirty-second "teasers" for the weekend before November 27. Anyone tuning in on Saturday or Sunday would know something was up. Then anyone seeing Monday's paper would know what it was.

Al also got things moving in-house. Placards for promoting the report on *News-Chronicle* coin boxes throughout the city were readied. House ads went into production. Thousands of extra copies of the November 27 newspaper were scheduled for the printing press. Dozens of "people places"—factory gates, coffee shops, shopping malls—were chosen for free distribution. Cut-rate subscriptions were agreed upon. Special advertising offers—two ads for the price of one, discounts for repeat ads, other inducements—were timed to break along with the report. With Al on the job, the elements were coming together. The Green Bay Project once again became a multipronged campaign.

Still missing, however, was an editorial overhaul for the *News-Chronicle*. This was outside Al's authority. Only Frank and his editor could act on it, but neither showed any inclination to do so. With the deadline closing in, their inertia grated. I had endless ideas for adding sparkle, life, vitality to the newspaper. My ideas had worked in Santa Fe, and they would work here. But Frank never was ready to discuss format changes.

And then one day I got it. Frank and his editor were *proud* of their newspaper. They believed in the mix they presented each day and called the *Green Bay News-Chronicle.* And they did not appreciate some know-it-all outsider telling them they were doing everything wrong. And yes, they had a point. Their *News-Chronicle* was in fact quite presentable. It measured up to the contemporary definition of an American newspaper. If it were the only paper in a small city anywhere, that city would be as well served as the next. It was the *News-Chronicle*'s misfortune to be the second paper in a Gannett town. But it was the *News-Chronicle*'s achievement to provide a genuine alternative, against all the odds.

That was the point I had missed. In my zeal for the *News-Chronicle* to do everything better, I had failed to honor all the things it was doing well—remarkably well under the circumstances. As for my ideas, well, maybe they would work and maybe they would not. Green Bay was not Santa Fe. I felt no bond with the people here. Why did I think I knew just what they needed?

Mostly it was ego, pumped up by the success I had enjoyed elsewhere. But Frank had hired me to try to save *his* newspaper, not replace it with one of my design. To the relief of all concerned I backed off, as November 27 drew ever nearer.

Now just a few pieces were not in place. Some were more worrisome than others, but time was running out on them all.

I made a list of the photographs needed for the report. There were twenty-five or thirty, but most were easy: buildings, people, and work scenes around Green Bay. They might take a day and a half to shoot. "Oh my God," groaned the editor. "How do you expect us to do all this and still put out the paper?" *You get it done,* I said silently, *by deciding to get it done. It's just another assignment. The key is the editor. He has to be behind a job—which you, my friend, obviously are not.* Grudgingly he agreed to try. *We are not all in this thing together,* I thought, thanking him for his sacrifice.

Even more troubling were Lyle Lahey's illustrations. Unlike the grumbling editor, he had been given ample notice. Yet he had not completed the work. His assignment was half a dozen illustrations to add impact to the national stories, and a few small graphics, to be sprinkled through the report. Each time I asked about his progress, there was not much. With November 27 just eleven days off and the Thanksgiving holiday in the interim, he had sketched just three pictures and finished none. Moreover, they were not very good.

His image of Gannett's questionable circulation claims had an Alice-in-Wonderland theme. It was clever, but lacked a dark tone. His concept of the Santa Fe trial was a generic courtroom scene, with no point. His take on the California price-fixing was bold, but it too missed. Its punks passing a wad of money under a billboard looked like drug dealers, not wheeler-dealers. The illustrations were a mixed bag. No theme connected them, to give the report a unified statement. Each was also a different shape, complicating the layout. They met the rock-bottom need of breaking up the gray type, but that was about it.

I was saddened as much as frustrated. Lahey's work was a sincere effort. If he and I were communicating better, we might be on the same wavelength, and his graphics might be powerful. Yet he had never warmed to me. Every word from his mouth was prickly. He rejected every suggestion I made, no matter how polite. His attitude was one part artistry, which I appreciated, but two parts resentment, two parts obstinacy, and two parts superiority. It added up to the very antithesis of editorial creativity.

In collaborative efforts of this sort, what usually works best is for people of different talents to strike sparks off each other, for a common goal. The process is sometimes bruising, but surpasses work done alone. If Lahey and I had broken through to that level, his effort might be in sync with mine. We had not, however. As a result, what I got was what he gave me. It could have been so much better.

Urgency was giving way to crisis. Disappointing as they were, I resigned myself to making do with the pictures in hand. But the missing ones alarmed me. I needed them all to calculate the final layout. And if they were unusable, there was almost no time for revisions. Most frightening of all, Lahey had not come up with an idea to use on Day One, November 27.

I was depending upon Lahey, the best and most iconoclastic talent at the *News-Chronicle.* But at the eleventh hour, he was not coming through. I felt a desperation, compounded by our testy relationship. Pushing him would be risky. But I had no choice. "The billboard is great," I fibbed. "I have mixed feelings about the others—I'm still thinking about them. But the one I need right away is the first day. What are chances of seeing a sketch tomorrow? And what's the status of the little stuff?"

"You seem to forget, Dick," Lahey replied, looking up from the draft of a cartoon, "that I have other work to do. I'll get to it as soon as I can. Now if you'll excuse me, I'm running late."

Barely suppressing my rage, I stormed back to my room. *What is wrong with these people?* I remembered working with Santa Fe illustrators, and the wonderful results. *What is going on here? Why do I have to put up with this shit?* Then came a revelation: *Maybe I don't have to put up with it.* In my file I found the name of Betsy James, the best and quickest illustrator I knew. She had done the Salem report and other crash assignments. She could handle this one too. "When in doubt," I recited, "turn to the *Santa Fe Reporter* Connection."

I dialed Betsy's number in New Mexico, praying she was there. She was. Quickly I explained the situation. Could she drop whatever she was doing and help me out? Already it was all but too late. Yet with Federal Express, we just might pull it off. I would rush her the stories today. She would get them tomorrow. If she could send me a first-day illustration on Monday, we could play out the others one by one, staying a day or two ahead. It would be like riding the crest of a wave.

"I ought to say no," she sighed, which meant she was going to say yes. "I'm doing children's books now, and I'm up to here in my own work. But to tell you the truth, I've missed this sort of thing. It has a sharper edge to it."

The following evening, Betsy and I conferred by phone. I had no good ideas, and wanted to hear hers. "I see something really dark," she said. "I see a recurring figure, a big, broad-shouldered man in a black, pin-striped business suit. In each illustration he would be doing something connected with the text. But his back would always be turned, and we would never see his face. Sinister, faceless, all-powerful yet still sophisticated—that's the image of Gannett I get from the stories."

My God, how I loved talking with Betsy about such things! I loved the way her mind worked, how she snapped onto the picture worth a thousand words. Just like in the old days. "It's now Friday," she said in closing. "I'll work over the weekend, and on Monday send you at least one graphic, maybe two. You'll get them on Tuesday. I'll send one a day after that."

On Monday morning I reapproached Lyle Lahey. "I have some good news," I said. "I do realize how busy you are, so I've made arrangements for someone else to illustrate the report. I'm sure this will be a relief to you."

"How about the little graphics?" he asked at length.

"Do whatever you think is best," I said. "I can get by without them. Make it easy on yourself."

"Well, if you were going to use another artist you could have told me before now," he sputtered, his hostility mixed with something else. "I've put a lot of work into this."

"I apologize for wasting your time," I said. "It won't happen again." Then I walked away, feeling good.

31

The Young Prince

So the Green Bay Project was going to happen after all. It had lawyers. It had an illustrator. It had advertising and circulation components, and an in-house honcho to get things done. It was in production. It had a deadline. But it did not have a name. My workaday label, the Green Bay Project, was not a flamboyant enough flag. The title must be short and strong, a phrase the man on the street would remember. On November 18, Frank and I met in my room to come up with it.

"Do you have any thoughts?" he asked.

"Yes, I do. But I'm not really happy with any of them. I haven't yet snapped my fingers and said 'That's it!' That's when you know it's right. But here's what I've come up with so far."

Knowing that none was *the* one, I presented my ideas: "A Matter of Life and Death," "Not Without a Fight," "We Want to Live!" Frank did not react to any of them. "How about '*News-Chronicle* Declares War on Gannett'?" he finally said.

"No, that's all wrong. It's too trite, it's too long, and there's not enough emotion in it. We need to kick the readers in the gut. The most powerful theme we have is life and death, and I think we should use it. How about 'We're Fighting for Our Life!' or even a direct appeal, like 'Please Help Us Live'?"

Frank did not like those, either. Nor could I blame him. My suggestions were getting worse, not better. But that was all right. It was all part of the process. Wild shots often were followed by a bull's-eye. The key was to get the juices flowing. And then the perfect phrase came to me. It was pithy, it accurately summed up the situation, it was easily remembered, it would arouse anyone's curiosity, it jumped off the page, and it kicked like a mule. "I've got it!" I exclaimed. "This is the one: 'It's Do or Die!' Yes, that's it: 'It's Do or Die!' "

Surprisingly, Frank was hesitant. "I'm not sure . . ."

"No, no, this is the one," I rushed on. "It does it all. It will be on everybody's lips: 'It's Do or Die!' "

"I guess I don't like the word 'die.' "

"But that's what makes it strong! Nothing is more emotional than death— and that is what we're talking about. If the *News-Chronicle* doesn't *do* something, it will *die*. It's that simple."

He remained unconvinced. "Let me think about it."

"Well, keep turning it over. But for now I'll consider it a working title. Up until the last minute, we can still change it. As far as I'm concerned, this one is fine. But if something better comes along, we'll switch. What do you say?" Reluctantly Frank agreed. Clearly he was not sold on "It's Do or Die!" But he would come around when he saw it in print.

Our task completed, Frank left. I pressed on with other things. A day or two later, the phone rang. The caller spoke just four words: " 'It's Now or Never!' "

"What?"

" 'It's Now or Never!' "

Then I recognized Frank's voice. He was presenting an alternative title. In a flash I understood. Like a callous doctor out of touch with a patient's fear, I had bludgeoned Frank with the word too terrible to contemplate: *death*. He could not attach this word to his *News-Chronicle,* and would not make an abject appeal for the town to save its life. He needed other words.

"That's great!" I almost shouted, as the phrase "It's Do or Die!" evaporated into nothing. "That's the finger-snapper. It's the one we were looking for all along. We've got ourselves a title!" Best of all, it was a title Frank could live with.

Even the Pack was adding to the momentum. The team had roared back from its slump, and was again in playoff contention. When the Packers overcame the hated Chicago Bears 14–13 with 32 seconds left, I too was swept up in the citywide delirium. But one key element of my project was still not accounted for. The missing part was not enough to derail us, but if it remained missing our chances of uniting the town behind us were slim. After almost two months in town, I could not yet mount a powerful local case against Gannett and its *Press-Gazette*.

I did know what they were doing. Their tactics were ones that had worked in Salem, in Santa Fe, in cities all across the land. Yet maddeningly, I had nailed down very little. Frank was no dummy, and the incidents he noted did add up to a systematic campaign to cut off his sources of revenue, large and small. But even after recovering from the flu, he could not provide the vital pieces of verifiable information needed to win his case in the court of public opinion.

I was not completely empty-handed. Frank had provided at least a few local stories strong enough to print. Others were tantalizingly close, needing only a crucial fact or confirmation to bring them home. But without those missing bits, they were unconvincing in some cases and unusable in others. This was the report's weakness. The national leg was firm, as was the portrait of Frank's company, showing why it was worth caring about. But if the report did not show that Gannett's dark force had been turned upon the *News-Chronicle,* it would not stir outrage. Unless it made people cheer for the paper like they cheered for the Pack, it would be limp.

"When the deadline comes, you take the best you have and go with it." In the end, this old journalistic axiom would determine what we presented. With weak material or strong, I would portray Gannett as aggressor and the *News-Chronicle* as victim. But I did not want to go with weak material. *What Gannett learned in Salem,* I remembered yet again, *is do what you did before, but don't document it next time.*

I felt horribly stymied. So near, and yet so far. If only I could fill in the gaps, my case would be strong. But there was nowhere to turn. Frank could not help me more than he had. Others in his company would not. And I did not know my way around well enough to pry out the evidence before November 27. But somebody else did.

Chris Wood returned from his honeymoon. Right away he checked in with me, to see how my project was going. "It's going well and not so well," I told him. "It will be breaking next Monday, come hell or high water. I'm sure it will get the town talking. But one part of it is still pretty weak."

"Which part?"

"The part about what Gannett is doing here. I've only got a few cases nailed down. On a few more I have enough to write something, but it won't be real strong. It could seem like name-calling, and I'm afraid a lot of readers won't buy it."

"Why is it so weak?"

"It's so weak," I said, annoyed by his naïveté, "because I wasn't able to get the evidence I need to make it stronger."

"Then let's get it."

And then, as I watched in grateful wonder, Chris proceeded in the next few days to do what I had been unable to do in all my weeks on the scene: He got the goods on Gannett in Green Bay. He called advertisers and casually got them talking about the *Press-Gazette*. He got answers for my questions. He went straight to records buried in obscure files. Within the company Chris went back to people who had sidestepped my requests, and got what I needed from them. He chatted up the staff, filling in the gaps in Frank's stories. Moreover, he expanded the list.

Chris and I devised subterfuges for getting information by telephone from the *Press-Gazette*. To avoid raising suspicions, he assigned Brown County Publishing workers to make the calls. He had people in the company call other newspapers throughout Wisconsin, to compare their policies with the *Press-Gazette*'s. Working early and late, over and above his regular job, Chris grew passionate in his determination to bring the project home.

"I know some advertisers will be pissed off when we name them," he said, not once but several times. "We'll probably never get them back. But I say to hell with it! There comes a time when you have to stand and fight, no matter what it costs!"

The hot-blooded prince, I mused, late at night in my room. *The old king is weary, but the young prince rises to give battle in his place. It is an old, old story. It is the way of the world.*

His fierce energy inspired me. It was cause for wonder, for Chris had suffered blows terrible enough to keep him down forever. In childhood he watched his best friend die under the wheels of a train as they were scurrying across the tracks. For years he lived in a fog of guilt and horror. When he finally emerged from it as a young man and tried to move on, he was diagnosed with terminal cancer.

He was told he would be dead within a year, and to make the necessary arrangements. Rejecting that advice, he underwent an experimental treatment. A requirement was that he "sign his life away"—agree in writing to hold the program blameless if the treatment killed him. Instead it worked. After two harrowing years and several gruesome operations, Chris was pronounced cured. With his new lease on life he returned to college, roamed the West and foreign lands, wrote songs, and started a career outside his father's company. Only after working in several other places did Chris join Brown County Publishing. Quickly he became its top salesman. Now he had just gotten married, to a fine, strong young woman who knew his history and chose to link her life with his.

If Chris Wood had strength enough for this fight, then by God, I did too. Two or three times a day we conferred. He kept feeding me facts, and I kept asking for more. I was still directing the investigation, but Chris had become the key.

The local component was gaining heft and credibility. Even with the new material, some stories remained just out of reach. But when I told Chris what element they still lacked, off he went in pursuit of it. By telephone he tracked down people who had moved to other states. He crammed ever more appointments and calls into his days, to secure one more fact, one more quote.

Moved by his example, I vowed to uphold my end. With the deadline ever nearer, I revised, upgraded, and wrote more stories. I wrestled with facts and figures, determined to shape them into telling accounts. Each day's output was zipped to the lawyers, and by telephone the next day we fixed anything that needed it. Not every article would be finished before the Monday launch, but that was all right. The evidence kept flowing in, and the report would keep unfolding for two weeks. As long as the lawyers and I stayed a day or two ahead, we could keep things rolling.

Just one week earlier I had all but despaired of the local leg. Now it was as strong as any other part. And more visceral. No, the tales from Green Bay were not as damning as those in the Salem exposé. Never again would Gannett provide anybody, anywhere, with a court file spelling out in lurid detail how the chain competes. But even without such a file, I now could reveal what was happening here.

I would not use all the stories I had heard. Some were still not pinned down. Some were repetitive. Some lacked drama. There was only a limited amount of time and space in which to tell the tale. In journalism, less can be more. Readers with short attention spans turn away when points are labored. I would make the case as swiftly and effectively as possible—then rest it, and hope that in the court of public opinion the verdict would be "guilty."

32

"We Will Not Sink That Low"

FOR MANY YEARS A STEADY source of revenue for the *News-Chronicle* was the publication of the City of Green Bay's official legal notices, council proceedings, and ordinances. But shortly before I came to help Frank Wood, he lost that source of revenue.

Set in tiny type amid the classified ads, these notices were not the flashiest part of the paper. But they were vitally important to the *News-Chronicle*. In 1987, however, Gannett took the city account away. Dropping its bid for the legal-notice contract by a startling 29 percent from the previous year, the *Press-Gazette* undercut the *News-Chronicle* by a fraction of a cent per line. Required by law to accept the lowest bid, the city gave Gannett the contract for the next full year.

Under Wisconsin law, the maximum rate that can be charged for printing legal notices is set by the state, calculated to cover costs and return a reasonable profit. Papers cannot bid higher than the state-imposed maximum, but are allowed to bid below it if they choose. Yet because the maximum is tied to costs, bids predictably come in close to the limit. And because big-circulation papers incur higher costs simply by printing more copies of the notices, they predictably charge higher rates than small papers.

For more than a decade before 1987, the eleven-thousand-circulation *News-Chronicle* routinely entered lower bids for the city contract than the fifty-five-thousand-circulation *Press-Gazette*. So losing the account was an unexpected blow, one the struggling paper could ill afford.

For the 1988 contract, Frank lowered his bid by 15 percent. At that rate there was not much profit, but there was some. His bid came in below Gannett's, and he got the account back, but at a sharply reduced margin. Yet even this victory was short-lived. The following year, in 1989, the *Press-Gazette* slashed its already reduced rate by an unheard-of additional 33 percent and regained the city contract. Gannett's 1989 price was barely half what it had bid for the same job in 1986. And it was barely half the price set by the state as reasonable. By Frank's calculations, the *Press-Gazette* was losing money on every city legal notice it printed.

Totaling less than fifty thousand dollars a year, the City of Green Bay account represented a minuscule fraction of the *Press-Gazette*'s tens of millions of dollars a year in revenues. But for the *News-Chronicle,* the account had been crucial, one of the few dependable sources of income it had in its fight to stay alive.

Just as it did in its campaign against the *Community Press* in Oregon, Gannett also used the telling of deliberate lies as a competitive tactic against the *Green Bay News-Chronicle.*

Late in 1988, Frank's company presented all its advertisers with an especially attractive offer: a series of thirteen full-page color ads for just $595 per page. The normal cost for such an ad would exceed $1,000. The drastic reduction cut out most of the profit, but Frank was growing desperate. Many advertisers eagerly accepted the offer. For others, however, the program was undermined by a lie spread by the *Press-Gazette* sales staff.

Frank first heard of the lie after one of his most faithful clients, a store called Furnitureland, turned the exceptional offer down flat. The reason, said the store's owners, was that a *Press-Gazette* representative had told them that instead of sticking to the $595-per-page price, the Chronicle papers were selling the program "for anything they can get for it."

Frank decided to confront the situation head-on. Driving to Furnitureland with his advertising director, who took notes, he met with the owners. They confirmed that a *Press-Gazette* staff member had told them that the special offer's rate "varied, depending on what the advertiser is willing to pay." At that point Frank produced a file of invoices showing that all participants in the program had been charged the same price. If more proof were needed, he would provide canceled checks. The store owners "were surprised and I think appalled," Frank said. "They didn't like being lied to by our competition." Within a week, Furnitureland signed up for the promotion.

Frank did not let the matter drop. Telephoning *Press-Gazette* publisher Michael Gage, he demanded that the story stop being told. Gage said he would look into the matter. Weeks passed, and then Gage called back, to admit that the lie had been spread by his paper. But now the staff had been instructed to stop telling it, he added. According to Frank's notes, the remark made by Gage to close the subject was: "It's been taken care of."

Another Gannett tactic was tempting Frank's few steadfast clients with incredibly attractive offers, difficult to refuse. One such target was a grocery group called Lindy's Markets. Lindy's was sharing its business with both papers. Frank's carried its midweek ads and the *Press-Gazette* distributed its Sunday circular, which was printed by Brown County Publishing. In both advertising and printing, Lindy's was one of Frank's largest clients, with an annual total of about $120,000. But Gannett was also doing well, with $70,000 of Lindy's budget.

Yet that was not enough. Seeking to get the full account, Gannett submitted, in writing, a rock-bottom bid for a package deal that would include all midweek advertising, all Sunday advertising, and all printing and distribution of circulars. The cost for this all-inclusive program was one hundred thousand dollars a year cheaper than the *Press-Gazette*'s published rates— and was also two hundred dollars a week cheaper than the joint program with both papers.

Because Gannett was not giving similar bargains to grocery stores that were not Frank's clients, Lindy's manager was told to keep it quiet. But through months of working together, Chris Wood and the manager had become friends. A copy of the remarkable proposal was given to Chris, who passed it on to me.

As the Green Bay Project neared its deadline, Lindy's was weighing the offer. The manager knew exactly why it was made, he told Chris, and knew that such offers would not come again if the competition folded. But it was a hell of a deal, he said, and he admitted he was considering it.

"I'll tell you, Dick," Frank had said as I pressed for cases, "what gets me worst of all is when we're used as a pissing post."

"What do you mean?" I asked. I thought I knew, but I was not familiar with the term. So he illustrated it for me.

Disturbed by a steep *Press-Gazette* rate increase in 1986, the J.C. Penney manager had asked Frank for help in holding the line on advertising costs. While leaving most of its budget with Gannett, the store began running a circular in the weekly *Brown County Chronicle,* which for two months provided this service. Had the program continued all year, it would have brought in thirty thousand dollars. But abruptly the circular went back to the *Press-Gazette.*

Upset by the loss of this significant account, Frank went to see the Penney manager. "He was very apologetic," Frank recalled. "He said the

Press-Gazette had made 'substantial concessions' to get his business back. He was getting good results with us, but gee, he just couldn't refuse this offer."

The manager acknowledged that Gannett had lowered his rates for one reason only: his use of the competition. But though he was grateful, he felt no need to maintain his program with the *News-Chronicle.* "We've frequently been used in this manner," Frank said. "Once they get what they want, they drop us. So now you know what a pissing post is."

Not content merely to pick off advertisers, Gannett also targeted Frank's printing plant. In September 1988, a letter from Gannett demanded changes in an arrangement that had been in place for years. Instead of continuing to take Tuesday delivery of circulars printed by Brown County Publishing for distribution in the Sunday *Press-Gazette,* Gannett insisted that, "effective immediately," it must have delivery by 10 A.M. on Mondays. Any later shipment would be subject to stiff additional charges.

The one-day change was crucial, especially in the volatile grocery business, where stores often do not know until only hours beforehand what items are available for special promotions. In the fresh-produce department, the time factor is extremely critical. The new deadline was bad news for any grocer using Brown County to print Sunday circulars going into the *Press-Gazette.* Stores that had to commit to Sunday prices a day earlier than usual would lose a competitive step on the chains that could wait—such as those whose circulars were printed by Gannett.

Yet the demand was phrased as though its purpose was to help the very clients it would hurt. As stated in the letter from advertising manager Roy F. Valitchka, the reason for the change was that the *Press-Gazette* "cannot afford to have our insert customers disadvantaged by late deliveries from their print house." The letter did not explain what "disadvantage" the old delivery schedule had caused. Nor did it acknowledge that the new deadline was itself a disadvantage to its insert customers.

The demand struck a double blow at Brown County Publishing. It created difficulties in holding on to longtime accounts. And it created difficulties in seeking new ones. The manager of one grocery chain told Chris Wood to not even submit a bid for her circulars, for the ability to make last-minute changes was critical.

Curiously, no other paper in Wisconsin seemed to feel that insert customers would be "disadvantaged" by deliveries after Monday morning.

Chris got for me insert-delivery schedules from eleven dailies around the state. Not one of them joined the *Press-Gazette* in demanding six full days before Sunday. One paper asked only a single day's advance delivery. Three wanted two days. One required three days. Three wanted inserts four days ahead of time. And a five-day advance was asked by the other three—including the other Gannett paper in Wisconsin.

Also curious was a statement made by a *Press-Gazette* loading dock worker to a Brown County Publishing driver rushing to meet the Monday deadline. Sunday circulars were not processed until late Tuesday, the worker said, and anything received on Tuesday morning—the previous schedule—could be accommodated with no problem.

When Gannett issued its ultimatum, a Brown County Publishing executive called officials at the *Press-Gazette* to ask for some flexibility. He was told there would be none. But when one of the customers paying to have the circulars printed called with the same request, the absolute Monday morning deadline was softened to Monday afternoon.

For more than a year, despite the hardship on its customers, Brown County Publishing met the Monday afternoon deadline. Just days before my arrival, however, an emergency caused unavoidable delays at the printing plant. Bypassing management, a Brown County Publishing official called directly to the *Press-Gazette* distribution center to plead for a Tuesday delivery. To his surprise, the foreman agreed.

Later that foreman was called again by Brown County Publishing. He was thanked for taking late delivery, and was asked if it had caused problems. He said it had not. He was asked if Tuesday delivery could be accepted every week. "That's fine for now," he replied. Then he was asked if Gannett had altered its policy on preprint delivery. "I have no knowledge of any policy change," he said.

Always scrambling for creative moneymakers, Brown County Publishing Company came up with a good one in the early 1980s. It was good for many reasons: It provided a service for Green Bay's major shopping centers. It provided a substantial source of revenue, as much as two hundred thousand dollars a year. It even generated business for the rival *Press-Gazette,* tens of thousands of dollars a year. But apparently Gannett could not live with an idea that also helped a competitor. First it found a way to squeeze unusual amounts of money from Brown County Publishing's novel program. Then it found a way to take over the program altogether.

In 1981 Brown County Publishing began marketing tabloid supplements for Green Bay's shopping malls, to be distributed in several papers in the area, including Gannett's. As the dominant daily, the *Press-Gazette* was a necessary part of the package. But Frank's company had no objection to sharing the business. By selling, producing, and printing the circulars, Brown County did most of the work and got most of the revenue. And though it got a smaller share, the *Press-Gazette* faced very little work and minimal expense. All it had to do was deliver the circulars.

But Gannett quickly converted this job into an exceptional amount of money. Instead of charging its standard delivery rates, the *Press-Gazette* devised a convoluted formula that more than doubled the fee for the circulars produced by Brown County. Hesitant to pass this sharp new cost on to clients, Frank's company absorbed the difference.

Despite the reduced margin, the mall program was valuable enough to continue. Through the mid-1980s the supplements ran regularly. At its peak, the program was bringing in two hundred thousand dollars a year in billings for Brown County Publishing. A full fourth of that total, fifty thousand dollars, was going to the *Press-Gazette,* just for distribution. But Gannett wanted everything. And so the *Press-Gazette* sent a one-sentence note to Brown County: "Effective August 15, 1986, the Green Bay *Press-Gazette* will not accept multi-store inserts which are not produced by the advertising department of the Green Bay *Press-Gazette. "*

Scrambling to hold on to the mall accounts, which he had built from scratch, Frank began delivering the supplements by mail. The cost was considerably higher, and it had to be passed on to the malls. Soon almost all had abandoned Brown County Publishing and were dealing directly with the *Press-Gazette* for circulars. Yet though Gannett now had the business, it had bitten off more than it could chew. The *Press-Gazette*'s printing press was much older than Brown County's, and it produced visibly poorer work. Accustomed to high standards, the malls found Gannett's workmanship unacceptable, and complained bitterly.

Brown County then made a bid to resume printing the circulars, even though it had lost the rest of the job. But Gannett took extraordinary steps to deny it even this role. Instead of printing the supplements locally in Frank's plant, Gannett farmed them out to the newspaper in Shawano, thirty-five miles away. Then while Frank's top-of-the-line press sat idle, the job over-whelmed the Shawano paper's capacity. Finding room for the circulars in an already crowded printing schedule proved tricky. Shawano needed from two to three weeks' lead time, a gap that caused big problems for the malls.

"To put it bluntly, I was really pissed off," said Steve Kennedy, a former Green Bay mall manager, whom my investigative associate Chris Wood reached in California by telephone. "I got tired of the *Press-Gazette*'s policy of making it harder to do decent advertising. They were really imposing on their customers." But in the end, Kennedy and the other managers gave up and endured the arrangement in Shawano. At least it resulted in a presentable product. "I had absolutely no use for the *Press-Gazette*'s printing capabilities," he said.

Even if it alienated customers, Gannett's strategy did shrink Brown County's once-lucrative program to a remnant of what it had been. From its previous $200,000 a year, Frank's company had just $21,500 in mall sections for fiscal 1988.

Still rankling under the nuisance of the out-of-town printing, the assistant manager of one mall asked the *Press-Gazette* in December 1988 to spell out its policy on circulars. The reply from advertising director Valitchka reiterated the refusal to accept any outside circulars "where we have the ability to sell, service or produce the product." Then he gave the official reason: "We want to maintain direct contact with our local advertisers," he wrote, "because their relationship with us is always a primary concern to us."

For Frank Wood, the worst aspect of the relentless campaign against him was watching one revenue source after another shrivel up and vanish. For his employees, however, the dreariest thing was the pettiness that had become part of the struggle.

Instead of simply working together on joint advertising accounts serviced by both newspapers, the *Press-Gazette* sales force had stalled, given excuses, "lost" ads, and failed to keep its end of agreements—not just a few times, but again and again. Gannett's tactics included: refusing to meet agreed-upon deadlines for handing over ads; "losing" ads when Chronicle Group representatives went to get them; giving newsprint copies of ads rather than crisp photostats to the *Chronicle,* necessitating a complete rebuilding of the ads; and delaying ads with tired excuses, such as: "I didn't have time," "The composing room didn't get it to me," "I don't know where it is," or "It hasn't been proofed."

Every one of these excuses was familiar to me. All had been used against the *Reporter* by the Gannett newspaper in Santa Fe. The *Chronicle* staff did not know whether Gannett's sales force had been instructed by management to behave in this manner, or if the salespeople had merely gotten into the spirit of the uneven competition in Green Bay. To them, it hardly mattered.

Individually minor, these actions created real problems, in a variety of ways. While waiting for misplaced ads, the *Chronicle* salespeople were not making calls. Rebuilding ads caused deadlines to be missed. The delays drove up labor costs for Brown County Publishing, both by downtime and overtime. The rough ads the *Chronicle* was forced to use in place of slicks were less attractive than the *Press-Gazette*'s, making Frank's papers look incompetent. And when in desperation *Chronicle* staffers went back to the client to get a new copy of an ad that had not been turned over as agreed, they, rather than Gannett, appeared to be the problem.

One of the most troublesome cases had occurred just the previous Mother's Day. A business association representing twenty-eight stores sold a media package to its members, and scheduled the ads to run in both the *Press-Gazette* and the *News-Chronicle*. It was a major promotion, and for Frank a transfusion of lifeblood.

The *Press-Gazette* sales rep suggested to her Brown County counterpart that they each pick up half the ad copy, thus saving work for them both. She also suggested that her paper build all the ads, and give copies to the *News-Chronicle*. Remembering past experiences, the *Chronicle* staffer insisted that her paper build its half of the ads. But for everyone's convenience, she did agree to service half the accounts, then swap finished products. As agreed, Brown County turned over professional-quality ads to the *Press-Gazette*. But Gannett waited until an hour before deadline, then provided not finished ads but raw copy, some in the handwriting of the client. The ads had to be built from scratch, and the *Chronicle*'s production schedule collapsed.

Gannett's tactics had demoralized Frank's workers, and left them frustrated and mad. At a staff meeting shortly before I came, the question of cooperating with the *Press-Gazette* came up. "Why the hell should we work with them?" asked one angry staffer. Many wanted to respond in the manner they had grown accustomed to in their dealings with Gannett. But Chris Wood, who presided over the meeting, refused. Giving firm instructions to maintain a professional attitude toward the shared work, he declared: "No matter what they do at the *Press-Gazette,* we will not sink to their level."

33

The Most Important Announcement

RIGHT ON SCHEDULE, FEDERAL EXPRESS brought the first of Betsy James's illustrations. But instead of just the one she had promised, three finished pieces were in the envelope, and the other three were sketched out. That was Betsy. Once her juices started flowing, she could not turn them off.

Her images were magnificent—powerful, dark, and scary. Like Gannett. Her hulking, faceless, pin-striped symbol of the chain dominated them all. In the first illustration he cast an ominous shadow over a typical American town. For the price-fixing case in California, he was shaking hands with a sleazy businessman. The strongest illustration showed the Gannett figure unleashing a ferocious Doberman pinscher upon people working at a small building labeled *Community Press.* The image was visceral, full of imminent savagery. It was also surgically precise, for the self-styled "Dobermans" were what Gannett had used to rip that newspaper apart.

As Al Rasmussen had become the Green Bay Project's strong right arm and Chris Wood its heart, Betsy James was now its stern, unblinking eyes. At this point, I was only its brain.

Early in the final week I presented Frank with a declaration I wrote for his byline. It began: "This is the most important statement this paper has made in its 17 years in Green Bay." In Frank's voice, it continued: "I now believe that our competition here, the Gannett Company, which owns the *Green Bay Press-Gazette,* intends to deprive this paper of its existence."

The piece described the struggle between the *News-Chronicle* and the *Press-Gazette.* It told what the "Now or Never" report would present: examples of Gannett's business practices, local and national, and a comparison with Brown County Publishing Company. It ended with a direct appeal to Green Bay:

"We are your neighbor. Home-owned, home-grown. We have lived the life of this community—hired its people, applauded its triumphs, pointed out its foibles and shortcomings, told its story. Now we are telling our story—ours and Gannett's.

"Green Bay is a community with a unique identity. It's the smallest city in the National Football League. It's a working-class city, a town of taverns and bowling alleys. It's a town of paper mills and packing plants. It's an honest town. This is a community with a heart. We like being here.

"Read 'It's Now or Never!' and see if you agree that the *Press-Gazette* should continue to have competition. We've done our homework. We want you to see it, and make up your own mind. Then if you agree with us, help us."

Frank gave the statement a quick read. He seemed pleased. The words "death," "die," and "dying" appeared nowhere in the text.

On the Tuesday before Thanksgiving I drove to *News-Chronicle* headquarters. Everyone at the paper knew by now that something big was up, but still they had only a vague idea of what it was. The time had come, however, for a step that would reveal my mission. For page one of "It's Now or Never!" I envisioned every staff member standing outside the *News-Chronicle*'s offices with arms defiantly crossed. I saw it as a visual statement of the paper's spirit to survive. I also could think of nothing else to lead with.

Each employee had received a notice to be present at 1 P.M. on Tuesday, November 21. The reason would be explained then, the notice said, and nobody was excused. When the hour came, some forty-five employees assembled in front of the old convent. Another dozen or so, however, were absent. Most prominent among them was Frank Wood. He was teaching a class. But these things no longer bothered me.

The scene at the photo session was a jumbled one. Puzzled employees, few of whom I had met, milled about, bundled up against the November chill. On a corner of the lawn, good old Al Rasmussen was covering up a "For Lease" sign advertising some vacant office space in the building. The photographer was positioning a ladder to provide the height and angle he needed to get all the faces.

"I guess I'm the guy behind all this," I said, introducing myself to him. "Good thinking on the ladder. It didn't even occur to me. I don't yet know what the layout's going to be, so I'll need both vertical and horizontal shots. And please get a lot of the building itself into the shot. It really adds character."

"I don't need anybody to tell me how to do my job," he snarled.

What is wrong with these people? I retreated, trying to understand. This was not the *Santa Fe Reporter,* where my authority was recognized. To the surly photographer and most of the others, I was a stranger. And nobody likes taking orders from a stranger.

"It might work best if you took charge," I said to the editor, drawing him aside. "Just say we're doing a story about competing with the *Press-Gazette,* and we want to show their determination to carry on. And could you make sure we get all the shots we need?"

"OK," said the editor, with his usual exasperation. "But let's get this over with as quickly as possible. It's taking us away from our work. Maybe that's all right for the news staff, but it's not for the advertising reps. If they're not out on the street, they're not making any money—for themselves or the paper."

What is wrong with these people?

"Oh yeah?" I had had enough. "Just when was the last time they sold five or six ads right after lunch? When was the last time they sold five or six ads, period? Maybe if they were selling more ads, there would be no need for this picture. But under the circumstances, we do need it—and nobody leaves until we get it."

"Hey, take it easy. No cause to get upset."

But I was upset. "You don't seem to understand something. I am here for one reason only: to try to help this newspaper. That means all the people standing here. Maybe my work will do some good and maybe it won't. We'll be finding out pretty soon. In the meantime, I have a job to do and I'm going to do it—with or without your help. I'd rather do it with your help, but that's up to you. Now if you don't mind, I need to get some pictures taken—with or without your help."

"Hey, don't take me wrong," he began in an unctuous tone. "I never meant—" He did not finish, for I just walked away.

He stood there a moment and then took command of the session. When it was over, all the shots I wanted had been taken. When the prints were delivered by company courier the next afternoon, they came with a bonus. Included in the package were all the pictures for the entire series. It seemed that fitting them into the photographer's busy schedule had not been so difficult after all. It also seemed that I should have popped off a long time ago.

Having the photos in hand was a real comfort. Right now I needed it, for alongside them on my table lay that morning's edition of the weekly *Brown*

County Chronicle, the sister paper of the *News-Chronicle.* It was opened to page three, which was dominated by a huge house ad that proclaimed: "On Monday, November 27, the *Green Bay News-Chronicle* will make the most important announcement in its history. DON'T MISS IT!"

34

A Performance of
the Symphony

WE HAD CROSSED OUR RUBICON. The house ad was a public commitment to the deadline day of November 27. Anyone seeing it, including anyone at the *Press-Gazette,* had to wonder what was up.

The time had come to stir up the public over our long-brewing secret project. We must make the *News-Chronicle* the equivalent of the Packers in the heart of Green Bay. The team was a shining civic symbol just then. On the previous Sunday it had scored the season's most stunning upset, a 21–17 road victory against professional football's best team, defending Super Bowl champion San Francisco. The Pack was only one game away from the division lead, and community feeling had not been running so high in years.

Green Bay's football franchise was, like Frank Wood's newspaper, an oddity. Unlike every other National Football League team, owned by huge companies or multimillionaire egotists, the Packers were a community resource, a nonprofit corporation owned by the citizens. It was the smallest unit in the league, and the least capitalized. Its tight finances were reflected in recent standings. The big-buck era of player salaries, endorsements, and media exposure had put Green Bay at a competitive disadvantage. Though it fielded a presentable team each year, each year the team got left behind—until this year. This year, as everybody in town was saying, "The Pack is back!" The Pack was a vibrant reminder that the little guy can sometimes win.

When the report broke on Monday, we wanted the town to rally behind its local newspaper like it rallied around its local team. And in the days before then, we wanted all of Green Bay wondering what was going on. But no one would be more curious than Gannett.

For all I knew, they already were aware of the project, and were ready with their counterattack. There had been plenty of chances for a leak. Now this announcement in the *Chronicle* all but tipped our hand. Still, there was potential for confusion. Maybe Gannett would think Frank was going to announce he was folding the *News-Chronicle,* or selling it, or filing a lawsuit. I hoped they would remain off guard until the last minute.

That last minute, however, was about to arrive. For the sake of responsible journalism, Frank had scheduled lunch on Friday with Michael Gage, publisher of the *Press-Gazette.* There Frank would reveal that he was going to accuse Gannett of purposely trying to drive the *News-Chronicle* out of business.

I was not sure Frank was the one to handle this matter. I was positive it should not be done over lunch. "This is not exactly a social occasion," I pointed out to him. All the "target interviews" in my experience had been tense and often hostile. But Frank felt a sense of propriety about this face-to-face encounter with his longtime adversary. He insisted on conducting it himself, and under genteel conditions.

However it was handled, the move was fraught with danger. Once alerted, Gannett would have all weekend to prepare a response, or even to deny in its big Sunday paper the charges we would make the next morning. But on the eve of publication, we could not avoid the risk. We had to give Gannett a chance to reply. The lunch was still two days away, but knuckle-biting time had already come.

Temporary relief was what I needed. Showing at the movies was one I wanted to see: *The Bear.* Reviewers had been beguiled by its concept, in which a grizzly cub's struggle to survive was shown from the bear's point of view. Off I went to the late show. *The Bear* was all I had hoped for—visually invigorating, conceptually provocative, and immensely satisfying in its story, which depicted the clash between the world of bears and the world of hunters. At the film's conclusion, a truce was struck between those worlds, and lives that seemed lost were spared. As I rose to leave the theater, *The Bear* worked one last piece of magic. It ended with a quotation from the naturalist J. O. Curwood: "The greatest thrill is not to kill, but to let live." The words echoed in my head. They were so true. If only Gannett understood them, none of this would have been necessary.

In my room, I tried to fit this phrase into the Green Bay Project. No, despite its truth it was not quite right. However, there might be other words waiting to be pressed into service. Down from the bookshelf came *Bartlett's Familiar Quotations,* which I had brought from Santa Fe. It had what I sought, in the words of Sir Andrew Browne Cunningham, a British naval officer: "We are so outnumbered there's only one thing to do. We must attack."

Then I remembered other words—not to print in the report but to deliver to Frank personally. Surprisingly, this passage was not in *Bartlett's*. So I went to the source. For the first time since coming to Wisconsin I opened a small brown Bible that was also on the shelf, a gift from a dear, born-again lady friend who prayed it would guide my way more than it had. In the First Book of Samuel I found the line. Yes, yes, it was just right. Word for word I took it down. Then I put it aside, for the time to present it had not come.

Thanksgiving brought a brief respite, with a festive dinner in Frank's home. At lunchtime the next day, however, I was gritting my teeth. Frank was with the Gannett publisher, and I was wondering if all four months of the Green Bay Project were about to go down the drain. Finally Frank returned, looking pleased with himself. "What did he say?" I asked. "I can't stand the suspense."

"He said, 'It's not true.' "

"What's not true?"

"That Gannett is trying to destroy the *News-Chronicle.*"

"Is that all he said?"

"Pretty much."

"C'mon, Frank, quit playing with me. Tell me what happened. Start from the beginning and don't leave anything out."

The showdown had gone better than I dared hope. After stalling through an awkward lunch, Frank had spoken plain. On Monday morning, Gannett and its Green Bay paper would be accused in print, in the first installment of a multiple-part series, of systematically seeking to destroy the *News-Chronicle*. The purpose of this meeting, he said, was to inform Gage what was happening, and to get whatever response he wished to make.

"That's not true!" was the Gannett publisher's reply. Frank asked if he wished to comment further. Gage thought it over, then reemphasized his earlier statement: "I know that it's not true." He refused to say anything else for publication. Gage never lost his composure. Leaving the restaurant, he even managed a chuckle. "With that announcement in Wednesday's shopper and then this lunch, I knew you were up to something," he told Frank. "But you know what I thought you were going to say? That you had sold the *Chronicle* to the *Milwaukee Journal*!" They then shook hands and separated amicably.

Even as Frank was making his report, I was certain that the unflappable Gage was burning up the wires to headquarters. He had to be. Nevertheless, I was vastly relieved. Short of a confession, a blanket denial was the best thing we could get. Gage's comment would be displayed prominently in the report, to challenge our assertions and show that Gannett had been given a chance to respond. Yet because of its brevity, the denial would not necessitate frantic revisions or a long additional story.

The cautious response was not surprising. As a Gannett functionary Gage had limited authority. The safe course was to run things up the corporate hierarchy until someone formulated an official response, which he would then represent. By quickly and tersely defending his employer and then seeking instructions from above, Gage was just doing what any prudent company man would do.

With this warning our foe was on guard, and readying a defense. Even so, I was glad the deed was done. I had been dreading it since the first days of the project. Now I need dread it no more. "Well, that's that," I said. "I guess we'll find out Sunday who fires the first shot, but there's nothing to do about it now. Speaking of Sunday, the first pages of 'It's Now or Never!' will be pasted up that evening. When do you want to have a look at them?"

"That's tricky," Frank said slowly. "I told one of my daughters I'd take her to Chicago on Sunday for a performance of the symphony."

A performance of the symphony! Just when I thought I had exhausted my capacity to be befuddled by anything Frank did, he fooled me again. With all that was riding on the Green Bay Project, it was inconceivable that he would not want to see the product itself, the instrument designed to give his *News-Chronicle* its one chance at life. But instead he would be keeping a promise to a daughter. I heard the low murmur of deep currents, which every family has and which must be navigated.

"Well, whatever works. The pages will be ready that evening. If you can make it, fine. If not, don't worry about it. You'll be seeing them Monday morning—like the rest of Green Bay."

"If you want me to, I'll try to get back early from Chicago."

If I want you to? Oh, Frank, that's not it, not it at all. Don't do it for me, do it for yourself. I personally would be incapable of not looking at the pages before they went to press. But you are wired differently. I never have really understood your connection to this project, and I guess I never will.

When Frank left I drafted a brief article presenting Gage's denial. A few minutes later it was in type. All the pieces for the first day's report were in hand. Returning to my room I passed Lyle Lahey's workstation. We had barely spoken since I replaced him with Betsy James, but now he called me over. "Here are the little graphics," he said, handing me a folder. Inside were three nicely crafted works. After his hurtful dismissal I had expected no further contribution from Lahey, and was prepared to get by without these illustrations. But how glad I was to have them. They were strong and bold and just right. They would indeed sharpen the report.

"Thanks, Lyle. These are terrific," I said without exaggeration. "They help a lot." After all this while, he had finally climbed aboard the Green Bay Project.

35

Five Smooth Stones

WELL INTO THE NIGHT I finalized layouts, headlines, and photo captions. When I went into production the next morning, not the smallest detail could be overlooked. Keeping me company was the radio. But this night it was tuned not to Wisconsin Public Radio but a Top 40 station, which every fifteen or twenty minutes sounded the message: "On Monday, November 27, the *Green Bay News-Chronicle* will make the most important announcement in its history. DON'T MISS IT!"

The same message was popping on half a dozen other stations and three television channels. It would continue to pop through the weekend. When Monday morning rolled around, the city should have a monstrous collective itch, which could be scratched only by the first day's installment of "It's Now or Never!"

By eight o'clock Saturday morning I was "on the boards"—newspaper lingo for the production paste-up tables. Because the *News-Chronicle* had no Sunday issue the production staff did not work Saturdays, so I had the big gloomy basement almost totally to myself. My only companion was the typesetter Floyd Ferdon, who was working on overtime to provide me with every last line of type I needed.

As always in the final production push, everything took longer than expected. Headlines did not quite fit. Typographical errors leaped embarrassingly from the galley proofs. Cutlines came out too long, or too short, to fit the pictures. Postponed details arose by the dozen, and every one had to be accounted for before Floyd left.

I had assured Floyd he would be finished by noon. As 2 P.M. came and went, with no break for lunch, his normally imperturbable disposition was fraying. Asking him to come back that evening was out of the question. The next day was even more impossible, for he was going deer hunting at dawn. So I racked my brains for one last list of things, thanked him for his exceptional services, and turned him loose at three o'clock.

Through a long afternoon and evening I found that my paste-up skills were rusty. But I still knew what I was doing. Under my slow hands the report finally assumed tangible form.

The paste-up process is a grown-up version of playing with paper dolls. Every item that the reader sees on the page—each story, headline, photograph, caption, box, border, graphic—begins as a separate piece of paper. Each piece is waxed to hold it in place, each black line is drawn with adhesive tape. Columns of text and illustrations are only as perfectly squared off as the paste-up technician makes them. The work is exacting. Specialists can fly through it. As an out-of-training semipro, I struggled.

When I knocked off at ten o'clock, the job was not finished. But I felt good about it. All four first-day pages were blocked out. Everything fit, headlines and graphics were in place, and apparently my final list to the typesetter had been complete. Most important, the pages looked good. Damn good. Many final touches remained undone. But that was Sunday's work.

I slept late the next morning, then tore through the Sunday *Press-Gazette,* to see if Gannett had tried to deflect the attack. Nothing, not a word. Perfect. I treated myself to a big truck-stop breakfast. Noon was near as I returned to the boards, but time was no problem. Three or four hours should wrap things up.

The moment I entered the basement I knew something was wrong. Water was standing on the floor and dripping from a dozen points overhead. A large, wet section of ceiling had collapsed onto the typesetting machines. The hiss of running water could be heard. My God, had Gannett sabotaged us? Instantly I dismissed the idea as preposterous. No, apparently a water pipe had burst in the night. But even if accidental, this could be disastrous. If water had dripped onto my pages, they would be ruined.

Everything—the type, the headlines, the photostats, the paste-up—would have to be redone from scratch. And there was no way to get it done that day. Floyd, the only typesetter with access to the "Now or Never" file, was off in the woods. If the water had found my pages, the "most important announcement in the history of the *Green Bay News-Chronicle*" would not come on Monday, November 27, as promised, but a mortifying day later. "It's Now or Never!" would make its entrance with a pratfall.

My work area was just ahead in the wet darkness. Afraid to switch on the lights for fear of sparking a fire, I approached the shadowed pages with trembling. They were dry! Running along beams, pipes, and ceiling frames, the water oozed and dripped all over the production room. But not upon "It's Now or Never!"

I called a maintenance man, from a number on a bulletin board. He quickly repaired the leak, which turned out to be minor. By late afternoon the pages were ready. As I reviewed them, the night production crew arrived. Most were women, working this low-wage job for a second income in the family. Two of them came over. "Mind if we have a look?"

And at long last, I did not mind. Nothing in the world is less secret than the front page of a newspaper, and that was where "It's Now or Never!" would be in a few hours. Later this very night, as the fiercely guarded report passed through the composing room and then the darkroom and finally the press room, there would be no way to keep Brown County Publishing Company's workers from seeing it and talking about it. Nor was there any reason to. The time for secrecy was, blessedly, over at last.

Word of my unveiled project flew through the production room. Within minutes every one of the dozen workers had checked it out. "Wow." "Strong stuff." "It's about time." "So that's what you've been working on." "Nice job." Praise flowed from these strangers, who until this moment had regarded me with suspicion. Even more surprisingly, they treated me as a fellow worker—although I did not know their names and they were not comfortable using mine.

I gave the pages to the night-crew chief, and withdrew to my room. Now the task hard at hand was publicity. The more publicity we could focus on "It's Now or Never!" the more effective it would be. I began addressing manila envelopes, to Wisconsin's major dailies, to the wire services, to national newspapers such as the *Wall Street Journal* and *New York Times,* to publishing-industry journals. Even to *Editor & Publisher.* Every story written about "It's Now or Never!" would spread the word about Gannett. Preparing the media kit was routine work: a cover letter, a list of contacts, photocopied clips for background—and tomorrow morning, I would enclose the first-day segment of "It's Now or Never!" After all that had gone before, this was a form of decompression.

The Green Bay Project was actually in place and locked down. Hard to believe. The only absent ingredient was a dispensable one, Frank Wood's stamp of approval on the finished product, the pages in the basement. Then he called. He was back from Chicago, and was at the printing plant down the street. A television news team had contacted him, and was doing a story on the ten o'clock news. Did I want to watch it with him and Agnes on the TV at the plant?

An icy slush was falling as I drove the familiar road. The news account excited us. Short on specifics, it played the "most important announcement" teaser spot, then predicted that "an old-fashioned newspaper war" was about to erupt. Interviewed on camera, Frank merely urged everyone not to miss tomorrow's paper. Skeletal as it was, the newscast was another confirmation that there was no turning back. "Well, the fat's in the fire now, and the shit's about to hit the fan," I chortled, in an outrageous mix of metaphors.

"The roads are getting bad," Frank said as he switched the TV off. "But I could still look at the pages if you want me to."

That phrase again. "No, I think they came out fine. We're all getting up early tomorrow, and you can see them then. Why don't you go home and get a good night's sleep in the meantime?"

"Well, that would be easier, if you don't mind."

The slush was crusting the roads as we walked to our cars. I handed Frank an envelope. "Don't open this right away," I said. "Wait until you get home, or until tomorrow morning."

He was puzzled, which was understandable, for I had sprung the envelope without warning. He might have thought it held my letter of resignation, or a rebuke for his lack of interest in the pages. It held neither, but I did not want to watch him open it. Inside was the passage I had found in First Samuel. Driving to my room, I tried to imagine Frank contemplating the verse:

> And he took his staff in his hand, and chose him five smooth stones out of the brook, and put them in a shepherd's bag which he had, even in a scrip; and his sling was in his hand: and he drew near to the Philistine.

36

"We Have Got a Fight on Our Hands!"

IN THE PREDAWN DARKNESS OF Monday, November 27, 1989, the street light outside my window illuminated a cold, white world. I pictured *News-Chronicle* delivery trucks skidding and crashing all over Green Bay on this "most important" day in the paper's history. But when I hit the roads at 5:30, I noted with relief that they were not frozen over, and the storm was dissipating.

The presses had rolled in the night. "It's Now or Never!" was ready for presentation to the world. All hands were under orders to assemble at the office at eight o'clock, but the circulation crew had to get going hours earlier. I decided to come in at six. After four months on the Green Bay Project, I could not miss this part of the show. Driving in, I learned by radio that yesterday's prelude to our event had turned out fine. The Packers had won by one point, and now were in first place. Playoff ticket orders were being taken.

The *News-Chronicle* was in a frenzy. Half a dozen delivery vans stood in rough formation while their drivers heaved bundles of newspapers aboard. Waiting in line were as many more unmarked cars and trucks, recruited for duty on this extraordinary morning. Each time a vehicle pulled out, another took its place. Inside the small wooden dispatch station, all was controlled bedlam. Big hand-lettered signs indicated delivery routes and the number of papers each needed. Workers jammed the cramped quarters, two big coffee pots percolated, and doughnuts were free for the taking.

I grabbed a loose copy of the paper to see the work my hands had wrought. It did come on strong. The four tabloid pages of the opening day's report "wrapped" the *News-Chronicle,* in a front and back cover. Page one was dominated by the photo of the staff, arms folded in defiance. Emblazoned above them in huge black letters was the battle cry "IT'S NOW

OR NEVER!" Then Frank Wood's voice: "I think the *Press-Gazette* is trying to destroy us."

The remaining three pages defined "It's Now or Never!" One article was about Gannett. Another gave the history of the *News-Chronicle*. Another told how the *Press-Gazette* gained the city printing contract. And a commentary posed the central question:

> The American economic system is based on competition: the idea that companies selling against each other will offer their goods and services at the best possible price, to hold their share of the market. In theory, this system provides the most good for the most people. But when the practices of a huge, nationwide, multi-billion-dollar conglomerate systematically cut off the few sources of revenue that a small, local competitor must have to even exist, is this good, clean, American business, or is it something sinister?

Frank was at the circulation shed. "It's overwhelming!" he said. "And the note you gave me—thank you. It meant a lot." *You're welcome, Frank,* I replied silently. *You're welcome. We are in this thing together at last, aren't we?* Al Rasmussen joined the bustle, and Chris Wood and Floyd Ferdon and Lyle Lahey. And the too-busy editor and workers who had cold-shouldered me, and company officers who had resisted the Green Bay Project. Each new arrival devoured the report, then complimented me.

The trucks and cars kept rolling. Newsstands received double or triple their normal quota of newspapers. Coin boxes all over town were packed, and emblazoned with an electric-blue placard proclaiming: "TODAY'S THE DAY! Read all about it!" Stacks of papers were dropped off at coffee shops and restaurants. At paper mills, packing plants, and factories, free copies were handed to workers arriving at eight or going home from the graveyard shift.

On a radio at the command post, the "newspaper war" was the top story on the seven o'clock news. The sketchy account, skimmed from "It's Now or Never!," sent a ripple through the crew. And through me. No doubt about it: We were wired. At eight o'clock scores of *News-Chronicle* and Brown County Publishing workers packed the newsroom, the only space large enough to hold them. The meeting started just a little late. Frank was on the telephone, fielding a call from United Press International.

When he took his place before his staff, there was fire in Frank's eyes. "My friends," he said, with a cutting edge to his soft voice. "We have got a fight on our hands!" And the hands of those who listened erupted in spontaneous applause.

"The *News-Chronicle* is fighting for its life. That is not an exaggeration. The *Press-Gazette* and Gannett are deliberately trying to make it impossible for us to survive in Green Bay. They've been doing it for years. And they've come pretty damn close to pulling it off. But now we have a little surprise for them: We're fed up, and we're not going to take it anymore!" There was more applause.

"You all have known that something special has been in the works for weeks. I know you've all been talking about it, and wondering what it was. I also know that you haven't liked the secrecy. 'That's not our way of doing business,' I know you've been saying. Well, you're right—it isn't, although there was a reason for it. But now the secret can be told. From now on, the battle is in the open. And we have all the ammunition we need to make it a good one! We have it because of one man."

Frank spoke my name, and called me to join him at the front of the room. I waved him off, and kept my place in the rear. This was not my moment, these were not my people, the *News-Chronicle* was not my newspaper, Green Bay was not my town. Now that Frank was taking full command, it was my turn to feel oddly detached from the project that had consumed me for so long. I was linked to it only by my work, which was out there for all to see. It must stand or fall on its own. Instead of an honored guest I felt like an outsider at this party. I waved Frank off a second time. He continued without me.

"This report will tell Green Bay what it needs to know about Gannett. And it will tell us what we need to know about Green Bay. If the town gets mad and rallies behind us, then we'll give the *Press-Gazette* a run for the money yet. But if no one gives a damn, if subscribers and advertisers don't respond to 'It's Now or Never!,' then that will be their message.

"But I say they will respond. I say we will pull this thing out. The key is right here in this room. It is you—all of you. This report should wake up Green Bay. But that is not a solution, only an opportunity. The rest is up to you. If we're going to survive, every one of you must do your job as though our life depended on it. Because it does.

"But let me tell you something: I know you can do it. I don't have any doubt. I know what you face each day at work: substandard pay, long hours, old equipment, an uphill struggle. But look what we've done in spite of it all! Now we have a chance to do better, to get the *News-Chronicle* back on its feet. It won't be easy—but what has ever been easy around here? Gannett will fight us every inch of the way. But we'll take whatever they throw at us, and keep fighting. And now, for once, we're the ones on the attack.

"It's like the headline says, my friends: It's now or never. But I say it's now, and I say we can win. We have got a fight on our hands, and this is all I ask: Lead, follow or get out of the way!" A final, sustained round of applause filled the room. Everyone seemed thrilled by Frank's call to arms. I knew I was. The old king had regained his powers, and woe betide his foe.

When Frank stopped speaking, Al Rasmussen moved through the assembled workers, giving each a round, two-inch metal badge that proclaimed "It's Now or Never!" in white letters on a field of black. Like a sheriff in a western movie, he was deputizing the townsfolk to ride in the posse. I laughed with pleasure when I got mine. I had not known they were coming.

Immediately afterward, Frank and I met with a reporter from the *Press-Gazette*. Frank knew him, and once had bought a weekly from him. I was glad the Gannett paper was covering "It's Now or Never!" I wanted this story to be the biggest one in Green Bay, impossible to ignore. Frank was still in fighting form. I let him do all the talking to the apologetic reporter. "It's Now or Never!" needed only one voice, and that voice was his, not mine.

The radio brought a fuller news account as I drove back to Denmark. Good. Getting the word out was the current item of business. The report went into the waiting media packages, which were shipped at once. As I left Federal Express the morning's euphoria was fading fast. But there was no rest for the weary: The next day's installment had to be pasted up that afternoon.

At lunch I read the Gannett paper's brief report, which had been rushed into print. "It's Our Job to Compete, *Press-Gazette* Publisher Says," stated the headline, and the story was defensive: "The *Green Bay Press-Gazette* is not trying to eliminate competition in the daily newspaper business, Publisher Michael Gage said today. 'It's simply not true. It's our job and our right to compete. That's what we've done and what we are going to continue to do,' Gage said."

Only after that confusing start did the eight-inch story reveal that the *News-Chronicle* had accused the Gannett paper of the things Gage denied. And that was the full article. It was exactly what I wanted on this first day. No preloaded counterattack and no surprises.

On the paste-up boards after lunch, everything was different. The room swarmed with workers, who smiled and welcomed me, and thanked me and offered to help with my work. But doing it myself was faster, and time was tight. Instead of two full days for this session, I had just the afternoon and evening. My work pace quickened.

The night crew came on, reporting that all the television stations had led with "It's Now or Never!" on the six o'clock news. To catch the ten o'clock wrap-ups, I hurried even faster. Our story remained atop the late-evening news, with both Frank Wood and Michael Gage on camera. "Wood declined to say how long the attack on his competitor would continue," the announcer intoned. "But he promised there was more to come."

37

"You're Greedy and Afraid"

THE NEXT MORNING'S PACKAGE DEMONSTRATED that because of the competition in Green Bay, the *Press-Gazette* was charging far lower advertising rates than any comparably sized paper in the chain; revealed what Gannett had done in Salem; noted the many awards won by the *News-Chronicle;* disclosed that deliberate lies had been planted by the *Press-Gazette;* and listed nine specific actions that readers could take to help the *News-Chronicle* survive. Yes, I felt, that should be enough to keep the ball rolling.

All through the week the ball kept gaining momentum. By the end of the second day, fourteen media outlets had been in touch. Among them were papers in Milwaukee, Madison, and other Wisconsin cities, as well as Milwaukee television stations, the Associated Press, and my own primary news source, Wisconsin Public Radio. National journalism trade journals began preparing stories for the next issue.

On the streets of Green Bay, the response was electric. "Everybody in town is talking!" Frank reported gleefully. And people were putting their money where their mouths were. Within two days the *News-Chronicle* gained more than eighty new subscribers, and half a dozen advertisers notified Frank that they would start using the paper. The most heartwarming call came from a bowling league president, proposing a subscription drive in all the city's lanes. Not even the calendar slowed things down. Green Bay seemed willing to put the Christmas season on hold.

On the evening of the second day, a student approached Frank at the college. He was a desk clerk at the Marriott Inn, and he thought Frank might want to know that five "top executives" from Gannett headquarters in Virginia had checked in that afternoon. Nervously we waited for Gannett's heavy boot to come down. But as more days passed without retaliation, we realized that despite the flying squad, the official response was going to be no response.

A spokeswoman at headquarters told Associated Press that the chain's policy was not to comment on the "local affairs" of its individual newspapers. She referred all inquiries to the Green Bay publisher, Gage, who insisted repeatedly that there was no attempt to drive the *News-Chronicle* under. Sometimes Gage expanded his remarks, taking a magnanimous tone that undoubtedly had been approved higher up. "I think it's a very unique competitive move," he characterized the *News-Chronicle* report to one interviewer. "I can take a pretty good punch, even if I bleed a little bit, and keep on competing. And that is what I am going to do—keep on competing."

As defender of his newspaper and his chain, Gage showed nimble footwork. Yes, he had once put a stop to lies being told by his staff against the *News-Chronicle*, he said, but he could not remember the details. The fact that his paper's rates were dramatically lower than Gannett's norm, he said, merely "displays what a good terrific buy we are in the marketplace." Gage criticized Frank and "It's Now or Never!" for examining Gannett nationwide: "Most of what he's run has to do with other things in other states. It hasn't much to do with Green Bay." Yet for the part that was local, Gage declared that he had no intention of issuing daily responses to the report's accusations.

I understood Gannett's strategy. Protesting "It's Now or Never!" from headquarters would only draw more attention to the struggle in Green Bay. By treating it as a tempest in a teapot, Gannett hoped to ignore it out of existence. This was the tactic used in Salem, and after some brief embarrassment it had worked.

I had mixed feelings about what was and was not happening. Part of me was scrapping for Gannett to take us on, in print or in court, to get our fight into the national spotlight. But I also was glad not to be dodging counterfire. In its absence the Green Bay Project could proceed as planned. Each new morning brought a new installment of "It's Now or Never!" Each day's package included a national story about Gannett's ways, a local story about Gannett's ways, and another chapter in the story of Brown County Publishing Company.

Was it good journalism? I wondered about that. Measured against the ideal of pure objectivity, it was not. This was not impartial and evenhanded reporting. This was journalism with an undisguised bias. Yet the information supporting the bias was true. "It's Now or Never!" was not disinterested reportage but a cause. Its cause was saving the *News-Chronicle*. It sought to provoke in those who read it three reactions: outrage at Gannett, compassion for the *News-Chronicle,* and a conclusion that the ways of the largest chain were unacceptable—in Green Bay or anywhere.

Evidence that the message was getting through mounted daily. Each new *News-Chronicle* subscriber or advertiser reconfirmed it. But the strongest proof appeared where least expected: on the pages of the *Press-Gazette*. Just days after "It's Now or Never!" broke, furious letters to the editor were swamping that newspaper's opinion section.

Like the non-response response to our accusations, printing these letters was a calculated gamble, no doubt approved at headquarters. Every inch of space given to irate critics of Gannett's Green Bay operation was fuel for the flames. Yet squelching the letters was untenable. Many had been sent in duplicate to both newspapers. If only the *News-Chronicle* ran them, Gannett would stand convicted of cowardice.

Clearly Gannett's best course was to acknowledge some criticism and weather the storm. It was also the right thing to do, which presumably was important to some members of the *Press-Gazette* staff—another factor in the call. Whatever the reasons, the paper gave full airing to several critics. I wondered how many other protests never saw print.

The letters came from all corners of Green Bay. With one exception I recognized none of the writers. Their syntax was unpolished and unprofessional, yet all cared enough to sign their names to a public testimonial. With satisfaction I read their homespun, eloquent expressions of concern:

> I am absolutely appalled to find out some of the things that have been printed about your paper recently. Even more appalling is the fact that I made some phone calls to check and see if those allegations are true—and they are.
>
> Lying, cheating and undermining your competition only makes you, the *Green Bay Press-Gazette,* appear to be afraid of the *Green Bay News-Chronicle.* Tell me, what is a paper with less than 10 percent of the market share going to do to you? It's hard to imagine why you would be afraid.
>
> Lying, cheating and undermining your competition only shows that your firm lacks the originality, confidence and fortitude it takes to survive in a competitive environment. You're greedy and afraid. Nothing I ever want to be a part of again.

> Shafting—that's what the *Green Bay Press-Gazette* has been doing ever since Gannett Co. has taken over. You keep raising your [subscription] rates because the revenue intake wasn't there. So—the daily subscriber is being used to keep revenue up, while the *Press* reduces their rates to advertisers in order to ruin competitors. Yet year after year, Gannett earnings have increased.

You sound like the little boy who kept crying wolf.

I do not like the tactics used by the Green Bay *Press-Gazette* in its bid to run the Green Bay *News-Chronicle* out of business. I had been approached with a sweet deal by the *Press-Gazette* myself, but turned it down because I felt the tactics being used to get my business from the *Chronicle* were in poor taste.

I decided to stick with the *Chronicle,* and the *Press-Gazette* forgot about me when they realized my business wasn't big enough for them anyway. I think it's funny how the *Press-Gazette* wouldn't even budge on their outrageous quote they gave me before I used the *Chronicle.* What a difference the *Chronicle* makes when dealing with the *Press-Gazette.*

I hope people realize how important it is to have competition, and support the Green Bay *News-Chronicle* in its struggle to survive against the Gannett *Gazette.*

This is an open letter to the *Green Bay Press-Gazette,* Gannett Co. Inc. and the *Press-Gazette*'s readers, editor and advertisers.

We believe that Gannett is attempting to build a newspaper monopoly in Green Bay by forcing the *News-Chronicle* out of business. Since we subscribe to the *News-Chronicle,* we'd like the *Gazette*'s readers to know that we feel our right to choose a source for local news is being infringed upon by the newspaper they support through their subscriptions. We want the businesses and services who advertise in the *Gazette* to know that their advertisements will not reach us if they advertise only in the *Gazette.* And we want the *Gazette*'s editor and Gannett to know that we detest the philosophy behind this attempt to limit our access to local news and services.

We will not purchase the *Press-Gazette* should it become the only local newspaper. And we would surely regret the loss of the independent voice that the *News-Chronicle* offers to this community should it be forced out.

I believe that Gannett, through the *Green Bay Press-Gazette,* is trying to bump off the *News-Chronicle.* As a result, I will not use your paper for advertising or anything else until the mess is cleared up and Gannett has made amends to the *News-Chronicle.* You might consider using some of your evil energy improving your paper, rather than attacking a competitor, as the main reason we left your fold was that you stank.

In closing, I would like to add that the only thing I hate worse than a bully is a greedy bully.

And on the letters went. I relished them all, but one stood out as my favorite—not for its vehemence, its rhetoric, or even its content, but for the identity of its writer.

> In view of the Gannett tactics being described in the *Green Bay News-Chronicle,* it'll be a sad day in Mudville if the *News-Chronicle* goes under. Brown County advertisers can expect to swallow substantially increased advertising costs which will almost certainly be reflected in their prices, and Brown County readers will face a journalistic future probably patterned after *USA Today.* A bleak prospect.

It was signed by Jack FitzGerald. Like Lyle Lahey before him, the stern lawyer who had been so sure that the Green Bay Project was a mistake could now be counted among its supporters.

38

"I Think We Have a Chance"

THE REST OF THE REPORT flew by so fast I could barely keep up. Every day Chris Wood brought something new. Now that they knew what was happening, Brown County Publishing employees were eager to talk of their dealings with Gannett. Their input toughened the report, but meant more rewrite, legal review, and typesetting. Each night I wrote late, each morning I was on the phone with the lawyers. Every afternoon and evening found me on the boards, pasting up the next installment. This part, however, had become fun. My skills improved daily, and the production workers embraced me into their boisterous camaraderie. No longer the resented outsider, I was now their pal. They rushed over to see my pages each night.

Monday through Friday, November 27 to December 1, the first week of "It's Now or Never!" hammered Gannett and the *Press-Gazette*. The weekend brought a welcome breather. The series was not going to run in Saturday's paper, and there was no Sunday edition. Yet I could not afford to rest. A second week was still to come, and an imperative need was disturbingly unaccounted for. The report had to end with a bang. Its summation must be strong enough to linger after "It's Now or Never!" was over. This was the most important piece. It had not yet been produced.

"It ought to be in your words, Frank," I insisted.

"Do you have any ideas?" he responded. "Maybe we could work together on it, like we did on the opening statement."

"No, Frank, not this time. This one really has to be you. You are the man who lives here, who loves this community, who built Brown County Publishing Company. You are the one to sum it up."

"I don't know what to say. I don't write much anymore."

"Then keep thinking about it. Go down deep, and don't come up until you have it. There has got to be some reason why you are spending all this money, taking all these risks, doing this thing that no one has ever done before. Just put that reason down on paper. When you do, we will have exactly what we need."

"I'll try. But why don't you keep thinking about it, too?"

If I had not already worked past it, my exasperation might have overcome me. One piece, one article from his own desk, was finally all I was asking Frank to give to the printed record of the Green Bay Project. Yet even that was a pledge he would not make. I was past the point of letting frustration deter the goal—which was to give "It's Now or Never!" a closing kick. Yet for reasons unclear to me, I was unwilling to write another statement for Frank's signature. Still, we had to close with something.

Words began building up. I went to my Smith-Corona. Like water overrunning a dam, they poured forth:

> Who are these people, these people from Gannett?
> What is it that drives them?
> Why do they want to destroy us?
> These are questions worth pondering.
>
> Clearly not for its own survival does the *Press-Gazette* need to take all our business away. We pose no danger to them. There is no way that a paper our size could threaten one 10 times larger, backed by the nation's biggest chain. This is not some clash-to-the-death between titans, from which only one can walk away. Nor have we prevented them from turning a profit, a multimillion-dollar profit, year after year. That's not it.
>
> So why do they want to destroy us?
>
> The most obvious reason is that Gannett wants a monopoly here, like it has in 81 other cities. No doubt about it, they can make even more money with us rubbed out. But is money so important that these people stop at nothing to get it? Is greed the only thing they know?
>
> Maybe money is not the only reason. Maybe they want to eliminate us for the sport of it, to say they beat somebody. But can they really think that closing down a company and throwing Green Bay people out of work is the same thing as the Packers beating the Bears?
>
> Can they take pride in defeating an opponent so much smaller? Did no one ever tell them they should pick on somebody their own size? Is the concept of fair play outside their understanding? Have they never heard of live and let live?
>
> Maybe they think of themselves as hunters, and are after us for the sheer love of the chase. Maybe we are just a trophy to them. Maybe these Gannett people gather at the corporate lodge and sip brandy in front of the corporate fireplace, bragging about the little companies they ran to earth and then put down.
>
> Perhaps we are an embarrassment. Maybe it's that simple. With only two non-monopoly newspapers in the whole Gannett chain, maybe the *Press-Gazette* has a hard time explaining why it is one of them.

We know that not everybody at the *Press Gazette* is out to get us. It's a big outfit over there, and most of its employees are decent and hard-working. So who are these others, who stalk our customers? Who figure out that our printing plant and country newspapers help the failing *News-Chronicle* survive, and so plot ways to break those operations too? Who will not rest until we're gone?

Do these people ever look into their hearts, and question the values they live by?

Who are these people from Gannett?

And why do they serve death, and not life?

The piece flowed out in one string. Usually this indicated a visit from the Muse, a touch of inspiration. But this time I was not sure. These words might be too hot. Over the weekend I let them cool down. Yet each time I came back, I liked them more. On Monday I gave them to the typesetter. "This was the best one yet," he said. His endorsement tipped the scales. Whatever Frank did or did not do, "It's Now or Never!" had its final punch.

I made a copy, but postponed giving it to Frank. I feared it might be too strong for his taste. In any event, it was not to run until Friday. No need for him to see it before Thursday.

Meanwhile, Green Bay kept responding. The *News-Chronicle*'s coin boxes kept selling out. New subscribers signed up daily. The paper's pages showed a surge of local advertising. Major accounts called to discuss programs in the next quarter. Other stores were now at least willing to make appointments to talk. And the Packers kept helping us, winning yet again, by just one point, for their best late-season record in fourteen years.

Frank reported comments from everyone he knew: students and faculty at St. Norbert College, business associates, church members, Agnes's friends, civic club leaders inviting him to speak at upcoming meetings. "All of them are on our side," he said. "They're saying this is the gutsiest thing they've ever seen."

In my smaller circles I too was noting a distinct reaction. Far beyond the paste-up area, Brown County Publishing Company now claimed me as its own. Wherever I went, smiles welcomed me—from the office staff, from the printing crew, from the darkroom, from the board of directors, from the pretty blonde in advertising and her fellow sales representatives. People I had not met introduced themselves, and thanked me. In the parking lot, strangers waved. Even in the village of Denmark there was a change. At the grocery, the gas station, and the quick-stop, people smiled and said hello.

On Thursday Frank surprised me. "Here's my piece," he said. I had by now assumed there would be nothing from him. My essay was ready to conclude the report. His contribution now seemed superfluous. And worse, what if it missed the mark entirely? But of course I had to take it. Moreover, it forced my hand. "Good, Frank. I knew you'd come through. Now here's something I did, to also appear on the last day. Let me know what you think."

As soon as Frank left I apprehensively skimmed his statement. But it was splendid. In his own language, from his heart, Frank had written down exactly what he wanted to say. He had accepted the challenge totally, and found inside himself the reason.

The phone rang. Frank was calling from the printing plant. "I just read your piece," he said. "I have real problems with it. It's really asking for trouble. I don't think we should use it."

"I don't know, Frank. I like it a lot." But I was not sure. I knew it pushed the line. And as of one moment ago, I also realized that his own statement, in its heartfelt simplicity, was more powerful than mine. He had caught me in a vulnerable moment. I did not know whether to fight for both or abandon mine in favor of his. Then Frank spared me the struggle.

"Well, if you feel that way about it, I won't object," he said. "With all you've invested in this project, you've got one coming. So let's go with it—and to hell with the consequences."

Like the opening segment, the final installment was a four-page wrap-around for the *News-Chronicle*. Highlighted in red ink, it recapped the entire report. Capsules of local cases filled one page. Betsy James's images lined up in dark formation on another. A reprise photo of the defiant staff shared the third page with my commentary. The last page showed Frank at his cluttered desk. Alongside the photo ran his closing statement.

> Well, here it is. Today brings the end of our 10-part look at Gannett, the *Press-Gazette* and the *News-Chronicle*. It has been a monumental piece of work, involving nearly four months of research and writing.
>
> At the beginning of the series I said it's now or never for this newspaper. It really is. We've done our best to tell you our story, in the belief that you would agree with us and care enough to help save this paper.
>
> I've lived in Brown County more than 36 years. My wife and I reared our eight kids here. We've all found it to be a good part of the world, a good community to grow up in. Agnes and I plan to live out our lives here.

American business has always had problems with where to draw the line between what is right and what is wrong. In recent years there have been many cases of corruption that surfaced in both business and government.

People working in either area are making moral and ethical judgments every day, and inevitably make some bad calls. But it is my belief that Gannett's way of business amounts to more than this. They not only don't know where the line is, they are too arrogant to care.

I've looked upon our industry as one with an extra dimension to it. I consider this paper a stewardship. I want it to continue. We might not make it. We'll see. If the response so far is any measure, we've got a chance. If it continues as it has begun, I believe we can make it.

And if we do, to paraphrase Mark Twain's comment upon hearing that he had died, "The reports of our death will have been greatly exaggerated."

After the final segment of "It's Now or Never!" Frank and I both were exhausted. Twenty-four full pages had been devoted to the special report, thirty-four different articles. We had shot our wad. "I've given this town everything I have," Frank said. "If the people of Green Bay don't care enough to help me now, then screw 'em!"

39

Vanity and Vexation of Spirit

PACKING TO LEAVE SEEMED TO take forever, and was a dreary process. It should have been a joyful time—my work was done, it had been pronounced worthy, and I was preparing to return to Santa Fe. Yet the sense of anticlimax was heavy in the days that followed "It's Now or Never!"

I crashed down hard after the last segment. Mind, body, and soul all seemed mired in a bog through the weekend that followed. But on Monday I was back at work, mopping up. The full twenty-four-page report had to be pulled back together, to be reprinted in the weekly *Brown County Chronicle*. Also, there were memos. As in the Green Bay Project's early days, long memos were again issuing from my desk. They now concerned follow-up, which seemed vital if "It's Now or Never!" was to have lasting effect.

Advertising promotions should come each month. Visits to headquarters of chain stores must be made. Numbers should be run for every Gannett advertiser, showing how much money the *News-Chronicle* was saving him or her. Circulation must be boosted. The bowling subscription drive should start at once. House ads must fan the flames. The news staff should keep tabs on Gannett's troubles elsewhere. Frank should speak at civic clubs.

But even as my fingers moved across the keyboard, a sense of futility oppressed me. Yes, the special report had stirred up more of a ruckus than I had expected. Yes, the results so far were heartening. Yes, the *News-Chronicle* had a better chance now than it had before. But the forces against it were too strong.

Though we had distracted Green Bay briefly from the holiday season, the Christmas rush would now return. In January the Super Bowl would dominate this football-crazy city, whether or not the Packers were in it—and now it looked like they would not be. Two days after "It's Now or Never!" ended, Green Bay was stomped by Kansas City, 21–3, the worst loss of the year. With the early defeats, that game all but ended Green Bay's hopes. Making the playoffs was still possible, but now depended as much on other teams losing games as the Pack winning its last two.

Reality was returning with a thud.

By the time the football season and the holidays were over, Frank Wood's valiant charge would be but a fading memory. Then the newspaper life of Green Bay would return to normal. Readers would again be preoccupied with their own problems. Advertisers would forget that Frank's paper was saving them millions of dollars, and would "economize" by cutting it out of the budget again.

Only an obsessive, never-flagging dedication to the struggle could deliver lasting results. Yet as I looked around Brown County Publishing, I did not see the necessary ardor. Frank was still swamped with other duties. Chris had the fire but not the experience. Al Rasmussen was needed elsewhere. Everyone in the company, in fact, already had too much to do. Moreover, these people were workers, not fighters. They brought energy and competence to their jobs, but not a zeal for battle.

Tellingly, two *News-Chronicle* workers took jobs at the *Press-Gazette* even while the report was running. Both gave the same reason for going: more money, more opportunity. When the chips are down, I mused, self-interest will beat a noble cause every time.

I looked at my lists of suggestions, certain that few would ever be implemented. Force of habit was powerful. Like the rest of Green Bay, Brown County Publishing would be falling back into its old patterns just about the same time my car hit the city limits.

I was discouraged also by the media. After the initial flurry of interest, the press had moved on to other things. Although more than two dozen news organizations—local, state, and national—had covered the struggle in Green Bay, not one had really dug into it. Without exception, the media had treated the story as "breaking news," to be covered on the run with little or no depth. Rather than using the report's disclosures as a starting point to look further into the largest newspaper company, the journalistic community contented itself with wrapping everything up at once, within the obvious David-and-Goliath metaphor.

In–a–highly–unusual–move–the–publisher–of–the–tiny–*Green–Bay–News–Chronicle*–has–charged–in–print–that–the–competing–*Green–Bay–Press–Gazette*–owned–by–the–huge–Gannett–chain–is–intentionally–trying–to–run–him–out–of–business, a typical story would report. When –reached–for–comment–the–Gannett–publisher–denied–the–charges–and –said–his–newspaper–was–merely–competing–fairly–and–aggressively–and–would–continue–to–do–so.

Although each account had individual touches, none deviated from this basic structure. Green Bay's newspaper war was treated like a neighborhood spat or routine court case. Both combatants got a chance to have their say, but there was no deeper inquiry. There, that's that, the media seemed to say, washing their hands of the matter. We've treated the story objectively and impartially, told both sides of it, and now must get on with tomorrow's news. Nobody checked out the report's accusations, or even spelled out what they were.

I knew that "It's Now or Never!" was by definition suspect, because it was blatantly self-serving. The case it made on its own behalf would need to withstand tough scrutiny to be advanced by other elements of the press. Yet despite these obstacles, I still was dismayed that not a single major news outlet found the nature of the nation's biggest chain worthy of further examination.

I had hoped that the independent Milwaukee newspapers, which considered themselves statewide, might assign an in-depth report for a Sunday issue. I thought perhaps the *New York Times* or *Wall Street Journal* might look into national implications. I expected only perfunctory coverage from *Editor & Publisher,* but hoped more aggressive journals like *Columbia Journalism Review* might do more. Perhaps because of its long-standing animosity toward Gannett, the *Washington Post* did send a writer to Green Bay. But although her story was fuller and better written than some of the others, it too failed to dig beyond the surface confrontation.

I recognized that the story was troublesome, professionally sensitive, nonfraternal. Nevertheless, I expected some editor, somewhere, to pick up our ball and run with it. But nobody did.

"It's Now or Never!" did generate bad publicity for Gannett. It did get my research on the record. Anyone investigating the chain in the future could find the report on microfilm in Green Bay. Yet in the short term, in the absence of major media follow-up, it amounted to a passing embarrassment. And what about Gannett in the long run? What effect, if any, would all this have on the biggest newspaper company?

Surely the *Press-Gazette* would be keeping its nose clean in Green Bay for a while. New sweetheart deals or whispering campaigns would be difficult to pull off while the memory of "It's Now or Never!" was fresh. But unlike Frank Wood, Gannett could wait. As soon as the coast was clear, the remorseless pressure would begin again. And in the end it would prevail. Though the end might now come later rather than sooner, the *News-Chronicle* would still be crushed by this giant that had never learned that the greatest thrill is not to kill, but to let live.

I pondered the questions that welled up at the end of the report. Who are these people? What makes Gannett the way it is? Money-lust was most of it, I imagined. But there was more. The adulation of Wall Street. An obsession with winning. The intoxication of power. The macho need to kick ass. The belief that the end justifies the means. Ego, personal and corporate. In short, Gannett embodied the ruling values in America.

Grudgingly I conceded that not everything about Gannett was bad. I knew it had an active program for the advancement of women and minorities. I knew Gannett had upgraded the quality of some dreadful newspapers it had bought, even as it was gutting excellent ones to meet profit goals. Though I generally dismissed Gannett's sound-bite journalism as lowest-common-denominator, I realized the chain was responsible for some of the most exciting graphic innovations in decades.

Because their papers had been bought into the fold, I knew that many of the country's most high-minded and dedicated journalists were now Gannett employees, and still were seeking to pursue their craft with idealism and integrity. I realized that alongside the fraud, price-fixing, lying, and ruthless elimination of competitors that defined Gannett as a company, the chain also did much honest, and even admirable, work.

Its scholarship, seminar, and advanced-studies programs made significant contributions to journalism, and to individual lives. Several of its papers—particularly the prestigious, recently acquired ones—worked diligently to expose wrongdoing. Just by being the biggest newspaper company, Gannett was a potent force for political debate, literacy, expression.

Mulling these contradictions, I kept coming back to a central question: If an organization is corrupt at its core, how do honorable individuals justify working in its service?

The question seemed crucial. The only hope for change at Gannett had to rise from within. Surely the majority of its thirty-seven thousand employees did not share the success-at-any-cost ethic of the few who set the moral tone. Most Gannett workers—those who answered the phone, kept the books, swept the floor, covered sports or politics, delivered the paper, ran the presses, sold ads—were decent people leading decent lives. They were nice to family and friends, gave to church and charity, voted, tried to do a good job, and had no wish to compromise their integrity.

If change were ever to come to Gannett, it must come from advertising salespeople refusing to spread lies or come off the rate card. It must come from assistant circulation managers refusing to falsify figures. It must come from reporters and editors demanding the same standard of conduct from their own company that they demand from the statehouse or the Pentagon. It must come from the board of directors, those high-profile, impressive men and women, imposing a code of ethics and insisting that it be observed at every link in Gannett's long, long chain.

Yet even as I nursed these hopes, they evaporated before me. Anyone waiting for change to well up in the ranks of Gannett's workforce would wait as long as the doomed Winston Smith waited in George Orwell's *1984* for the downtrodden "proles" to rise up and overthrow the system that shaped them. When the chips are down, self-interest beats a noble cause every time.

As long as seven-figure paychecks at headquarters depended on maximizing profits, there would be no code of ethics. As long as reporters and editors could win their awards, advance their careers, and salve their social consciences without risking job security, they would continue to find their exposés elsewhere. As long as publishers kept winning promotions by bumping off the competition, small competitors would continue to die.

As long as its employees could say "I was only following orders" and "that's just business," they would continue to do what they were told to do in the name of Gannett. The few who objected would quit or get squeezed out, and the rest would carry on.

Such were the thoughts that oppressed me as I packed, in the second week of December 1989. They did nothing to speed the job. Somehow I seemed to have twice as much stuff to haul back home as I had brought. How many trips down the long stairway would be needed to lug it all to the car? Fifteen? Twenty? I felt like going back to bed. But bed would come very late, for the production crew was taking me out for a farewell beer at midnight, after locking down the paper. No, better to keep at it, to get the car half loaded before tomorrow, my last day in Denmark, Wisconsin.

Darkness had fallen, though the hour was not yet 5 P.M. The early gloom only deepened my melancholy. Instead of fighting on, Frank should start making plans to lay the *News-Chronicle* to rest. It had no chance of surviving. In essence, nothing had changed.

What Frank should do was not go down with his ship, but go out with a winner. While "It's Now or Never" still pulsed, he should shut down the *News-Chronicle* with grace and dignity. He could take lasting pride that with his meager forces he had mounted an amazing assault upon the invincible Gannett. His valor had gone above and beyond the call. Now he could, with honor, withdraw from the field. It was not necessary for him to die there.

In the third load I picked up to take to the car was the brown Bible. Again it reminded me of some reflections to leave with Frank. I found them in Ecclesiastes, and typed them out:

> For my heart rejoiced in all my labour: and this was the portion of all my labour.
>
> Then I looked on all the works that my hands had wrought, and on the labour that I had laboured to do: and behold, all was vanity and vexation of spirit, and there was no profit under the sun.
>
> One generation passeth away, and another generation cometh: but the earth abideth forever. Better is the end of a thing than the beginning thereof.

I folded the ancient words into an envelope. Then I continued loading the car. Just before it closed, I arranged for Denmark's lone florist shop to send Floyd Ferdon a bouquet at his typesetting station after I left. I suspected he had not gotten many flowers.

Four hours before midnight, my stomach told me lunch had worn off. I drove to the quick-stop for a sandwich. As I pulled up, Denmark's police cruiser slipped in behind me. The purposefulness in its movement told me that I had again been targeted, again for reasons I did not understand. Well, I would bluff it out.

"Excuse me, sir."

"Are you talking to me?"

"Yes, sir, I am," the young officer replied. "Did you know that one of your taillights has burned out?"

"No, I didn't. But is it really a problem? In New Mexico the law requires only one red light at the rear of a vehicle."

"Well, sir, it's different in Wisconsin. Our law is very clear. A vehicle must have two functional rear lights."

With my car half-packed to leave, they had finally nailed me. For a taillight. Sure, I'll pay your stupid fine, I thought, suppressing the impulse to hold out my wrists for the handcuffs.

"It's hard to get foreign parts around here. But there's a place on Lime Kiln Road where you might be able to find your bulb."

A couple of beats passed before I comprehended that the cop was giving me not a ticket but friendly advice. "I'll go there tomorrow," I said, thanking him. "I'm leaving the next day."

Then he blurted out: "Look, I'm sorry about that ticket for snow parking, OK? It's the law, but I should have issued a warning."

"Don't worry about it. It taught me a good lesson—to read the street signs. That was worth the three bucks."

"Well, thanks for taking it that way," he said. "And thanks for helping out the newspaper. That was really something."

40

As Though I Had Not Come

THE BEER PARTY WAS FUN, yet also sad. I was going to miss this raucous female gang that pasted the *News-Chronicle* together night after night in that dingy basement. When they knocked off at midnight we took over the tavern below my window, the one where big Hubert and little Sammy got tanked up for their name-calling showdown in the street. But in this night's tanking up there was no ill will. Each time my stein was drained it was refilled at once, and I was not allowed to pay for anything.

As the alcohol hit I drifted toward moroseness, reflecting upon the piddling wages and tenuous job security of my hosts. But they would have none of it—bawdy was their idea of the appropriate tone. Soon we were competing to see who could tell the most obscene, repulsive jokes. My repertoire had always fared well in such contests, but these corn-fed Wisconsin farm girls sent me running for cover. When last call came, they presented me with a pinhole peep-show that a few years ago might have landed its bearer in jail.

The next morning my head was throbbing, my throat was raw, and my bowels were shaky. I had forgotten how bad a beer hangover can be. Time passed in slow motion. Each trip down the stairs with another box or suitcase seemed to take half an hour, and when I got back to the room I had to rest. Like my body, my mind too seemed unplugged from its energy source. And so it drifted.

Tonight I was having an early dinner with Frank and Agnes. Tomorrow morning I was hitting the road. And then the Green Bay Project would be history. What had it all added up to?

In lasting terms, probably not much. Through the murk of the hangover, I saw no reason to revise my outlook for the *News-Chronicle*. Maybe "It's Now or Never!" had bought it a few more months—or at best, a few more years—of life. But in the end, it had no chance of surviving as a home-owned paper in a Gannett town. History itself was flowing against Frank

Wood. It was a force against which he could not stand. And yet, by God, he was trying.

The will to live. The most basic of all instincts. Was that why Frank fought on? No, that was not quite it. His own survival was not at stake. He could shut down the paper tomorrow and be well-off for the rest of his days. In fact, keeping it going was the real threat, for it could bring down both him and his company.

So his motive was something else. It was the love of a parent for a child. Yes, that was it. Maybe the *News-Chronicle* was not the smartest child in the class, or the best-looking or the most popular—but it was Frank's child, and he loved it without condition. This big good man, father to all he surveyed, was constitutionally incapable of stepping aside while his child was put to death before his eyes. Before he would do that, he would defy the forces of hell. He had no choice. The alternative was simply not acceptable.

And so he would fight on, until his great heart got broken or gave out. Only then would he endure the unacceptable alternative. But acceptable or not, the alternative was what awaited us all. Thus the value was in the fight itself. That was where Frank could be proud. With little more than his bare fists he was slugging it out with an armed and armored giant, determined to slay his child. And so the giant would, ultimately. But for now, Frank had stayed the killer's hand. He had won this round.

And what of me? What, if anything, had I won? Very little that I could see. I had answered Frank's call, acquitted myself well in his service. But the *News-Chronicle* was not my child, and saving it was not my fight. I had come to Wisconsin not to make a stand, just to lend a hand. I was just passing through. Unlike Frank's, my heart had limits. I had loved some things, but somehow had let go of them all. Now I was just a hired gun.

I looked back over my time in Wisconsin, and regretted the lack of understanding that had marred so many days. No, this was not my country, these were not my people, this was not my paper—yet I had sought to bend everything to fit my expectations. As a stranger and outsider I was quick to find fault, slow to give credit. I had honored neither Frank nor what he had built. I had refused to acknowledge that he and Brown County Publishing must be doing something right. No wonder the time had been so difficult. Judge not, that ye be not judged.

This was the lesson I had learned in Green Bay. Yet I had already learned it, many times. I seemed trapped within my own parameters. Assigned a job, I was a highly proficient technician. My work would be exceptional. But in the heart, where the real work takes place, I was losing ground. And time was running out.

But what difference did it make? We live our lives, do our work, serve our gods, fight our mighty battles, and so quickly it passes, until nothing is left and no one remembers.

The packing was all done. Dinner with Frank and Agnes was the Green Bay Project's last unfinished business. The time to meet them drew near. Heavy footsteps, taking the stairs two at a time, startled me. Someone must be lost. Except for Frank and Chris and Al, visitors to my room had been nonexistent. But the knock on my door was firm, directed. I opened it to find Lyle Lahey.

"Frank said you're leaving tomorrow."

"That's right, Lyle. First thing in the morning. Come on in. I must say, this is an unexpected pleasure."

"No, I'm on my way somewhere." He was clearly ill at ease, this gaunt, lopsided man to whom I had never found the key.

"Well, I'm heading out, too, to meet Frank for dinner."

"In Wisconsin, we call it supper," he said, grinning. "I just wanted to say good-bye." He thrust out his big, gifted hand. "And I also wanted to say this: You done good."

I joined Frank and Agnes at the Union Hotel. Throughout the meal we made small talk, as though no one was comfortable with farewells. In my jacket pocket were the doleful lines from Ecclesiastes. After dinner Frank ordered champagne.

"Here's to you, Dick. For doing 'It's Now or Never!' "

"No, Frank, that's not accurate. I've been thinking about it a lot, and I've come to realize something. I'm not the one who did 'It's Now or Never!' You are."

"What do you mean? You did all the work."

"Yes, I did the work, but that's all I did. It goes deeper than that. Whenever something important gets done, it usually traces to one cause. And you caused 'It's Now or Never!' to happen."

He looked at me with a little smile. I went on.

"You had the idea, and the determination. You paid for it. Hell, you named it too. You did what was needed to convert it into reality—and that includes getting me to do the work. I was only an instrument, and a difficult one at that. If it had been up to me, there never would have been a Green

Bay Project. None of it would have happened. No, Frank, you're the one who did it."

"Well, then," he replied, lifting his glass again, "let's put it this way: We couldn't have done it without you."

"That's right, Frank. You couldn't have. I'll drink to that."

Agnes had grown quiet when the talk turned to business. But as we clinked I caught her eyes, and they were warm.

In the silence that followed, I felt a need for confession. "I was mad at you a long time, Frank. You knew, didn't you?"

He looked at me with his mild blue eyes, saying nothing.

"I felt you had hung me out to dry, had tricked me into coming up here, then left me on my own. It was real hard on me."

His little smile did not change. He let me finish.

"But I'm not mad anymore. I haven't been for two or three weeks. I know you didn't abandon me on purpose. And in the end, you came through. You just had too much other stuff going on."

"That's about to change."

"What do you mean?"

"I've cut down my teaching load next semester to one course. All my extra time will go into selling advertising. And if I do say so myself, nobody in Green Bay can sell ads like I can, when I put my mind to it. I've proved it before, and I'll prove it again."

"That's good, Frank. I wish you luck."

"I don't think you realize, Dick, how much of an impact 'It's Now or Never!' has had. But I do. I see it every day, everywhere I go. The town is up in arms. It'll be a long time before this dies down. In the meantime, we're going to make the most of it!"

"That's terrific. You know I wish you well."

"Tell me, Dick. Do you think we're going to make it?"

"If there's one thing I've learned about you, Frank, it's to never count you out. Let's leave it like that."

"Well, we just might surprise you."

In the lobby there were hugs all around. In Frank's bearlike embrace the envelope in my pocket crinkled. Until this moment I was not sure whether to leave it with him. But now I decided. Whatever awaited my friend, I wanted the ruminations of the Old Testament Preacher to be part of his thinking. And whatever the outcome in Green Bay, I wanted to remind him that the earth would abide.

"Remember how I gave you something just before 'It's Now or Never!' broke, and asked you to wait before reading it? Well, I want to do the same thing again," I said, handing him the envelope. "Don't open it until tomorrow, when I'm gone."

"I won't if you won't," he replied. From his own pocket he took out a small, square package, which fit easily into my palm. Both of us, it seemed, had saved one thing till the end.

A sharp, cold wind flecked with moisture was blowing from the east as I drove back for my last night in Denmark.

I awoke at dawn, to the sounds of slush. I jumped to the window with alarm. Snow was flying, the wind was whistling, and cars were skidding over white streets. On Sunday, December 17, the winter of 1989 had finally arrived in Wisconsin.

The radio said a storm was blowing in off Lake Michigan. There was turbulence throughout the Great Lakes region. Two inches of snow had fallen, and Green Bay would get at least a foot more. Subzero temperatures were just behind the snow. How I had longed for an arctic blast to break the monotony of the dead gray skies. Yet now that it had come, this storm was not welcome. I could not bear the thought of another day in this place. The Green Bay Project was over. It must be left behind.

Without shower or shave I flew down the stairs to my car. I muscled snow and ice off the windshield, then spun away. Sipping a huge cup of coffee from the quick-stop, I steered through Green Bay on the interstate. West of the city, with Lake Michigan ever more distant, the storm slacked off. So despite a warning voice I did what I always do, and left the freeway for smaller roads. The driven snow gave way to frequent flurries. Each one threatened to cut short my getaway, and send me scurrying for shelter in the next town. I did not expect to get far this day. But I was on the road again, and my blood was flowing faster.

In the state's midsection the squalls lessened in force and frequency, while my boldness grew stronger. At a crossroads I turned north instead of south. At the highest tip of Wisconsin was a place on the map that I wanted to see: Apostle Islands National Lakeshore. This was not the best timing, but I might not pass this way again. Through the lake region and the north woods, I closed in on the Apostles, named by early French trappers to honor the disciples of Christ. Only an occasional blast of snow slowed me. But the wind was high, and the temperature had dropped below zero.

State Route 13 was the lone road leading to the site, on a peninsula jutting into Lake Superior. Route 13 was ninety-four miles long from the points where it left and rejoined U.S. Highway 2, and the map showed only a couple of settlements along its path. It was a risky detour. But no snow had fallen for two or three hours, and sunlight was breaking through the clouds. There seemed to be less to the storm than predicted, and the afternoon was young. I would check out the Apostles, return to U.S. 2, and bed down in a highway motel at nightfall.

Route 13 passed through a resort area, but winter had closed it down. Boarded-up motels, cottages, restaurants, and fast-food stands lined the deserted roadway, slick with ice and snow. The national lakeshore visitor center told of the Indians, trappers, rugged pioneers, and others who had wandered through long ago on their own journeys to oblivion. The only way to see the islands was by boat, but none would be going until summer.

Nothing but winter, however, loomed outside. The cold air burned my lungs as I went to my car. Black clouds had erased the sun once more, and the wind was rising. Though the hour was just four in the afternoon, darkness was settling in. As swiftly as I dared, I headed down the ice-encrusted road back toward civilization.

Snow began to fall, softly at first but soon furiously. Without transition, afternoon became night. Bouncing off the snowflakes, my headlights blinded me. The roadway ahead was as white as the fields. There was almost no telling one from the other. I had to find shelter. But where? U.S. 2 was at least thirty miles ahead, and the lakeshore community was almost as far behind. I should have stayed there. I sure as shit should have. No tracks indicated that other vehicles were out in the storm. I goosed the engine, but slipped into a skid. I corrected it, then held a grimmer pace.

The car radio reported that the snow would fall all night, and the temperature would bottom out at fifteen below zero. There was one bright piece of news: the Packers had beaten the Bears, to keep their playoff hopes alive. But now staying alive had become my goal as well. The fuel gauge showed plenty to get me back to Highway 2, but not enough to keep the engine and heater going until dawn.

Oh boy, Dick, I rebuked myself, *you've really done it this time. You pushed things just a little too far, and this time it caught up with you. Nobody ever plans to, but people really do freeze to death in their cars. This is the real thing.*

There was nothing to do but press on. Shuttered motels mocked me. Nowhere in this white world did a light seem to be on. Slow panic was rising. But still I felt the irony. What a time to go, just hours after wrapping up the Green Bay Project. It was as good a time as any. At least the job was finished. Then up ahead a beacon pierced the storm. A gas station! It seemed I would not die just yet after all. I would sleep on the floor of the station if need be, or at worst fill my tank and ride out the night in the lot. But first I would do the sensible thing.

"Is there an open motel anywhere near here?"

"Sure is, mister, just a couple of miles down the road. Only one around that stays open all year. But it ain't fancy."

The motel did not look open, much less fancy. Its sign was not lighted, and the only illumination came from a red neon beer emblem in the office window. The parking lot was under a foot of snow. If I pulled in, I might not be coming out. But what the hell. My gas tank was now full, and one lot was as good as another.

Presiding over the office was a hard-bitten old woman. Yes, she had a room, twenty-two dollars, cash only. I was saved. The key to room 18 was superfluous, for the door was not locked. Nor was the bed made. Its dirty sheets were piled atop the stained mattress. The electric heater did not seem to work, and a rough wooden board lay across the bowl of the toilet, which held no water in its tank.

Under the circumstances, I did not want to be particular. But surely there was a better room than this. Starting back to the office, I noticed that other doors were also unlocked. Like room 18, the next three had dirty sheets. But the heaters and toilets worked. The fourth was the one I sought: clean bed, functional plumbing, and a flow of warmth when I turned on the heater. The manager just shrugged when I said I wanted to swap.

In the room I remembered I had eaten only a sandwich all day. Looking for a restaurant was impossible, so I rummaged in the car and came up with cheese and crackers, a candy bar, and the dregs of a bottle of brandy. Supping on this feast, I suddenly realized the obvious: My haven was a hot-mattress roadhouse, which sold more rooms by the hour than by the night. I laughed aloud, while the wind howled outside. Never before had I fully appreciated the old saying "any port in a storm." Yes, any port in a storm.

After a while the room was warm enough to take off my coat. It was time to turn in. Tomorrow I would continue the long homeward slide. But now I would sleep, with every expectation of waking up.

A bulge swelled the coat's lower pocket. It was the package Frank Wood had given me, just the night before. How long ago that night seemed—

that night and all those in Green Bay that had come before it. Yet this very day I had climbed out of bed in the one-room apartment at Brown County Publishing Company. In the frenzy of the storm, I had forgotten the unopened package. Except when afraid of dying in the cold, I had scarcely given a thought all day to Frank, the *News-Chronicle,* or the Green Bay Project. But now that I was safe and warm, it all rushed back. Too much, too much. Absorbing it would take a while.

Yet here in my hand was one small package, proof that it had all been real, and had seemed important enough to do, in its time. That time had already passed, blown away by the wind and the snow, and the inexorable march of the seasons. Only this package remained, unwrapped, unknown.

I wondered if Frank had picked his way through the words of the Preacher: "Then I looked on all the works that my hands had wrought, and on the labour that I had laboured to do: and behold, all was vanity and vexation of spirit, and there was no profit under the sun." I was sure that he had.

I wondered if his course would be altered by those words. I was sure it would not. After a while we are who we are, and that is just the way it is. I was gone from Green Bay now, as though I had never come. But Frank remained in place—yesterday, today, and tomorrow.

I wondered what was in this little package. Beneath the wrapping paper was a blue velvet box, inscribed with the name of a Green Bay jeweler. Inside the box was a single object, one inch long. It was a silver bullet.

Epilogue

THE PACKERS DID NOT MAKE it to the playoffs that year. They finished strong, beating the Dallas Cowboys on the season's final Sunday, for their highest victory total since 1972. But Minnesota refused to cooperate, defeating Cincinnati and taking the slot that might have gone to Green Bay. The team sank back into the league's lower echelons the next year. In 1993 and again in 1994 the Pack did squeeze into the playoffs, but was eliminated early both times. The 1995 season, however, saw the Packers advance almost to the Super Bowl. They won their division title, then lost the conference championship game. Winning it would have returned them to football's premier event.

The Christmas advertising season that immediately followed "It's Now or Never!" was the best ever for the *Green Bay News-Chronicle*. Strong gains continued throughout the next year. In 1990 the paper had 40 percent more advertising volume than it had had in 1989. Most of the increase was on the local level.

Circulation also improved, but less dramatically. More than one thousand new subscribers signed up for the *News-Chronicle* after "It's Now or Never!," an 11 percent gain. The single most significant response was a $1.7 million printing contract awarded to Brown County Publishing Company by a major national retailer. The executive in charge said he was impressed by Frank Wood's stand.

A few other chain stores also began substantial programs with the Chronicle Group. But most major merchandisers in Green Bay were unmoved by "It's Now or Never!" While some ran token advertising for a month or two after the report, the majority stuck to business as usual. Citing the larger circulation of the *Press-Gazette* and the nuisance of dealing with two papers, the chains dismissed whatever benefits that competition might be bringing, and continued to give all their business to Gannett.

The *News-Chronicle*'s increased revenues were absorbed quickly by pressing internal needs. Delivery was improved, salaries were raised, overdue bills were paid, equipment was upgraded. A year after the Green Bay

Project, the paper had a more solid financial footing and fewer crises. But its losses were undiminished.

To carry on the fight Frank sold one of his other papers, a thriving twice-weekly in a town forty miles south of Green Bay. With the cash infusion he moved boldly—and perhaps ill-advisedly—to turn the corner once and for all. With much fanfare on St. Patrick's Day of 1991 he launched a Sunday *News-Chronicle.*

The new product was a hybrid with few if any precedents in daily journalism. With news, sports, columns, syndicated features, and color comics, it had the heft and look of a full-service Sunday paper. But it was delivered free. Although technically it was just one more edition of the 12,000-circulation *News-Chronicle,* it also went to 60,000 nonsubscriber homes in Green Bay. With one stroke Frank was seeking to overcome the two most common reasons given by major advertisers for not using the *News-Chronicle:* that its circulation could not match the *Press-Gazette's* 55,000, and that Sunday was essential to a full advertising program.

The Sunday paper became at once both an asset and a liability. It did succeed in attracting several chain retailers: supermarkets, discount stores, general merchandisers. It also generated enormous new expenses: in printing, in staffing, in distribution. With the long national recession eroding his other divisions' ability to cover *News-Chronicle* losses, Frank announced in January 1992 the first layoffs in his company's thirty-nine-year history. Although many workers accepted reduced hours or unpaid vacations to cushion the blow on others, thirty full- and part-time jobs were eliminated.

In November 1992 the *News-Chronicle* celebrated its twentieth anniversary. That occasion was noted by Wisconsin's largest paper, the *Milwaukee Journal,* with a long article in its Sunday magazine. Frank admitted to the writer that in 1991, the first year of the Sunday *News-Chronicle,* "we lost our tail on it"—more than nine hundred thousand dollars. But things were getting better, he said, and he had no plans to quit.

Over the next two years things did improve. The *News-Chronicle* continued to lose money, but smaller sums. The 1994–1995 fiscal year was the best ever, overall, for Brown County Publishing Company; every employee was given a two-hundred-dollar bonus, all in two-dollar bills. But unprecedented increases in the cost of newsprint—which rose 76 percent over a twenty-two-month period—undercut the firm's subsequent profitability, which at the end of 1995 was again precarious.

In the *News-Chronicle's* twenty-third anniversary issue, in November 1995, Frank Wood acknowledged that the paper's unending losses had imposed a "fearsome cost" on Brown County Publishing. "Other parts of the company have been dismayed by how much it's been taking from what they've been earning to pay the bills here in Green Bay," he said. And he admitted that the *News-Chronicle*'s future was unclear. "I don't know," he said. "Some way or another, we have to get this publication to the break-even point."

Despite the skills he developed in Salem, N. S. "Buddy" Hayden was unable to prevent the collapse of the *Philadelphia Daily News,* which he served as its final publisher. Later he sought to save another failing metropolitan daily, the *Los Angeles Herald-Examiner.* It too ceased publication under him. In April 1992 Hayden announced the formation of Capital Development Associates, a newsletter-publishing, direct-marketing, and public-relations firm in Fair Lawn, New Jersey, which he would serve as chief executive officer. Late in 1995, no such company was listed in Fair Lawn's telephone information directory.

Hayden's advertising director in Salem, Wayne Vann, who later became president of the *Santa Fe New Mexican,* was transferred in 1985 to Gannett's western regional headquarters in Reno, Nevada, to assume unspecified duties. Late in 1995 he was no longer working there.

After the 1982 collapse of the *Albuquerque Sun,* former *Santa Fe Reporter* advertising director Didier Raven bought a fashion-industry journal in New York. In 1986 he sold it and moved to Paris, France, where he opened a Mexican restaurant called Rio Grande, on the Right Bank of the Seine. Late in 1995 he continued to preside over the Rio Grande.

Allen H. Neuharth retired as Gannett chairman in 1989. His successor was a company man named John Curley. Six months after Neuharth left, the monumental losses of *USA Today,* plus an aborted television show that he modeled after *USA Today,* plus the ongoing newspaper war in Little Rock, gave the chain its first quarterly drop in earnings in more than twenty years. Although Neuharth's decisions made the dip inevitable, the timing of his departure enabled him to say it did not come on his watch.

Neuharth's first project in retirement was the publication of his autobiography, *Confessions of an S.O.B.* Then he turned his attention to the Gannett Foundation, which he continued to head. In 1990 he announced plans to sell all the foundation's Gannett stock, which at 10 percent of the total shares was the largest single block in the company. His stated reason was that he was not satisfied with Gannett's dividend performance.

Neuharth's move had the effect of putting Gannett in play for corporate raiders. To prevent a takeover, the chain bought back all the foundation's stock for $670 million, after a previous offer of $540 million, based on book value, was rejected by Neuharth. To meet the huge cash outlay, Gannett was forced to borrow, which further undermined its standing on Wall Street. Drawing a Gannett pension of $300,000 a year for life, and enjoying the proceeds of $5.1 million in company stock given to him upon his retirement, Neuharth infuriated former colleagues with his "ingratitude." However, none of them would comment for the record. "They loathe him and don't want to say so," an executive with *Washington Journalism Review* told *Time* magazine.

Neuharth quickly gave them further reason to detest him. In 1991 the renamed Freedom Forum (his new title for the foundation) led a highly publicized effort to force Gannett to swallow $29 million in debt to save the failing *Oakland Tribune* in California, the only major black-owned daily in America. With no more stake in the chain's bottom line, Neuharth now found more merit in preserving newspapers than in forcing them out of business.

Another change that Neuharth wrought in the former Gannett Foundation was diverting its largess away from gratitude-building donations to local charities in the dozens of cities where the chain ran newspapers. Now that his income was not pegged to those papers' prosperity, the former chairman defined a new mission. From now on, he announced, the Freedom Forum would focus primarily on grand conceptual issues regarding the First Amendment, both in this country and in others that had no First Amendment. To advance this new mission, the foundation adopted a new slogan, "Fostering First Amendment Freedoms."

Some observers sneered that what Neuharth was really fostering was his own image as a journalistic visionary—or, as press critic Ben Bagdikian might say, his own myth. Among the Freedom Forum's early projects were a task force to poll newly liberated Eastern Europeans on their feelings about democracy, funding for a group of black journalism educators, a conference of Soviet reporters and editors, and a grant to monitor gender issues in the media.

Neuharth's overhaul included raising his pay as part-time chairman from $39,000 to $71,000 a year. He also hired several close associates as officers, at annual salaries ranging from $114,000 to $167,000. Administrative expenses soared from $5.9 million in 1985 to $19.3 million in 1989. Meanwhile, revenues dispensed in grants dipped below 50 percent, as compared to a National Council on Foundations average of almost 80 percent.

One Freedom Forum board member resigned to protest the "lavish" expenses. And a former Internal Revenue Service commissioner specializing in nonprofit tax law in Washington told *Editor & Publisher:* "I don't think high-style living belongs in a charitable foundation. I do not think managers and directors of foundations should treat foundations the way some CEOs direct their corporations—as cash cows for their own fulfillment, including limousines and other perks."

Meanwhile, Neuharth proceeded with his $15 million plans for moving the foundation into baronial new offices, across the street from Gannett headquarters. Among the touches: a million-dollar art collection, a $5 million high-tech conference center on the roof, carved stone staircases, suede-covered filing cabinets, an eighty-thousand-dollar boardroom table, and a forty-thousand-dollar desk for Neuharth.

News reports (notably in the *Washington Post*) of such expenditures touched off an investigation by the New York attorney general's office, which had standing in the matter because the foundation was relocating from that state to Virginia. In January 1995 Neuharth and the Freedom Forum's trustees agreed to make restitution of nearly $175,000 to the foundation to settle the case.

The investigation cited a long list of improprieties. Among them were: "the selection of unnecessarily expensive custom furniture for executive offices"; "an absence of adequate cost controls"; the purchase of personal exercise equipment and a massage table for Neuharth at foundation expense; the assignment of lucrative and noncompetitive contracts, without the knowledge of the board, to a design consultant whom Neuharth was dating; the convening of costly board meetings in resorts such as Puerto Vallarta, Mexico, and in American cities hosting the NCAA basketball finals and the Super Bowl; the unwarranted expenditure of thirty thousand dollars for buying two thousand copies of Neuharth's book at retail-store prices instead of at half-price from the publisher, and for events promoting the book.

Wrapped into the settlement was a strict set of new financial policy guidelines for the Freedom Forum. Included were a ban on most first-class and chartered-airplane travel, an almost total ban on limousines, prohibitions on luxury rooms and suites in hotels, limits and procedures for meal reimbursements, and a stipulation that travel expenses for spouses and other family members would not be reimbursed unless those persons participated directly in foundation business during the trip.

In accepting the settlement, the Freedom Forum made no admission of wrongdoing. "The settlement involves nothing illegal or unethical but simply deals with matters of judgment on expenditures," said the foundation's president, Charles Overby. Neuharth was blunter. The restitution was, he said, "utter nonsense."

Meanwhile, week after week, hardly an issue of *Editor & Publisher* appeared without two or three, or more, notations that the Freedom Forum had awarded scholarships to journalism students, or sponsored a symposium on business coverage, or funded a doctoral program at a major university, or initiated a study of sex or race bias in the media. In the midst of its troubles, the former Gannett Foundation was doing much good work—and building a long list of influential professionals indebted to it, and unlikely to find fault with its ways.

In his 1989 book *Confessions of an S.O.B.,* Al Neuharth had a supremely confident vision of Gannett's future in Detroit, where he and the Knight-Ridder chain were negotiating their controversial joint operating agreement. "If approved," he wrote of the JOA, "we have a 100-year guarantee of a highly profitable newspaper partnership. If denied, we'll have the only game in town in the USA's sixth-biggest market. The *Detroit News,* undervalued and underappreciated, is on the verge of generating mega-million earnings for years to come."

The years that came, however, saw a different reality.

From the start, the agreement failed to deliver the touted profits. The first year's losses were dismissed as one-time adjustments, quickly to be left behind. To hasten the "mega-million earnings" foreseen by Neuharth, the merged Detroit Newspaper Agency, or DNA, which now ran business operations for both the *News* and the *Free Press,* began implementing the measures that always had been predicted if the JOA were put into place.

Delivery to outlying areas of Michigan, where circulation costs were high and advertising income nonexistent, was abruptly cut off, leaving longtime readers without a metro daily. Readers in and around Detroit, who had grown accustomed to artificially low subscription rates during the long-drawn-out "war" that was prelude to the JOA, were hit with dramatic increases. The same fate befell advertisers, who now were dealing with a two-pronged monopoly.

Yet for once this time-tested road to riches took a surprising turn. Grown cynical during the highly suspect and highly publicized JOA drive, readers and advertisers alike declined to swallow the sharp hikes imposed upon them. Circulation at both papers plummeted, with the fall at the Gannett-owned *News* by far the most precipitous. From a pre-JOA average daily circulation of 690,422, the *News* dropped to just 359,057 by mid-1994. Over the same period Knight-Ridder's *Free Press* fell from 626,434 to 551,650. As had happened in almost every other American city, the morning paper was proving dominant over the evening paper—despite both chains' insistence in their JOA bid that the morning *Free Press* was failing and the evening *News* would be the lone survivor.

As a second and then a third year passed without a profit, the frustrated JOA newspapers escalated their efforts. According to the publisher of two small dailies and thirteen weeklies in Detroit's suburbs, the tactics they turned to were ones familiar to Gannett. "Having reconciled their efforts to eliminate each other, the combined Detroit dailies have directed their unified attention to eliminating their suburban competitors," wrote J. Gene Chambers, president of a company called Independent Newspapers, in a letter to the Antitrust Division of the U.S. Department of Justice.

"Accompanying this letter," he continued, "you will find several examples of predatory pricing and other unlawful practices directed against the *Macomb Daily* by the DNA." In his list of twenty examples, Chambers contended that the advertisers of his papers—even small, one-location suburban stores—had been targeted by the DNA, with "unbelievable offers" impossible to turn down. Invoices sent to the Antitrust Division showed discounts as high as 86 percent below the printed rate card. In one case, Chambers said, an ad priced at $3,200 on the card was offered to one of his advertisers for $250.

"The advertisers are not ones that are going to make or break the DNA," Chambers told *Editor & Publisher,* "but they are advertisers who can make or break us." He estimated his past year's losses to predatory pricing at $1 million. "When they were at each others' throats, they were cutting each other," he went on. "But now that the *News* and *Free Press* have joined together, what it's done is pretty much given them a license to kill off all the suburban publishers."

His cry was heard in Congress. Early in 1994 two Michigan Democrats in the House of Representatives, David Bonoir, then the majority whip, and William Ford, took up Chambers's call for a Justice Department investigation. "We have been presented with compelling evidence that DNA is violating antitrust laws as well as the Newspaper Preservation Act by deliberately trying to take advertising away from suburban Detroit newspapers," they wrote the head of the Antitrust Division. "If predatory pricing forces these smaller papers out of business, then the JOA will actually reduce the editorial voices in southeastern Michigan—the exact opposite of what the JOA originally intended," their jointly signed letter stated. Two months later, Democratic U.S. Senator Carl Levin of Michigan sent his own letter asking the Antitrust Division to investigate.

The DNA response to Chambers's allegations was terse. Refusing to comment on specific cases, president and chief executive officer Frank Vega stated: "The only thing I can say is we are very confident we have not engaged in predatory pricing."

The Antitrust Division, headed by lawyer Anne Bingaman, the wife of a Democratic senator from New Mexico, snapped into action after the letters from Congress. Division investigators interviewed Chambers for three hours, and in June 1994 Bingaman wrote Senator Levin: "You may be assured that when we have completed our investigation, we will take any further action that may be appropriate." In the November 1994 elections Republicans won control of both houses of Congress. Soon the Detroit investigation had dropped out of sight. In a September 1995 update, the Antitrust Division reported it was "reviewing" the case.

Paper Losses: A Modern Epic of Greed and Betrayal at America's Two Largest Newspaper Companies was the title of a 1993 book by Bryan Gruley, a business reporter at the *Detroit News.* In meticulous detail he spelled out the beginning, middle, and up-to-the-moment status of the JOA in that city. He asserted that both of the chains had deceived their employees, and, further, that the heads of both had emerged from the deal as losers.

Author Gruley and one of those "losers," Neuharth, clashed face-to-face in January 1994 at a Freedom Forum–sponsored discussion of the Detroit JOA. The Knight-Ridder chief, Alvah Chapman, declined to appear. With his trademark biting wit, Neuharth reported: "I called Alvah and said he really should reconsider. But he told me, 'I don't really think it's necessary. I think you can display enough greed and betrayal for us both.'"

In the debate, Gruley argued that one of the Detroit papers should have been allowed to die in the early 1980s, and that the "insane practices" of the pre-JOA war had left both vulnerable to "new competition ranging from suburban papers to CNN." Gruley maintained that going into the negotiations, Neuharth held the upper hand, but squandered it by allowing the *News* to be the afternoon paper—the one most likely to fold if the JOA continued to flop. "What was it, Mr. Neuharth," he asked the former head of Gannett, "did you screw up or did you just not care—or was this your plan all along?"

In full combative form, Neuharth replied: "Had I known that one of these papers should have died, I would have conducted myself better. As it is, these greedy, greedy businesspeople saved two newspapers for the city of Detroit—even if one of the best reporters, like Bryan Gruley, wanted one of those papers to die." Waving away the idea that either paper would fail, Neuharth declared: "The JOA's OK. Detroit will have two newspapers for at least 96 years."

After months of bitter and fruitless negotiations, six unions—from the Newspaper Guild of writers and editors to the Teamsters—went out on strike against the Detroit newspapers in July 1995. "This is something we saw coming two years ago," said a picketing Teamster. "This is Phase II of the JOA, with Phase III being the shutting down of one of the papers."

According to the unions, the DNA had purposely refused to bargain in good faith, in an effort to break the unions at the papers. A regional office of the National Labor Relations Board agreed, and issued an unfair labor practice complaint against the DNA. But DNA management routinely denied any wrongdoing, and proceeded to publish a combined issue of the *News* and *Free Press* starting on the strike's second day. Thin on news and advertising, the strike paper at first had less than a fourth of the papers' normal circulation. But as weeks passed, the unverifiable and contested figures rose to well over half the usual total.

Sporadic violence punctuated the strike, particularly at DNA's main production facility in the Detroit suburb of Sterling Heights. At times helicopters were used to bypass militants in the streets, determined to block the paper's distribution. When some $480,000 in contributions from DNA to the Sterling Heights city government—for police overtime in keeping the plant open—became known, city council members sympathetic to the strike forced the city manager to resign. But the DNA held tough, and striking workers began slipping back into their jobs. By late October some 340 former strikers reportedly had gone back to work, and a coalition of six unions had offered to return under the terms of their old contracts, with certain adjustments. The offer was turned down flat by Gannett's Detroit publisher.

One intense observer of the Detroit newspaper scene, John K. Hartman, a Central Michigan University journalism educator and the author of a 1992 book titled *The* USA Today *Way,* predicted the folding of the *News* as a fallout of the strike. "I think Gannett has pretty much had its fill of the Detroit JOA," he told *Editor & Publisher.* "They lost money there for the first three years, then they went through three CEOs until they found one who has at least made a modest profit. I think [the surviving paper] is most likely to be the *Free Press,* which has the most circulation and probably the most prestige around the state." In his book, Hartman argued that Gannett had bought the *News* primarily to gain automotive advertising for *USA Today.*

Spokesmen for the DNA denied any plan to close the *News.*

By its tenth birthday in 1992, *USA Today* had not once shown an annual profit. Losses for the previous year topped $20 million, and its total cumulative deficit was a staggering $800 million. Al Neuharth's cocky promise that it would be making money within five years had been washed down the drain with red ink, and analysts now were saying "The Nation's Newspaper" might never be profitable.

The problem lay in *USA Today*'s very identity. As a nationwide publication, it had no local base for classified ads or retail merchandisers. Its circulation was huge, 1.8 million, second only to the *Wall Street Journal* among daily newspapers. But its real competition for advertising came from national news magazines such as *Time* and *Newsweek,* whose circulation was twice as large and which had a shelf life of a week instead of a day. "It's here today, it's wrapping fish tomorrow," sniffed one advertising agency executive on the occasion of the tenth anniversary.

Only 27 percent of *USA Today*'s vast circulation was home delivery. Moreover, in cities served by excellent papers, such as New York and Chicago, *USA Today*'s numbers were abysmal. "It isn't seen as a primary read," explained the same executive to *Newsweek.* "It's something you pick up as a supplement, or read on the plane." Consequently, *USA Today* was not considered a prestige buy by corporate purchasers of national advertising.

Yet in its first decade the paper had steadily improved its journalism, and solidified its presence in American life. Its articles got better as well as longer, its reviews had national impact, its graphics continued to set the pace for other papers. In terms of professional esteem, said the chairman of the American Society of Newspaper Editors Future of Newspapers Committee, "the paper has made Gannett a company to be reckoned with."

Nevertheless, at Gannett's annual shareholders meeting in April 1992, a disgruntled stockholder introduced a proposal to fold or sell *USA Today,* to improve the chain's profits. "Present entrenched management," said his resolution, "has shown its incompetence by wasting talent and huge sums of money, in an amount that will never be recovered, on fantasies and personal agendas such as continuing *USA Today,* which management has run for about nine years and which will never recoup its losses in the next 10 years."

"Entrenched management" resisted the proposal, which was voted down overwhelmingly. An argument against it was Gannett's just-reported first-quarter performance. For the full chain, both revenue and profits were up from the previous year's first quarter. Despite *USA Today*'s bottomless losses, the financial bloodbath in Little Rock, and the debt incurred by buying out the foundation, Gannett's "flexibility" in the eighty cities where it ran monopolies had enabled it to increase earnings yet again.

And then, at the end of 1993, *USA Today* logged its first small operating profit, after eleven years of existence.

The Battle of Little Rock was won by Walter Hussman. In October 1991, almost six years after entering the market, Gannett abandoned "the oldest newspaper west of the Mississippi."

Technically, Gannett sold its *Arkansas Gazette* to Hussman's *Arkansas Democrat,* for $69 million. After the sale, Little Rock's lone daily paper was rechristened the *Arkansas Democrat-Gazette.* But the hyphenated name was only a sop to the Pulitzer Prize heritage of the once-illustrious and once-dominant *Gazette.* In style, staffing, management, and corporate identity, the surviving paper was all *Arkansas Democrat.*

Before the end came, the deficits suffered by both papers were astronomical. Gannett admitted to losses of $50 million in the last two years alone; and unconfirmed estimates put the *Gazette*'s total during the full six-year war at more than $85 million. Hussman refused to put a figure on his losses, but told an interviewer that the *Gazette* had outspent the *Democrat* by $10 million a year for the last five years.

In forcing the nation's largest chain out of the Little Rock market, Hussman had achieved a "stunning feat," according to *Editor & Publisher.* And as he admitted in a speech in 1992, Hussman himself had felt at times that he was bound to lose. In a postmortem analysis of why he won instead, Hussman said the outcome turned on a monumental blunder by Gannett.

By cutting the home-delivery cost of the *Gazette* from two dollars a week to eighty-five cents, the chain figured to either surge past its rival in circulation or force the *Democrat* to lower its own rates and suffer ruinous drops in revenue. But neither happened. When cold calculations showed Hussman he could not afford to follow suit, he kept his higher rates and waited for the worst. Instead, Arkansans saw the slash as a sign of declining quality at the *Gazette,* and turned it down. Meanwhile, the reduced rates cost Gannett millions of dollars in income from existing subscribers.

Other factors in the *Gazette*'s demise, Hussman said, included high turnover of key executives; an editorial package based on Gannett's norm rather than Arkansas tastes; and, ironically, too much money to toss around. While *Gazette* employees felt protected by the chain's vast wealth, he explained, his own workers knew they were fighting to hold onto their paychecks. "Job security was a luxury we never had at the *Arkansas Democrat.*"

Finally, Hussman prevailed by adopting a long-range strategy of mere survival. "We clearly understood we could not overwhelm or rout Gannett. They simply had too much money and firepower. But we realized we did have a chance at survival—and that if we did survive, Gannett could not win, because our survival would not accommodate their profitability goals in Little Rock."

Hindsight also proved useful to other observers looking back to see where Gannett went wrong in Little Rock. Robert Picard, editor of the *Journal of Media Economics,* blamed the chain for "a certain amount of corporate conceit, perhaps arrogance, that allowed them to believe they could walk in and dominate." But Picard was quick to add that Walter Hussman's victory was little short of miraculous. "Nobody could have projected that the *Democrat* was going to be able to fight back the way it did," he said. "There is probably no other independent publisher in the country today who would be willing and able to make the financial sacrifice Hussman made."

After the fall of the *Arkansas Gazette,* just sixteen American cities were left with competing daily newspapers. In the entire Gannett chain only one competitive market remained: Green Bay, Wisconsin.

I got a copy of the lawsuit filed in October 1992 against Gannett in Rockford, Illinois, by its weekly competition there, Rock Valley Community Press Inc. This company published a number of free newspapers in communities covered by Gannett's dominant daily, the *Register Star.* The complaint alleged that Gannett had embarked upon an extensive, deliberate campaign of lying about the circulation, distribution, and auditing of the weekly papers.

According to the lawsuit, Gannett had claimed falsely that: the circulation of the Community Press papers was not audited; the Community Press papers were not distributed in several specific villages and suburbs; the circulation of the Community Press papers was much lower than it actually was; the Community Press papers were promising delivery to thousands of households that they did not reach; the Community Press papers were charging higher advertising rates than their circulation warranted; the majority of the Community Press papers were delivered on racks instead of by home delivery; the Community Press papers were inconsistently delivered, and frequently "dumped" in lieu of delivery; the Community Press papers were published on an infrequent or irregular basis; and, conversely, that Gannett had made false claims about the circulation of its own *Register Star,* stating figures much higher than actual.

The alleged "false, deceptive, and defamatory statements" had been made verbally by representatives of the Gannett paper and in printed circulars distributed to advertisers in the area, the complaint contended. The language of the circulars, which were attached to the complaint as exhibits, included:

"They're guessing. Remember that numbers lie. The [Community Press] newspapers tell you the total they print and call it circulation. Whether littering city sidewalks or passed by in store racks, the newspapers actually opened and read is undeterminable. That is why the [Community Press papers] *choose* not to be audited. The numbers would not substantiate the claims." Another flourish was: "NICE AD, TOO BAD . . ." on the cover of a circular, which continued inside " . . . YOUR AD MISSED 2,300 HOUSEHOLDS THAT YOU PAID TO RECEIVE!" It then declared: "They aren't giving you your money's worth." The Community Press lawsuit concluded:

> The oral and written false, deceptive, and defamatory statements about Plaintiff and Plaintiff's newspapers constitute a concerted campaign by Defendant to drive Plaintiff out of business as a publisher in the Rockford metropolitan area. This campaign has seriously damaged Plaintiff in its business. As a direct result of the false, deceptive, and defamatory statements described above, existing advertisers have reduced or terminated their advertising purchases from Plaintiff, and future and prospective advertisers have refused to do business with

Plaintiff. Some of those advertisers or prospective advertisers have mentioned or quoted the false, deceptive, and defamatory statements of Defendants to Plaintiff's employees and agents as the basis or as part of the basis for their refusal to do business with Plaintiff. Plaintiff's goodwill and reputation among advertisers and readers in the Rockford area have been seriously damaged or destroyed. Plaintiff's past, present, and future profits have been seriously damaged.

Although Gannett refused to comment on the lawsuit filed against it in Rockford, it responded with a counterclaim, suing the Community Press company for allegedly making inaccurate statements in a leaflet it had distributed. Late in 1995 a Community Press lawyer told me by telephone that the case had bogged down. "It's just in the system," he said. "I can't give you a very good prediction when it might be resolved."

Was it true, I asked him, what I had heard: that Gannett's campaign against the Community Press papers had been given the in-house title "M.A.S.H."—for "Make A Shopper History"?

"There are documents showing that that was the case," he said. "But I can't get into that. I don't want to disclose information that is covered by the court's protective order."

"It's Now or Never!" was a 1990 winner of the Gerald Loeb Award for Distinguished Business and Financial Journalism, the nation's most prestigious business-writing prize. Seven publications were honored that year, and the *News-Chronicle* was by far the smallest. The others were the *Washington Post, Crain's New York Business,* the *Los Angeles Times, Forbes* magazine, the *Arizona Republic,* and the *Wall Street Journal.* Because the Green Bay entry fit no standard definition of journalism, it was singled out for a Special Recognition Award, independent of the contest's regular categories. "Marvelous," said one judge, "but I couldn't make it fit in with the other entries."

The Loeb Awards judges, thirty-two in all, were drawn from prominent posts in the worlds of finance, academia, and journalism. The final panel included representatives of the University of California at Los Angeles, the Draper Fund, CNN Business News, *Forbes, Business Week, Money* magazine, the *Los Angeles Times,* and the *Wall Street Journal.* None of the judges was affiliated with Gannett.

In naming "It's Now or Never!" a prizewinner, the judges were generous with their praise. "Terrific!" one of them wrote. "As compelling a piece as I've read in a long time. It reached down and grabbed my gut. My ignorance was salved by this piece." Other comments were equally forceful: "Classic David-and-Goliath story. Needed to be said and they did." "Informs the public in an area that a small newspaper rarely addresses." "This piece is scrappy and self-serving. It is right at the roots of what journalism is all about." "The story *was* accurate as reported." My favorite accolade declared: "In the age of monopoly newspapers, it's nice that someone fought."

I was notified by telephone in May, from the Loeb Foundation office at the graduate school of business at UCLA, that "It's Now or Never!" had won the prestigious award. The thrill was keen, for three reasons: I was pleased for myself, I was pleased for Frank Wood and his besieged paper—and I was pleased that this account of Gannett had been absorbed by some of the most influential journalists in the country: the contest judges. These were people who needed to be aware of its content. Even more important, the announcement of the awards would draw nationwide attention and credibility to our exposé of the nation's biggest chain. The seeds we had planted were beginning to sprout.

The prize would be presented at a banquet in Los Angeles in June. Happily I made plans to attend. I urged Frank and Agnes to alter their vacation schedule to come also. "This is the payoff for all you did, Frank," I insisted. "You've got to be there." With some difficulty he made the necessary adjustments, and I was glad.

But the gladness wilted.

Under a balmy Southern California sky, the awards evening began with cocktails under a yellow-and-white-striped canopy at the posh Four Seasons Hotel in Beverly Hills. At the reception table the attendant recognized my name immediately. "Oh, you're one of the winners," she smiled, and pinned a white corsage to my lapel. The Loeb Foundation had urged prize winners to invite guests to share this special occasion of high professional recognition. In addition to Frank and Agnes, my circle that evening included the former *Santa Fe Reporter* writer now at the *Los Angeles Times,* a Los Angeles–based son of the *Reporter*'s new owner, and a lady friend who was a Hollywood screenwriter. After cocktails the assemblage moved into a grand dining room, where a designated table awaited the *News-Chronicle* entourage. A program of the evening's festivities lay folded on each plate. A quick scan told me all I needed to know.

The large triple-folded program held much information. The six winners in the competition's standard categories were featured in bold type, and twenty-two additional finalists were also listed. For all twenty-eight of these entries, the name of the journal's publisher accompanied those of the award-winning writers.

The program also stated the subject of each honored entry. Descriptions were brief but specific: "Coverage of the Eastern Airlines strike," "Coverage of the collapse of Lincoln Savings and Loan," "Coverage of the takeover battle for UAL Corp.," "Coverage of the problems surrounding the Wyoming Department of Insurance," "Articles on the failed merger efforts between First Hospital Corp. and Comprehensive Care Corp." The extensive program, stylishly designed with lots of white space, also gave a concise history of the Loeb Awards, noted the credentials of the six people with official duties during the evening's ceremonies, and listed the name, title, and affiliation of all thirty-two contest judges.

Notably missing from the Loeb Awards program was any mention of the *Green Bay News-Chronicle,* Frank Wood, Richard McCord, Gannett, or "It's Now or Never!"

Of course I knew why. Most of the competition's judges were working journalists, who were alarmed and horrified by the Green Bay report. But when they bestowed a prize upon "It's Now or Never!" it was the Loeb Foundation's turn to be alarmed and horrified. Rejecting the judges' choice would surely touch off one of those awards scandals that periodically embarrass the journalism fraternity. But honoring an attack on Gannett could antagonize the nation's most powerful chain. The Gannett Foundation might rule out future cash payments to the Loeb Awards program—or even to UCLA.

A diplomatic compromise was needed. So the Loeb Foundation found one. If the award could be presented unobtrusively, with little or no reference to Gannett, the situation might pass quietly, without flaring into an incident. As much as possible, the *News-Chronicle*'s award presentation should be kept verbal, so that the written record would bear no trace of it. Yes, that was the way to avoid offending Gannett.

Through an exquisite dinner and a lively address by "Adam Smith" of television fame, I stewed silently. The Club had closed ranks once again. Everyone at our table raised an eyebrow at the program's curious omission, but we did not discuss it. My friends were embarrassed for me, and I felt bad for Frank. This was the first major national award ever won by the *News-Chronicle,* but realpolitik had conspired to deprive him of its luster. After cutting short his vacation and flying to the coast at his own expense, he did not even get to see his name in print.

At the evening's climax the awards were presented. One by one the achievements of the six recognized winners were lauded. In turn the writers strode to the podium to get a handshake, a certificate, a thousand-dollar check, an engraved letter opener with a Waterford Crystal handle, and a round of applause.

An air of adjournment followed the presentation of the last officially noted prize. But master of ceremonies Shelby Coffey, editor of the *Los Angeles Times,* cut through it. One more honor remained, he said, a Special Recognition Award for a small paper in Green Bay, Wisconsin, that was competing with a larger Gannett newspaper. The word "Gannett" did not again pass his lips. Citing none of the methods used to squelch competition in Green Bay or elsewhere, the emcee quoted some generic compliments from the judges. No listener not already familiar with "It's Now or Never!" could possibly have guessed its content. My name was spoken, and I went up for the loot. Then the festivities were over.

The thousand-dollar check was negotiable, I assumed, and the shiny letter opener would undoubtedly do its job. But across the annals of the nation's most influential business-writing competition, the Green Bay Project had left no tracks.

Two writers from another winning publication rushed up to me. "Thank you, thank you, for what you did," said one, a young woman. "We heard about your work in Green Bay. We were working in Detroit when Gannett and Knight-Ridder pulled off that phony joint operating agreement. It was awful what they did. Every bad prediction of the results has come true. That's why we left. It's good that someone stood up to Gannett at last. Thank you so much." Others in the room offered congratulations. But the name of Gannett was not uttered by anyone else. As we left I thought I heard a huge sigh and the whispered words "It worked!" rising from the Loeb Foundation table. But probably I only imagined that.

A UCLA press release announced the Loeb Award winners. The *News-Chronicle*'s prize was duly noted, but in careful words that made no mention of Gannett. The reference to "It's Now or Never!" stated, in its entirety: "This entry was cited for its stylish and persuasive treatment of an important local issue—the struggle of a small-town newspaper to survive and remain independent."

UCLA need not have been so careful. *Editor & Publisher*'s account of the Loeb Awards did not even mention the *News-Chronicle,* while citing every other winner. Whether or not the word *Gannett* was deleted from the press release, "The Only Independent Weekly Journal of Newspapering" was not about to recognize an effort that took the name of its biggest advertiser in vain.

In the years after "It's Now or Never!" won the prize, recipients of Special Recognition Awards in the Gerald Loeb competition were listed in the banquet program with the other winners.

On a crisp April morning my phone rang in Santa Fe. The caller was a man from Gainesville, Georgia, a small city in my home state. Until recently, he said, he had been publisher of a weekly competitor to the Gannett daily in Gainesville. But he had just been driven out of business, and was convinced that the chain had acted deliberately to eliminate him. In fact, he had been told so, off the record, by former employees of the Gannett newspaper. Now he was considering an antitrust lawsuit.

The caller had read about Green Bay, and was wondering if I could help. I said I was not available. But I wished him well.

Index